A GUIDE FOR HIGH RANKING INTERVIEWS

A GUIDE FOR HIGH RANKING INTERVIEWS

S.K. TARAFDER

ATLANTIC
PUBLISHERS & DISTRIBUTORS

Published by
ATLANTIC PUBLISHERS AND DISTRIBUTORS
B-2, Vishal Enclave, Opp. Rajouri Garden, New Delhi-110027
Phones : 25413460, 25429987, 25466842

Sales Office
7/22, Ansari Road, Darya Ganj, New Delhi-110002
Phones : 23273880, 23275880, 23280451
Fax : 91-11-23285873
web : www.atlanticbooks.com
e-mail : info@atlanticbooks.com

ISBN 81-269-0383-X

Printed in India at
Nice Printing Press, Delhi

Preface

This book, *A Guide for High Ranking Interviews,* has been designed to meet the requirements of the candidates appearing in competitive examinations for obtaining exalted positions including other sophisticated employment. The book serves dual purposes—one for written test and the other for *viva voce* test. The answers to the questions, both written and *viva voce* are very interesting and well adapted to practical themes. This book is a panacea to embellish the mental faculties of the candidates preparing to come out with flying colours in high ranking employments.

An ideal attempt has been made in this comprehensive book to widen the candidates' periphery of knowledge to a large extend. With this purpose in view, I have also focussed on the international events in this book, although in majority of the cases answers to the questions for written test have been dwelt on the glimpses of India. The answers to the questions for written test and also for viva as stipulated in this book are wide ranging based on practical aspects.

For laymen this book is significant to quench their thirst for knowledge and hence it will serve the purpose both for the candidates aspiring for exalted positions and the others who are voracious readers of books for enriching their knowledge.

A number of books for helping the candidates for appearing in competitive examinations for high ranking positions are available in the market, but this book serves as a better substitute for other such books as a large number of topics are conspicuous by their absence in those books. I am pretty sure that the readers of this book—either for enriching their knowledge or for acquiring distinguished employment—will be fully convinced that this book will be a treasure for them. Another important feature of this book is that it has dealt with the topics of a diversified nature.

Personality of the candidates plays an important role to attain success in life. This book has analysed threadbare as to what a personality is in true sense of the term, and as to how to practise the traits of personality, which is no doubt a lengthy process to attain. Other instructions to the candidates as embodied in this book are also very important which the candidates have to follow in toto.

I am extremely grateful to the publishers through whom this book will be widely circulated throughout the country for the benefits of the readers and candidates appearing for test and interview in civil services and other high ranking positions.

S.K. TARAFDER

CONTENTS

1

Guidelines to the Candidates Appearing at Interviews for Civil Service and other High Ranking Positions

Embodiment of the following traits is essentially needed by the candidates appearing before interviewers for civil service posts and other high ranking positions:

(a) Candidates must have good communication ability and listening skills backed by relevant educational background.

(b) Candidates must have intelligence, patience, in-depth and up-to-date knowledge of current affairs in particular.

(c) Candidates must be analytical, sensitive, perceptive and committed, but at the same time should not be emotional.

(d) Candidates must have self-confidence and receptivity.

(e) Candidates must have presentation of skills for appearing before interviewers.

(f) The candidates must have physical fitness, as healthy body and healthy mind go hand in hand.

(g) The candidates must have honesty, mental alertness, presence of mind and straightforwardness.

(h) The candidates must be well dressed and cheerful.

(i) The candidates must have perseverance and firm determination.

(j) The candidates must have maturity of thought.

(k) The candidates must not have negative attitude.

(l) The candidates must show to the interviewers grace and courtesy and when seated in the chair before the interviewers must look relaxed and comfortable, but remain alert. When answering questions speak freely exchanging ideas and offering comments, wherever necessary.

For fresh candidates destined to achieve success in Civil Service examinations or the other, it is always desirable to take guidance from the persons who are experienced. Candidates desiring to appear before Civil Service examinations must start preparations in right earnest at least before one year of commencement of such examinations. The candidates must bear in mind that personal interview is not a question-answer session, but it is a personality test.

Personality of the candidates appearing at interviews plays a very important role as a deciding factor for attaining success in getting employment. It is also an essential ingredient which the candidates have to maintain in the interest of their rising high in service career during the course of employment. Personality does not mean that a person is essentially required to be good looking. Appearance and other factors are considered to determine personality of a person. The traits of personality a person should have are mentioned below:

(i) Self-confidence

(ii) Fixity of mind

(iii) Capacity to influence others

(iv) Clarity of expression

(v) Not to be fickle minded

(vi) Capacity of quick understanding

(vii) Wearing of well fitted costume

(viii) Positive approach on matters

(ix) Cleanliness

(x) Gravity

(xi) Proper dressing of hair

(xii) Steadiness in walking

(xiii) Sense of etiquette

(xiv) Good manners
(xv) Will power
(xvi) Gentleness
(xvii) Good behaviour
(xviii) Deportment
(xix) Soft spoken
(xx) Cool temperament
(xxi) Loveable habits

Writing skill of the candidates is very important for scoring good marks in written examination. Candidates should practise writing of essays for developing the writing skill.

The candidates should collect all the reading materials at a time for preparation so that precious time is not squandered in looking for materials here and there in order to avoid disturbing the mind. It is also pertinent to note that the candidates must procure the previous years' question papers with syllabus for Civil Service examinations. This will help the candidates immensely, as it will be made known to them about the nature/trend/pattern of questions to be answered.

Witty answers to the questions asked in the interview Board are very important. It displays the mental make-up and intelligence of the candidates for Civil Service examinations and other high ranking positions. It should be noted that questions in the interviews are generally asked in respect of the candidates' districts, state, hobby, current affairs, other socio-political and economic issues. The answers to be given must be straightforward and to the point.

The candidates have to bear in mind that the interviewers in the Interview Board especially keep eyes on certain main traits of the candidates, such as their honesty, truthfulness, communication skills, mental alertness, Intelligence Quotient (I.Q.) and presence of mind.

2

Purpose of Personal Interviews and the Prerequisites to be maintained by the Candidates before the Interview Board

Before the personal interview takes place, the depth of knowledge as well as the writing capacity of the candidates qualified in the objective and written tests is already put to proof. Therefore, in the personal interview the Board is more concerned with the approach, reaction, response, attitude, reasoning, grasping power, clarity of expression and convincing ability of the candidates. Keeping in view of the above in respect of the candidates, questions are asked in the personal interviews by the Board relating mostly to general knowledge and current affairs. The interview board consists of Chairman and other 4/5 qualified members. The first and foremost prerequisites for attaining success in the interview is to express things freely, fluently and effectively by the candidates. The candidates ought to have thorough knowledge and ideas which will give them confidence to stand in the interview without being nervous and down-hearted. The candidates must always bear in mind that interview is a Personality Test. Personality traits of a candidate have already been discussed thoroughly in the foregoing.

Embodiment of the qualities as enumerated therein is an index of pleasing personality which is very important to win success. The candidates should, therefore, inculcate the personality traits by regular systematic practice.

3

Formalities to be observed by the Candidates before the Interview Board

In the interview the candidates have to keep in mind the following points:

(1) It is always desirable that the candidates must reach the place of interview at least half an hour before the appointed time of interview. This will help the candidates to get themselves adjusted with the new environment with calm and ease. While waiting at the interview centre, the candidates can spend time usefully in exchanging information with other candidates.

(2) The candidates should make sure that they observe etiquette and manners and that they should also be cheerful smiling and polite to the members of the Interview Board.

(3) If any of the answers to the questions are not known to the candidates, it is to be said frankly, "I am sorry, Sir/Madam." The candidates must not try to bluff. There is no cause for worry if answers are not known.

(4) Before entering the interview room the candidate should knock at the door 3/4 times and then push the door gently to proceed to the Board with confident steps. Next he/she will greet the Chairman and Members of the Board in a cheerful, pleasant and enthusiastic manner. A file containing his/her educational certificates and testimonials, in original should also be in his/her hand. The candidate should also take with him/her a note pad and a pen.

(5) The candidate should not take his/her seat in the chair unless he/she is asked to sit in and during the course of sitting he/she will say, "Thank you Sir/ Madam".

(6) The voice of the candidate must not crack while giving replies to the questions. He/she should not also gulp while giving answers as it is a sign of weakness, nervousness and fear. He/she should not stretch/extend hands while answering questions, as it looks unbecoming in the Interview Board.

(7) Before the interviewers the candidate must not give false statement in respect of the answers to the questions, otherwise, the candidate will be in false position in the midst of volley of questions asked by the interviewers subsequently.

(8) The candidate should not interrupt during the course of asking questions by the interviewers. He/she should not jerk his/her legs while sitting in the chair in front of the interviewers.

(9) The best attire for the male candidate will be complete suit-pant with tie during the winter season and in summer season wearing of complete suit-pant may be avoided. Hair of the candidate should be properly dressed and he must have fresh shave if he is not keeping beard. Socks should be matching with the colour of the pant he wears. Shoes should also be well polished. In case of the female candidates light coloured costume is preferable.

(10) On the previous night of the interview, the candidate must have sound sleep so as to keep himself/herself fit in the interview Board.

(11) Before the interviewers the candidates must not answer more than what is required.

(12) Showing oversmartness by the candidate is not desirable as it exhibits his/her artificiality.

(13) Sometimes candidates are asked questions simultaneously by the interviewers for replies with the object of puzzling the candidates. In that case,

the candidates have to listen to such questions with patience and very carefully and give replies one by one beginning from the first question asked.

(14) At the end of the interview and at the time of leaving the interview room the candidate should say with a smile, "Thank you, Sir/Madam." The candidate should not extend his/her hands towards the interviewers for a handshake, unless otherwise any of the interviewers comes forward for a handshake. The handshake should be with firm hold and also with a smile.

(15) After completion of the interview the candidate should not turn his/her eyes back towards the interviewers in the mid-way of moving forward towards the door.

The above formalities should also be observed in the case of other candidates appearing before the Interview Board for other high ranking positions.

4

What the Candidates Have to Know the Minds of the Interviewers in the Matter of Selection

Interview is a selection device. Therefore, the candidates have to be meticulous while appearing for personal interviews. It will be very much helpful to the candidates to attain success in the interview if they are in the know of the minds of the interviewers in the matter of selection of prospective candidates for the posts they would be interviewed. The interviewers decide as follows in most of the cases while interviewing the candidates:

(1) Interviewing prospective candidates calls for keen judgement of character, talent and skills of the candidates.

(2) Interviewing involves gathering of past information about a candidate in making upright selection. On this basis, the interviewers can surmise future performance of the candidates.

(3) Before the actual question-answer session begins in the interview, the interviewers believe in introduction which is devoted generally for five minutes or so to put the candidates at ease. When the interview closes, the interviewers make additional note of the candidates while leaving the room.

(4) The candidates should also know that the interviewers focus on the following aspects during an interview:

(a) Social skills *i.e.*, how far the candidates get well with others and create good impression and rapprochement.

(b) How far the candidates are motivating *i.e.*, taking initiative and actively participating.

(c) Whether the candidates have quick thinking power and also presence of mind.

(d) Specific knowledge of job profile.

(e) How far the candidates can imprint first impression in the minds of the interviewers.

While appearing for interviews the candidates should also bear in mind that their candidature for the post is liable to be rejected on the following counts:

(a) Poor personal appearance

(b) Lack of interest and enthusiasm

(c) Failure to keep eye contact

(d) Arriving late for the interview

(e) Lack of leadership quality

(f) Non-interest in extra curricular activities

The candidates should, therefore, bear in mind that the interviewers attach importance to these criteria also while considering selection of the candidates.

5

Group Discussion

WHAT IS GROUP DISCUSSION?

Group discussion is not a debate. It is a formal selection or employment interview. In the Group Discussion generally two members of the Interview Board remain present. When the group discussion starts they become the silent observers and do not participate in the discussion. In a group discussion maximum ten candidates in a single batch are asked to participate. The group is divided into two categories—one who speaks for the motion and the other against the motion. The candidates taking part in the group discussion should bear in mind that they are rivals to one another, as they all compete for selection to limited vacancies of appointments. The candidates endowed with natural and effective leadership qualities are destined to emerge successful in the group discussion.

The candidates in a group discussion are seated in chairs placed in semicircle way facilitating them to face each other for discussion. Each candidate is allotted separate Roll numbers and they are called by numbers only and not by name. As for the subject of discussion, the observers/examiners may put forward two or three topics and ask the group to select any one of them and then proceed to discuss the same. The subject of discussion may be sports, politics, economics, unemployment, films and so forth. It may also be the topic of the day which has appeared in the headlines of the newspapers. Group discussion is quite time consuming and is restricted to a single candidate at a time. The candidates in a group will have full freedom to express their views the way they like with a definite time limit fixed—one for the motion and the other against the motion. During the course of speaking the candidates must not get exasperated and criticise other's view points in anger but place their own opinion in convincing way. Before eliciting views the candidates have to listen to the points of argument of others with rapt attention.

AIM AND OBJECTIVE OF GROUP DISCUSSION

Group discussion test is a selection technique for employment of candidates for higher positions. It offers an excellent opportunity to the observers to judge the leadership qualities of the candidates by their way of speaking, gesticulation, motivation, facial expression and argumentative capacity. This selection interview is an assessment of the personality of the candidates and determines his/her suitability to the job. Group discussion is also a device superior to personal interview. Group discussion is extremely important in the modern competitive selection. The technique of group discussion serves as an effective preliminary screen to weed out dull and negative oriented candidates. Therefore, the chances of getting employment by the candidates coming out flying colours in group discussion are brightened. As far as the language for discussion in the group is concerned, the commercial organisations for executive cadre posts want the discussion to be conducted in English. The same medium is also followed in most UPSC tests and Service Selection Board. In State Public Service Commissions, the language of the State may be followed in certain states, especially in respect of non-gazetted appointments.

6

GENERAL TOPICS

Q.1. What is the future of India?

Ans. It is an admitted fact that after Independence India has leaped forward towards various developmental activities and the tempo of race in this direction has been continuing unabated except of course in the case of certain occasional and temporary set-back in the developmental process on account of ephemeral installation of governments in the centre.

India is still not considered an affluent country taking into account that about 35% of the total population of India are living below poverty line. The reason is not far to seek. The developmental process so far achieved by India in the field of economy has not percolated to the downtrodden. Otherwise, the poverty of the people could have been eliminated long back and India would have become a welfare state by now. 21st century has been ushered in an upbeat mood for all-round development and naturally it has thrown a challenge for India to keep pace with the other fast developing and already developed countries of the world. World focus is towards India for its consistent developmental process. Western leaders are no doubt keenly awaiting to see that India emerges as one of the big powers in the world after attaining all-round development utilising properly the loans in billions of dollars taken from different financial institutions of the world.

On account of encouraging foreign policy of the government of India, cordial relations with other countries of the world have been established and India is placed in high esteem by them for its pragmatic approach to the issues. India has a voice to the world. She is no doubt in congenial position for further all-round development in the not too distant future, if healthy economic policy is pursued. To sum up, India has already had the achievements, such as:

(a) India has become the sixth atomic power of the world.
(b) India has to its credit become one of the ten industrialised nations of the world.
(c) Standard of living of the people in general has been attained.
(d) In the matter of food production India has achieved self-sufficiency enabling to feed its more than 100 crores of people without depending on foreign imports.
(e) Scientific progress is spectacular.
(f) Indian engineers are second to none in the world.
(g) Non-dependence on foreign manufactured goods.
(h) Self-sufficiency in warfare and military power.
(i) India has produced galaxy of intellectuals and creative persons especially scientists of first water.
(j) Racial clashes are practically nil.
(k) India has become a unity in diversity.

India is of course beset with certain knotty problems standing in the way of speedy progress. They are:

(a) Mushroom increase in the number of children among the ruralites on account lack of education and foresightedness.
(b) Continuance of child marriages in the villages.
(c) Unavoidable increases in the prices of commodities on account of increase of crude oil prices effected by OPEC (Organisation of Petroleum Exporting Countries).
(d) Widening financial gap between the rich and the poor.

(e) Ever increasing unemployment problem in the country.

(f) Terrorism is a very big threat impeding progress.

(g) Rising oil prices and the somewhat ambivalent behaviour of the foreign institutional investors means that our foreign exchange position is not as comfortable as it may seem.

The above are still the hindrances in the way of speedy development of India. The government should, therefore, take concerted efforts to annihilate the problems and in doing so India will continue to march forward to become a welfare state and here lies the rosy future of India in the comity of nations.

Q.2. In what way illiteracy has a direct bearing in the matter of mushroom growth of population in the country and the consequences emanated from growth of such population?

Ans. Illiteracy is a bane and a stigma. These illiterate people are in the dark and never tested the modernities of life. They are the parasites of the nation. They have no prudence. If these people are talked about the imperative need of family planning, they turn a deaf ear. For them multiplicity of children is the benediction of God. This notion prompts them to go on producing offspring without any planning. The result becomes alarming and apprehensive. Country becomes poorer and poorer. A section of the affluents living in the towns and cities is not the true replica of the country. If the society is swarmed with poor people spiced with illiteracy, society becomes degenerated. The number of such people outweigh the affluents and here lies the true picture of the country. All developmental activities centre round the educated people only who have foresightedness and the number of children are minimal in their families. India is an agro-based country and in absence of enlightenment among the ruralites in absence of education the number of uneducated children are multiplying at an alarming proportion and it becomes beyond the capacity of the government to stem the tide and the human resource development poses a challenge.

Q.3. We are now in the 21st century. When the whole world is poised for all-round developments what are the components which we require most to keep pace with the developments and prosperity of our country?

Ans. Ours is a very big country with bounties of resources. With such rich and abundant storage, our country can march forward to all-round development and prosperity in the not too distant future if we pursue the steps such as:

(a) There should not be political wranglings. The policies of the government should be corrected, if wrongs are there, through constructive criticism. No political party should think of toppling the government which is installed for a full term of five years. The citizens should also not be misled by violent criticisms by other political parties for their partisan interests.

(b) Population control is a dire necessity through strong family planning programme so that the majority of the population can become the assets of the country rather than wastage and can be put to use for developments of the country.

(c) Education should be disseminated in every nook and corner of the country, so that the people at large can develop their mental faculty and understanding capacity.

(d) People should have nationalistic spirit as well as they should have feelings of brotherhood and fraternity. There should be cooperation amongst the people. Selfishness is a bane which should be shunned. Arrogant and unparliamentary behaviour should not be resorted to at any point of time.

(e) Through moratorium there should not be gheraos, strikes, lock-outs and bundh in the country, so that congenial industrial climate is maintained.

(f) In an agro-based country like India priority should be given for rural developments.

(g) Terrorism should be quelled with iron hand.

These are the principal ingredients which will help the country march forward to the path of rapid developments and prosperity.

Q.4. Unemployment problem has aggravated in India. What are the ways to contain it?

Ans. Unemployment problem is the burning question of India. With the passing of years it is being aggravated to an alarming proportion with the mushroom growth of population unabated year after year. Consequently, India is being divided into two groups—Haves and Havenots. Middle class people are on the process of extinction resulting in the abrupt increase in prices of commodities owing to steep hike in the crude oil prices effected by the Organisation of Petroleum Exporting Countries. Under the circumstances, if the standard of living of the people in general could be ameliorated by way of widening the scope of employment amongst the educated adolescents, the situation will be arrested from going bad to worse. Now, the question crops up as to how the situation could be improved upon by way of generating employment scenario in the country. Employment has two aspects—one is direct employment and the other self-employment. Direct employment is for those who work in the Organisations for which they get salary/wages in return of work rendered by them.

Employment situation in the country could be improved upon by the following steps:

(1) India is an agro-based country. It will be, therefore, in the fitness of things if setting up of agro-based industries is given preference in most of the rural areas. This will ensure employment amongst the educated ruralites. This will tend to reduce the pressure of influx of such ruralites to cities and towns.

(2) Mushroom growth of population amongst the ruralites has to be curbed to ease the unemployment problem, for which they have to

be educated about the paramount need to limit the size of family. Family planning programme must be made stringent.

(3) In pursuance of the five-year Plans industries are to be set up expeditiously in the areas where infrastructural facilities are abundantly in existence. With the setting up of heavy industries, ancillary industries will automatically spring up in and around such industries and accordingly employment potentiality in the areas will expand.

(4) Vocational training Institutes are to be set up in sufficient number so that the candidates intending to go for white collar jobs lean towards technical jobs. There is imperative need for technical hands for development of the country. Technical jobs offer better salary/wages and the scope of technical job is more than the white collar job.

(5) All sick industries in the country are to be revitalised. BIFR (Board for Industrial and Financial Reconstruction) should play a vital role in this respect. Unemployment problem will be arrested if the industries/organisations run smoothly.

(6) Militancy of Labour Union is to be eschewed, so that even the well run industries/organisations in the country are not closed down by declaring lock-out by the Management.

(7) It is to be ensured that all the existing industries run on optimum level so that the question of trimming of employees working there does not arise.

(8) Work culture amongst the employees is to be maintained. They should be sincere and hard working for efficient running of the establishments. This will avoid laying off of the employees and unemployment problem will not ensue.

(9) Generation of electricity to the optimum level is the prime factor for industrialisation which eradicates unemployment problem. Government should, therefore, give utmost preference to setting

up generating units to recoup shortfall in the supply of electricity with the intention of rapid industrialisation of the country.

(10) Special facilities are to be provided to the non-residential Indians who are the financial giants to lure them to set up industries in the country.

(11) Side by side with the direct employment, government should also encourage self-employment for the educated people to set up their own small scale enterprises by providing them loan on easy terms. This will help solve unemployment problem in the country to a large extent, as a sizeable number of people will be employed in such enterprises.

(12) India should opt for labour-intensive sectors like agriculture, agro-processing industries, horticulture, floriculture, tourism, small-scale industries and setting up of more industries from urban to rural areas.

Q.5. What will be the impact arising out of the acute unemployment problem in the country?

Ans. Employment potentiality has a direct bearing with the economic growth of a country. Economic sluggishness is the result of non-industrialisation and very slow technological progress. Number of educated adolescents are increasing year after year in alarming proportion. But, these educated youths are practically finding no source of gainful employment due to retardation of economic progress which has been accentuated owing to world-wide economic recession. Application of Voluntary Retirement Scheme (VRS) has also hastened unemployment problem. Of course, employment potentiality would have improved if there would have been new recruits against the vacancies created due to VRS, which is not taking place. Industries are becoming sick and ultimately they are being closed down throwing sizeable number of employees working in such Organisations out of employment. Inflation in the country is no doubt coming down but nevertheless prices of essential commodities are still increasing consistently year after year. Bank interest rate is slashing down as a result of which there is squeeze in the amount of interest against the deposited amount with the bank. Many families are, therefore, finding it extremely difficult to defray expenses with the reduced interest amount. Although there is slashing down of birth rate, yet there is no appreciable decrease in the growth of population because of the persistent fall in the death rate. This has also heightened unemployment problem in the country.

When this is the true replica of the country in the economic field vis-a-vis unemployment problem, the educated youths in general aspiring for gainful employment are now very much down hearted and in most of the cases they have become the liabilities of their old parents. Very few educated youths have tested the economic liberalisation. Unemployment is rampant mostly amongst the middle class educated youths. This has created adverse effects in the society. Such idle brains are the devil's workshops. They practically have no assured future, since the doors of employment for them are virtually closed. The vitals of most of the middle class educated youths are being eroded like the fire in the powdery wood. These young people, who are the future of the nation, with no employment have become very much restive and their sense of respectability towards the elders has been evaporating fast. There is also distinct mark of social disorder as the health of the society is emaciating as a result. As far as the educated young women are concerned, they are also not finding suitable partners for marriage, as the educated male youths for want of employment are outnumbering. This is another problem society is fraught with due to increase in the number of unemployed youths. Obviously, the old parents are disquieted very much for crossing the marriageable age of their daughters for want of suitable bride-grooms settled in life after getting employment.

Thus, unemployment problem in the country is creating far-reaching consequences and the normal lives of the people mostly amongst the middle class families are being thrown into confusion.

Q.6. What effects are there in the society on account of downsizing of the Govt. organisations by way of reducing the staff strength by the adoption of VRS?

Ans. On account of Fifth Pay Commission report salary/wages of the government employees have increased very high. In most organisations it has been seen that more than 70% of the budget goes as salary/wages and very little funds are available to secure the objective of the organisations for which such a large workforce is recruited. Apart from this, by way of increase in Dearness Allowance, every employee working in the government organisations gets the benefit of increase in their salary/wages to the tune of Rs. 1000/- per year or so on an average by way of quarterly increase in dearness allowance. This is in addition to normal annual increment. Such an abnormal spurt in the salary/wages of the employees has no doubt put the government exchequer into disarray. When the salary/wages of the employees increased as a result of the Fifth Pay Commission report, it was felt that the work culture of the government employees would be improved considerably due to higher range of salary/wages but it was contrary to the expectation. It is an admitted fact that most of the government organisations are not working with maximum efficiency/commensurate with the increased salary structure of the employees and as a result financial viability of the organisations has been dwindling. Now, in order to get rid of the economic malaise of many government organisations it has been felt an absolute necessity to downsizing the organisations by reducing the staff strength by offering VRS. While bulk of the employees are being thrown out of employment on account of application of VRS, new recruits to such organisations are obviously stopped, excepting in a few departments, aggravating unemployment problem in the country to a considerable extent.

Due to acute unemployment problem number of earning members in most of the middle class families have been reduced and accordingly scant income of these families are not keeping pace with the present-day high cost of living and accordingly members of such families are becoming impoverished, which has a tremendous impact in social order, which needs no elucidation. Recruitment in bulk of the private organisations has also been downsized, aggravating the employment arena furthermore, taking into consideration that the government employees constitute 2 to 3% of the total population of the country, whereas the employees strength in private organisations is much more than that of the government employees. Therefore, when the source of employment in both the sectors is being squeezed with ever increasing population of the country there cannot be check in the social degeneration in future years to come, if the employment situation in the country continues to become dismal.

Q.7. What is all about dowry system?

Ans. One of the greatest social evils of the day is dowry system. Even the anti-dowry law and the stringent penal provision initiated by the National Commission for Women (NCW) has virtually become infructuous.

Non-fulfilment of promised dowry by the parents of the brides has led to the increase in bride-burning cases year after year which has now increased ten-fold during the last fifteen years. Peace in the families after marriage of the sons has been seriously disturbed in most of the cases due to non-fulfilment of the heavy demands of dowry by the in-laws and the brides have become the enemies of the families and are subjected to untold torture and persecution. The ill system of dowry is nothing but a sale of the brides in the market against heavy ransom. Ironically, even the highly educated and the affluence people are not exceptions from demanding dowry and that they come forward first to set conditions for dowry before the marriage is finalised. It is a fact that many if not all highly placed bride-grooms either in their business or in highly lucrative employment are the fortunate ones in getting sumptuous dowry in terms of lakhs of rupees at the cost of impoverising the parents of the brides. Cases are plenty that thousands of brides are compelled to commit suicide in different parts of the country just because their parents have failed to meet the demands of dowry by the in-laws of the bride-grooms. The demands of dowry system have become rampant in society on account of disbalancing in the male and female ratio in the field of marriage. Well placed bride-grooms are not plenty as compared to the number of availability of marriageable girls.

Grown up girls with sound education have now understood very clearly that they are no longer prepared to play into the hands of uncertain destiny after their marriage on account of non-fulfilment of heavy demands of dowry by their parents. The first thing required to overcome this evil practice of dowry is to do away with the male dominated society. Marriage is a union of two souls and that it should not at all be bargained with dowry. Grown up daughters are now very much conscious of themselves and it is a happy augury that female education has been spreading by leaps and bounds. Women are now moving shoulder to shoulder with their male counterparts. Sizeable number of educated women are creditably competing in competitive examinations and are settling in the society on their own feet. They are not the parasites of society. Government should fix up compulsory reservation of seats for the educated women contenders for employment. The annihilation of difference between men and women in the matter of education and employment will automatically wipe out the evil of dowry system from society and the enactment of anti-dowry law initiated by National Commission for Women will not help the purpose.

Q.8. What are the differences in respect of Internet, Fax and Electronic mail (e-mail)?

Ans. *Internet*: Internet is a medium through which people at large all over the world are communicated in the matter of various information. Internet can be browsed through a computer which is connected to a modem. The information that can be disseminated through Internet includes scientific data, advertising, government documents, databases, getting the latest news from around the world, conducting business negotiations, exchanging information with others, providing vital information to the customers and many more. Millions of people around the world make use of Internet today.

Fax: Fax is an instrument through which information is transmitted through telecommunication network. Fax is a common name for 'facsmile transmission' or 'telefax'. Copy of original message as also photographs so transmitted are received by the Fax installed at the other end. Fax machine is connected to a telephone number. The user has to dial from his Fax machine in order to send required document/message to the other end.

Electronic mail (e-mail): E-mail has become a key part of the communications networks of most modern offices. Data and messages can be transmitted from one computer to another using telephone lines, microwave-links, communications satellite or other telecommunications equipment. The same message can be sent to a number of different addresses. E-mail is sent through a company's own local area network or beyond, through a nationwide or worldwide communications network. E-mail services use a central computer to store messages and data and to route them to their intended destination. With a subscription to a public e-mail network, an individual PC user needs only a modem and a telephone to send and receive written or vocal messages. Because of the huge amount of e-mail that can be generated, systems have been developed to screen mail for individual users.

Q.9. What are the important factors impeding poverty alleviation in India?

Ans. The most important factor hindering poverty alleviation in India today is the mushroom population growth. The population increasing at a high rate of 2.1 per cent per year reminds us of the Malthusian caution. India was perhaps the first among the developing nations of the world to launch its family planning programme dating back in 1951. Since then India has already spent Rs. 50 billion on family planning alone with practically no abatement in the growth of population. Whereas other countries in Asia introducing family planning programme much later than India have achieved encouraging result.

The following are the tangible reasons leading to the high rate of growth of population in India:

(a) There is national apathy towards the family planning.

(b) Lack of education amongst the ruralites.

(c) Growth of population amongst the Muslim community is comparatively high as Islamic Shariat advocates marriage of more than one woman, as also permits a girl to get married when she attains puberty. The All-India Muslim Personal Law Board has decided to go to the court seeking exemption for Muslims from the Act restraining child marriages. They say Shariat Law is final and non-negotiable. But, in view of the imperative need to check growth of population, Bangladesh, an Islamic country, has implemented family planning programmes without fearing adverse reactions from the religious establishment of the country.

(d) Illiterate people of India think that multiplicity of children means more earning members who will sustain the old parents at the fag end of their lives.

(e) Mental diversions of the ruralites are practically absent, as they have no source of entertainments in the villages. Child production is, therefore, more amongst the villagers as their enjoyments are squeezed outside their houses.

There is no denying the fact that India's huge population has marred India's image in the eyes of the world. Since the poverty alleviation of India has direct link with the population growth, it is of paramount necessity to control growth of population. The check in the growth of population must be on the national agenda. China has the highest number of population in the world. Since Chinese Government has taken the issue on national agenda, the growth of population has been checked there thus increasing the quality of lives of the people of China. A time has come for India, which is poised for all-round development keeping pace with other developed nations of the world in the 21st century, to control growth of population. What is needed most in the future years to come is that India does not need multiplicity of unwanted population like swarm of bees but quality people with abatement in the growth of population.

Simply earmarking money by the government of India for the Family Planning Programme will not help the purpose. India's whole approach to Family Planning lacks a scientific basis. Following actions are advocated to make the family planning a complete success:

(a) 65 per cent of the total population of India are living in villages. They are still ignorant of the ray of development which is the result of non-dissemination of education to them. Spread of education amongst the villagers will awaken them and help them achieve foresightedness and they will be made to think that arrival of new mouths is not the gift of God. Among all the Indian states the percentage of literacy of the Keralites is the highest and this is the reason of the lowest growth rate of population there.

(b) Vice-chancellors of over 200 universities in India must think of introducing course on population dynamics. Also the students unions have to take up the issue of possible population explosion that would directly or indirectly affect their future.

(c) Mobile van of family planning personnel must move from village to village to educate the villagers about the danger of multiplicity of children and how it is robbing of them from testing the quality of life.

(d) The family planning programme must be put on national agenda. The political parties and bureaucracy must take up the issue of population control with all seriousness it requires. Scores of seminars on Family Planning must be organised at regular intervals.

(e) The Government must take stringent action like China to contain growth of population irrespective of different religions and philosophy.

If the Family Planning Programme is neglected India can never be expected to become one of the developed nations of the world but will continue to become a developing country for all the future years to come which will never end and in turn poverty cannot be conquered to give the people of India better way of life.

Q.10. The number of cases of divorce are increasing now-a-days. What are the probable reasons for the same?

Ans. The reasons for increase in the number of divorce now-a-days are not far to seek. If we take into account the pragmatic view of the same, the reasons could be analysed as per point Nos. (i) and (ii) below:

Of late, joint family system in our society is mostly not in vogue. Present trend is that young couple prefers to live separately from their parents and in-laws as also other members of family in their own interest only. Also with the increase in the number of population housing problem reigns supreme and this leads to fragmentation of joint family system. In the earlier days when the couple were staying combinedly with other members of family with the availability of plenty of accommodation, there was complete cohesion and sweet relations among all the members of family staying together as also there was no mistrust in the dealings. Since there was real pleasure in staying altogether in joint family looking after the interest of all equally, the question of divorce was a remote possibility.

(i) In earlier days this was the system that parents were negotiating and fixing up marriages of their sons and daughters by finding out suitable boys/ girls in conformity with the status and other factors of the families. But, now in most of the cases the boys after attaining their maturity and economic liberalisation choose the girls for marriage of their own choice and selection even without looking to the uniformity of status of the family in most of the cases in flagrant disapproval of their parents. The ultimate result of such marriage does not augur well. In due course of time it is observed that there is rift, misadjustment and mistrust between the couple owing to the disuniformity in the mental make-up and ultimately this leads to divorce.

(ii) Girls are now educated and they in many cases want to supplement the income of the family by virtue of their education and also for economic necessity, by working in offices and elsewhere. When the spouse are mostly engaged in money earning activity there is a little scope of maintaining sweet and harmonious relations, as they are separated most of the time from each other, which is aggravated by the fact that the wife on many occasions returns home late willy-nilly and this leads to suspicions, displeasure and mistrust in the minds of the husband and consequently the relation between them start becoming sour. This ultimately leads to separation.

Although these are the main reasons for separation between the spouse, yet it should not be taken into account for divorce in all cases, as there may be other factors which would determine sweet relations between the husband and the wife thus avoiding divorce.

Q.11. What is *bundh*?

Ans. The legal position regarding *bundh* is clear from the Supreme Court's 12th November, 1997 decision. It upheld a landmark judgement of the Kerala High Court which ruled that a strike, or a *bundh* undermines freedoms and rights and declared *bundhs* to be "unconstitutional" and "illegal", as they violated the fundamental rights of citizens guaranteed by Articles 19(1) (a) and 21 in addition to causing national loss.

The Communist Party of India (Marxist) and the Communist Party of India had filed counter-affidavits after this. They argued that holding a *bundh* was a spontaneous expression of protest against a national calamity or against the exploitation of the people, and that this was the fundamental right of a political party calling for a *bundh*.

The Kerala High Court quashed this argument, saying that political parties had the right to protest against an erroneous policy or exploitation but not to call a *bundh* on the plea that it was an expression of their freedom of speech and felt that political parties and organisations which call *bundhs* and enforce them should compensate the government and citizens for the losses sustained by them during *bundhs*. If a political party feels compelled to call a *bundh* to protest against a government policy which goes against the interests of the people, it should be done only after allowing the government a reasonable time to redress the people's problems.

In the Constitution there is no such thing as a fundamental right of a political party. A political party, therefore, cannot impose *bundhs* on people who are not in agreement with it. It can only call general strike on condition that they will not use muscle power and coercion to enforce them.

Q.12. Print media was thrown open to foreign capital as announced by Mrs. Sushma Swaraj, the then Information and Broadcasting Minister on 25th June, 2002. What is all about this?

Ans. Mrs. Sushma Swaraj, the then Information and Broadcasting Minister, pushed through her proposal on 25th June, 2002—the Cabinet accepted it in full—that allows Foreign Direct Investment (FDI) of upto 26 per cent in print media Companies running news and current affairs publications and upto 74 per cent foreign investment in running non-news and non-current affairs publications. The 1955 Cabinet resolution prohibiting foreign investment in print media, which was reversed by the Cabinet, was nothing more than a historical curiosity. It would not be an exaggeration to suggest that the Cabinet decision inaugurates a new era in the history of the Indian print media. The NDA government must be applauded for opening up a window of opportunity before the print media of the country. While announcing this breaking news she guaranteed the following safeguards:

(a) The majority shareholder in a Company accepting FDI must be an Indian resident holding significantly more than 26 per cent.

(b) At least three-quarters of the Board members of a Company accepting FDI must be Indian residents and its Managing Director must also be an Indian resident.

(c) Key posts on editorial boards are to be held by Indian residents.

(d) Credentials of foreign investor is subject to verification by Home and I&B ministries.

(e) Permission of I&B ministry will be needed for a change in shareholding pattern.

The decision to throw open the print media to foreign capital is a very bold and well-thought-out one. The advantages that would flow from the decision are not difficult to pinpoint. The advantages and benefits are:

(i) The step will help publications challenge market leaders and encourage competition. This will automatically raise standards and thus benefit readers.

(ii) In taking this decision the Cabinet has ensured that editorial and managerial control of publications remains in the hands of the Indians.

(iii) By this decision it would enable print publications to access funds especially from financial institutions that had foreign equity.

(iv) The step would provide a means for publishers to improve the quality of publications by enabling easier access of funds.

(v) Indian newspapers and magazines will have access to international capitals and, therefore, to more advanced technology.

(vi) The decision would reflect the growing official confidence in Indian journals and editors.

(vii) The standards of editing and reporting would have a great deal of maturity and sophistication.

(viii) Throwing open of the print media to foreign capital would obviously increase the pages of the newspapers and magazines and this translates into more job opportunities and better pay packets.

Q.13. What is primary education system of West Bengal as stipulated in the 'Pratichi Trust Education Report' released by the Nobel Laureate, Prof. Amartya Sen?

Ans. Professor Amartya Sen, the Nobel Laureate released his 'Pratichi Trust Education Report' on 16th August, 2002 pinpointing several lacunae in the primary education system of West Bengal based on his intensive investigation of education in 18 conventional primary schools and 17 Sishu Siksha Kendras in Birbhum, Purulia and Midnapore. It also highlighted some positive aspects of the system and suggested radical reforms to remove the lacunae.

The positive aspects of the primary education system, as mentioned in his report are:

(i) The rise in enthusiasm among parents to send their sons and daughters to schools.

(ii) The success of lady teachers in Sishu Siksha Kendras.

(iii) The spurt in the number of registration in schools.

The negative aspects of the primary education system as depicted in his report are:

(i) Free primary education has ceased to exist in the face of private tuition, which is a violation of the basic right guaranteed by the constitution. It has, therefore, resulted in an immensely discriminating system against the interests of children from the poor and less-privileged families. The poor feel deprived when they are unable to take tuition. In fact, in the primary stage of education why should there be need at all to continue with the system of private tuition?

(ii) On an average, as much as 20 per cent primary school teachers have been found to be absent. As far as absenteeism in respect of the students is concerned, 49 per cent among primary school students and 36 per cent in the Sishu Siksha Kendras have been found absent.

(iii) There is the existence of class-based disadvantages and absence of infrastructure in the institution.

(iv) There is the failure of the mid-day meal programme.

(v) Amongst the students there is racial or class discrimination.

Releasing the 'Pratichi Trust Education Report' the Nobel Laureate announced that he would set up 'Pratichi Bhavan' in the city of Kolkata, which would function as a centre of "research for action" to remove the human deprivation in the primary education system. The report's suggestions included the need to set up parents-teachers committees in schools and endow them with legal power to bring about radical reform in the primary school system. It also proposed offering proper representation to parents from different backgrounds.

The Government of West Bengal has hailed the 'Pratichi Trust Education Report' of Prof. Amartya Sen and vowed to take immediate corrective actions on the following:

(i) Re-introduction of mid-day meals to encourage poor students to study and be healthy,

(ii) The improvement of infrastructure,

(iii) Drive to enrol 89 lakh children in the 5-11 age group in schools,

(iv) To set-up 9000 primary school buildings and fill around 80,000 vacant posts of primary teachers,

(v) An amount of Rs. 450 crores will be allocated to help remove inadequacies in the state delivered education system, of which 25 per cent will go towards primary school education,

(vi) Absenteeism of the teachers and students will have to be tackled.

Q.14. Production and consumption of steel in India are very poor. Why?

Ans. As far as steel production in India is concerned, its rank is 9th as compared to the following countries:

Singapore	...	1st rank
Taiwan	...	2nd rank
S. Korea	...	3rd rank
Japan	...	4th rank
Malaysia	...	5th rank
Hongkong	...	6th rank
Thailand	...	7th rank
China	...	8th rank
India	...	9th rank

This is due to the very low consumption of steel in the country. It is worthwhile to mention here that in the early 1960s production and consumption of steel in China and India were almost the same. But now India has gone down both in terms of production and consumption to sixteen times as compared to that of China. Unless the consumption of steel is increased, its production cannot be boosted. For this reason, most of the steel industries under the aegis of Steel Authority of India Ltd. of late present a dismal look.

Steel consumption will increase only when soaring prices of the steel can be arrested and kept low to match the buying capacity of the people in rural India. The prices of steel have gone high consequently reducing its consumption on account of the following reasons:

(i) The prices of raw materials of steel re-rolling mills have risen high since 1992. The main source of supply of raw material that is billet is Steel Authority of India Ltd. The price of billets in 1982 was Rs. 3,490/- per tonne. Now, the price of the same has been increased abnormally to Rs. 12,500/- per tonne.

(ii) Railway freight charges for transportation of steel are high which has led to the increase in the prices of steel.

The following actions taken by the Government will help reduce the price of steel resulting in substantial increase in its consumption *paripassu* increase in production and due to lower price of steel, export of the same could also be boosted up thereby earning more foreign exchange for making the country viable from the economic point of view:

(i) Customs duty has to be slashed down substantially on billets and other re-rollable materials from 25 per cent to 5 per cent.

(ii) Railways should allow special concessional freight charges for transportation of steel to ensure cheaper price of the same.

On account of lower prices of steel for taking the above actions an increase in housing and other construction activities in rural areas will help rise the per capita consumption of steel. Consequently, the working of the Steel Industries will also be viable.

Q.15. What are the possible reasons for the distress of the ruralites of India?

Ans. It is no doubt a happy augury that India is heading towards attaining global power in IT and other technological fields, but the superstructure should be on a sound socio-economic base. Otherwise, there is inherent danger of the collapse of this superstructure on weak foundation. India is an agro-based country. True replica of India lies in the prosperity of the ruralites who are the backbone and architects of the nation. What is distressing is that the executives at the helm of affairs of India have to all intents and purposes lost their sensitivity to feel the pulse of the countrymen. They do not want to hear the cries of the distressed who have gone emaciated due to multifarious burning problems being faced by them. Starvation and starvation deaths are still there in many parts of India although there is Green Revolution.

The reason for the starvation and starvation deaths is the overall bad planning of the executives. There is no shortage of food in the country rather it is surplus. The bungling in the Public Distribution System owes greater onus of responsibility for miserable plight of the ruralites. Huge stocks of food grains stored in the godowns of Food Corporation of India across the country are rotting, but no attention is practically being taken for proper and systematic distribution as a result of which all have not the access to food. What is the fun in telling about the achievement of Green Revolution when there are malnourished children, women and men in the villages?

Q.16. In multiple cases, Governments are employing persons on contract service for certain years rather than on regular service. What are the reasons for the same?

Ans. Fifth Pay Commission Report recommended abnormal hike in the salaries of the existing employees as also of the new recruits. Such increase in the salaries was almost three-fold than what it was before implementation of the Fifth Pay Commission Report.

This unusual spurt in the salaries and consequent impact on the payment of bonus, leave travel concession, unavailed leave salary, pension, etc. in one go has told upon the government exchequer to a very great extent. It is an admitted fact that with the increase in the salaries and the related financial implications, there has been no improvement in the work culture of the employees and on the other hand this abnormal increase in the salaries of the employees and the teachers has led to the increase in the prices of commodities because of more circulation of money in their hands. The spurt in the salaries of the government employees and the teachers has also adversely affected the standard of living of the general categories of employees working in the private sectors, as there has been no proportionate increase in their salaries and practically they are hard hit for increase in the prices of the commodities.

Consequent upon almost three-fold increase in the salaries of the government employees and the related financial implications, Government has now started experiencing extreme difficulty in making provision for mitigating such a huge wage bill, which is further precipitated when the employees are paid lacs of rupees after they are superannuated. Therefore, in order to get rid of this impasse, the Government has devised ways and means to employ persons on contract basis in many cases, as this way of recruitment of hands will not have much strains on the government exchequer. It is pertinent to mention here that the government will not have any obligation to make payment of pension to such employees including the teachers as they are not on permanent cadre. Payment of pension is a permanent liability from which the government will be exonerated. There is no denying the fact that many state governments have also colossal financial indebtedness for which they are gasping. Government, therefore, as a means to get rid of this financial crunch, has also adopted this stratagem of new recruits. Privatisation of many government organisations is also a part of this policy. By this process, the government will not have any liabilities of the employees.

Q.17. Whether India should export arms and ammunitions since huge investments in Ordnance factories are lying unutilised and are not giving returns.

Ans. Jammu & Kashmir has become the scramble for Pakistan. They have vowed to snatch the state either by cross border terrorism or by military operation against India for which they have become frantic to procure arms and ammunitions from their friendly countries. Under the circumstances, India cannot remain a silent spectator of arms build-up in Pakistan. India is five times bigger than Pakistan and in consideration of its large territory India's military strength must be at least three times bigger than Pakistan for any eventual war with Pakistan on Jammu & Kashmir and accordingly India has to prepare herself fully in defence preparedness by procuring modern warfare from her friendly countries and hence at the present situation, India cannot think of exporting arms and ammunition, although huge investments in Ordnance factories are lying unutilised and are not giving returns.

India has been fully successful in launching missiles and has become a No. 1 missile power. India is now capable to pierce missile market. The Brah-Mos (named after the Brahmaputra and Moskva rivers) is set to launch India as a player in the global missle market. The Defence Research and Development Organisation (DRDO) has begun marketing Indian missile to representatives of Asian and African countries at Defexpo-2002. Even before the exposition the DRDO has been sounding out potential buyers, among them the United Arab Emirates and Malayasia. While finalising deal in selling missile, India has to become extra-careful, making it clear that the missile is for sale only to friendly countries. It has been estimated that India's anti-ship cruise missile market will generate more than \$7 billion in revenue in the next ten-year period,

2001-2010. Hence, the extra revenue arising out of sale of cruise missile will make India very strong in South Asian countries in defence preparedness which is absolutely necessary in view of the belligerent attitude of Pakistan towards India.

Therefore, India has to export its indigenously manufactured cruise missile at the present moment and not the other arms and ammunitions.

Q.18. What is the prospect of human resource development in India?

Ans. In order to attain prosperity of a country human resource development is an absolute necessity. Development process of a country is directly interlinked with the participation of resourceful human beings. A country will go on continuing to become a developing country for considerable years if human resource is not fully developed.

Human resource development thrives mainly under three factors:

(i) Politics matter for human development because people everywhere want to be free to determine their destinies, express their views and participate in the decisions that shape their lives. It is, therefore, essential to establish democratic governance systems and expand political freedoms that advance the human development of all people. Therefore, authoritarian rule—either military, as in Pakistan or pseudo-democratic, as in Zimbabwe cannot be conducive to human development.

(ii) Economic liberalisation of people plays a vital role in shaping human resource development. If people are free from economic subjugation and have square meals a day, they can devote more fully in widening their activities without any scarce and anxieties and these activities conduce them to attain human development. Optimistic estimates suggest that 3.7 per cent annual growth in per capita incomes is needed in developing countries.

(iii) Spread of mass education is also an important element for attaining human resource development. Dissemination of primary education every nook and corner of the country as well as gender equity in access to education is a first step to develop human resource.

In view of the above factors which are the main conditions of human resource development of a country, analyses will reveal how far India has been successful in human resource development.

As far as democratisation of India is concerned, the country is very much congenial for human resource development, as India is the largest democratic country in the world where people are free to determine their destinies, express their views and participate in the decisions that shape their lives.

With regard to economic liberalisation and primary education, India has yet to go a long way in brining overall economic solvency and spreading primary education amongst the ruralites. While the Government of India has already taken these two aspects on national level and when the objectives will be fulfilled, it will be an easy task for the Government to develop human resource throughout the length and breadth of the country.

Q.19. What is the fate of the educated adolescents of India stored for them in future?

Ans. Growth of population is a continuous phenomenon. The year, 2020 has been set to develop India fully, when the total population of India is estimated to be at least one hundred and thirty crores. Real development of a country is reflected by the increase in the per capita income of the people with the industrialisation of the country and flourishing of trade and business, which lead to slashing down of the unemployment problem, thus arresting restlessness amongst the general category of the educated adolescents in particular.

Although India has become one of the tenth industrialised countries of the world, yet it has failed to contain unemployment problem in the country. General categories of the educated adolescents of the country, which are inflating year after year are far in excess of requirement in respect of their absorbility in organisations and the problem of unemployment is being accentuated alarmingly by way of closure of establishments, execution of Voluntary Retirement Scheme, lay-offs and closure of the door of employment. When the already employed persons are denied employment by way of enforcement of Voluntary Retirement Scheme on them, their sons and daughters are still in the making while continuing their studies in schools and colleges in most of the cases.

This sudden taboo in their employment creates far-reaching adverse effects in the minds of the growing up sons and daughters who lose interest in moulding their career thinking that they have also no assured future even when the country is set to develop by the year, 2020 and, therefore, the alienation between the country and its growing population will continue to persist.

Under the circumstances, the educated adolescents who are the future of the nation will remain unutilised and in such case human resource development will be infructuous. Unemployment of these educated adolescents will also pose social disorder as also the educated young girls will find difficulty to get suitable partners in the field of marriage, as the well-settled educated young boys will be few and far between virtually for want of employment and in such case both the educated boys and girls will be advancing in their age without getting married in most of the cases and the result, as is known, will be disastrous posing incurable social problems.

Another important fact is that the haves and have-nots will continue to widen for rising unemployment problem in the country and it will naturally axe on the country's real development. Therefore, the top-most priority of the government must be to take measures to contain unemployment problem in the interest of the real development of the country by the year, 2020.

Q.20. What is the dispute between Karnataka and Tamil Nadu arising out of sharing of water from Cauvery?

Ans. Sharing of water from Cauvery river has been continuing to become a long standing dispute between Karnataka and Tamil Nadu. Requirement of water by both states has no doubt increased consequent upon bringing more land under cultivation by deforestation. Accordingly, sharing of water by the two states from Cauvery river on increased scale has posed a problem, because it has gone beyond the capacity of the river to meet the requirements except during rainy season.

In the first week of September, 2002, Supreme Court had asked Karnataka to release 1.25 tmcft. (thousand million cubic feet) of water per day to Tamil Nadu till the Cauvery River Authority decided on a distress sharing formula, which they slashed to 0.8 tmcft per day subsequently. Supply of this reduced quantum of water as decided by the Cauvery River Authority irked Tamil Nadu Government under the Chief Ministership of J. Jayalalitha, who again went to the Supreme Court with the Cauvery dispute and asked them to issue show cause notice to Karnataka Government for the contravention of the Supreme Court directive to release required quantity of water to Tamil Nadu. In the earlier regime of Jayalalitha also, the Apex Court forced Karnataka to release stipulated quantum of water to Tamil Nadu.

It was observed that the directives of the Supreme Court in this direction time and again could not solve the problem of Cauvery water dispute on permanent basis. In order, therefore, to solve the dispute once and for all, both the states should consider as follows and then only durable solution to the problem would be a possibility:

(a) In consideration to the limited capacity of the Cauvery river to meet the requirements of water, both Karnataka and Tamil Nadu should opt to the crops like cotton, fruits, pulses, millets and oil seeds which do not require much water, in the Cauvery river basin.

(b) Another most feasible solution lies in the fact that while Tamil Nadu gets monsoon twice every year, there must be arrangement to preserve more water during the rainy season by making water reservoirs and this water could be properly utilised during dry season, when the Karnataka Government would not be in a position to release the required quantum of water from Cauvery to Tamil Nadu.

The above pragmatic considerations are very important to arrive at a durable solution to the Cauvery dispute between Karnataka and Tamil Nadu instead of enkindling the problem from the political point of view as also moving to the Supreme Court every now and then.

Q.21. We are now in the 21st century. When the whole world is poised for all-round developments what are the components which we require most to keep pace with the developments and prosperity of our country?

Ans. Ours is a very big country with bounties of resources. With such rich and abundant storage our country can march forward to all-round developments and prosperity in the not too distant future if we pursue the steps such as:

(a) There should not be political wranglings. The policies of the government should be corrected, if wrongs are there, through constructive criticism. No political party should think of toppling the government which is installed for a full term of five years. The citizens should also not be misled by violent criticisms by other political parties for their partisan interests.

(b) Population control is a dire necessity through strong family planning programme so that the majority of the population can become the assets of the country rather than wastage and can be put to use for developments of the country.

(c) People should have nationalistic spirit as well as they should have feelings of brotherhood and fraternity. There should be cooperation amongst the people. Selfishness is a bane which should be shunned. Arrogant and unparliamentary behaviour should not be resorted to at any point of time.

(d) Education should be disseminated every nook and corner of the country, so that the people at large can develop their mental faculty and understanding capacity.

(e) Through moratorium there should not be gheraos, strikes, lock-outs and bundh in the country, so that congenial industrial climate is maintained.

(f) In an agro-based country like India priority should be given for rural development.

These are the principal ingredients which will help the country march forward to the path of rapid development and prosperity.

Q.22. In what way has terrorism become rampant in India and what consequences have India been facing out of it?

Ans. Terrorism is a stigma and a menace posing global threat. Terrorism is an instrument to wreck destruction in a clandestine method and is distinctive than that of a declared war. When war breaks out it entails heavy expenses by way of cost of fuel for mobility of tanks, war planes and other military vehicles, loss of war equipment as also army and increase in the price of food-stuff affecting the populace of the country. Also when war breaks out, country's development process is halted. The sequel to the war is impoverishment and deceleration of the countries involved in war for another 15/20 years and the innocent people have to bear the brunt of fury of war causing destruction all around. But, all these things are conspicuous by its absence in the case of terrorism. In another form terrorism is an undeclared war wrecking havoc and destruction to men and property virtually without incurring any expenditure by the country fomenting terrorism and this war continues unabated for years together. Thus, terrorism is the cheapest way of wrecking havoc to a country.

India has become the victim of terrorism and it has posed a challenge to the country. Pakistan was the epi-centre and hot-bed of terrorism. When Kashmir could not be acceded to by Pakistan despite waging four wars with India and also by not getting support of foreign powers in the matter of Kashmir issue, Pakistan embarked upon a stratagem of fomenting terrorism in India by patronising the terrorist outfits such as — Al-Qaida, Jaish-e-Mohammad, Lashker-e-Toiba and Hizbul Mujahideen.

While the main target of terrorism was Jammu and Kashmir as also western parts of India including Delhi, it spread other parts of India and also lately its eastern part too through Bangladesh where I.S.I. and Al-Qaida raised their heads. Series of terrorist activities in India were clear testimony that India has to be weakened and tortured by suspense and anxiety, so that its developmental activities are derailed and the commitment of India is not implemented to become one of the world powers swaying suzerainty over its neighbouring countries of Asia. Most unfortunately, the United States of America committing to stamp out terrorism internationally after the demolition of world Trade Center and Pentagon in New York and Washington respectively on 11th September, 2001 have shown disinclination to quell terrorism in India as a result of which Pakistan being their best ally got fresh impetus to wreck destruction in India through terrorist outfits operated from their soil and patronised by them.

India has been emboldened to crush terrorism with an iron hand and is committed to march forward undeterred to its destination of becoming one of the powerful states of the world notwithstanding the ineffectual attempts made by one of its neighbouring countries to destabilise the state.

Q.23. The exalted vision of Dr. A.P.J. Abdul Kalam, President of India was to make India a prosperous country by the year, 2020. What were the objectives needed for attaining this goal, as announced by the President on the 54th Republic Day-eve address to the nation?

Ans. When the foundation of a country's democracy is strong and deep-rooted, it is not unthinkable and an impossibility on the part of that country to attain prosperity in the future years to come. It is no doubt applicable to India when it was proved to the world once again after the Jammu and Kashmir as also Gujarat elections. The President called upon the following objectives for implementation to attain all-round prosperity by India by the year, 2020:

(a) The President urged the nation to put together again a second green revolution to increase agricultural yield similar to that of 1960s. On the basis of ever increasing population in this country, this green revolution has to attain target of 30-crore tonnes of food grains. Achievement of this target is no doubt a challenge particularly when the agricultural arable land for food production would be reduced to 10-crore hectares from 17-crore hectares due to pressure of increasing population and construction of houses for dwelling purpose.

(b) In his vision of India, Dr. Kalam called for a 'mega mission' to reach the urban ameneties to rural areas. This would require connectivity at the level of physical infrastructure, roads and communication networks.

(c) The students have to go on literacy mission as also the government should upgrade the small-scale industries technologically.

(d) India has to face the challenge in the context of continued degradation of the environment and pressures of increasing population on the land.

(e) The President urged the nation to take the light of progress to the teeming villages throughout the country.

(f) The defence scientists have to prove their excellence further by increasing the nation's defence capabilities with electronic warfare skills.

Q.24. What are the impediments for the speedy development of India?

Ans. Admittedly, India is pregnant with resources. Still then the sluggish development of the country holds the onus of responsibility for the following reasons, in particular:

(i) Seventy per cent of the total population of India are ruralites. Light of education has not practically impregnated in the remote villages and the lack of education is the stumbling block of speedy development of the country.

(ii) There is no check in the growth of population amongst the village people. Villagers have still nurtured the idea that multiplicity of children is the benediction of God. This idea of theirs is due to lack of education. Multitudinous people is the cause of derailment in the speedy growth of India.

(iii) Country's speedy development largely depends upon availability of oil of its own of which India is suffering from bereavement. This has resulted in the importation of oil from other countries to meet up its requirement, amounting to Rs. 80,000/- crores per year.

(iv) Huge amount of money is squandered for defence preparedness at the cost of speedy development of the country, arising out of the bellicose attitude of the neighbouring country.

(v) The wars with Pakistan in the years, 1965, 1971 and 1999 in particular had an impact on the economy of India leading to sluggishness in the development of the country.

(vi) Terrorism has become wide-spread in the country which is responsible for the reversal of country's speedy development.

(vii) Illegal infiltration to the tune of 20 million people from the then East Pakistan and Bangladesh has told upon the economy mainly of the country's eastern states which is one of the reasons for retardation of India's speedy development.

(viii) India is the largest democratic country in the world consisting of 28 states. Huge amount of money is spent in holding assembly as also general elections almost every year on successive stages thus creating impacts on the economy of the country.

(ix) Patriotism is almost in extinction from many of the Indian citizens. They are mostly found self-centered in their self-aggrandisement at the cost of country's speedy development.

(x) Lust for power by the political parties as also recrimination and wrangling in intra-party levels are upsetting rapid development.

(xi) Subsidy granted by the government for a number of items is affecting the exchequer.

(xii) Repayment of huge loans taken from the International Monetary Fund and World Bank is causing reversal of country's speedy development.

(xiii) Government has to spend huge amount of money arising out of the devastations caused due to vagaries of nature such as floods, cyclones and drought.

(xiv) Criminal background as well as dishonesty and corruption which have become the life-blood of many are the steps in the back foot of country's speedy development.

(xv) Extravagance in the expenses of government departments is causing rift in the exchequer.

(xvi) Thefts are taking place in bulk in many government organisations such as Railways, Octroi, Narcotics, construction departments, etc.

(xvii) There is the theft of electricity to the tune of Rs. 25,000/- crores per year.

(xviii) Thousands of crores of rupees advanced to the entrepreneurs by the banks have been lying unrealised for years together as a result of which speedy development of the country could not be undertaken for non-availability of funds for its remaining out of circulation.

(xix) The scams and frauds taken place in Unit Trust of India to the tune of thousands of crores of rupees have rebuffed the speedy development of the country.

Notwithstanding all these constraints India's development so far achieved is no doubt spectacular, India has committed to implement its pledge to become a prosperous state by the year, 2020.

Q.25. Admission of foreign students to Indian Universities is showing downward trend rapidly. What steps are to be taken to lure large number of foreign students for admission to the Universities?

Ans. The Ministry of Higher Education of the Government of India is very much concerned at the sharp decline in the number of foreign students enrolling in Indian Universities from 11,888 in 1995 to 6,988 students in 2000 with a steady fall in the inflow from neighbouring countries like Bangladesh and Nepal. This indicates that in a span of five years the number of foreign students getting admitted in Indian Universities was almost reduced to half. The fall in numbers could be ascribed to the laxity in transmitting abroad the educational facilities available in Indian Universities.

Apart from the already available facilities in the Indian Universities, following steps have to be taken to lure the foreign students for admission to the Indian Universities in large number:

(a) The course of study should be updated and diversified.

(b) The admission process should be streamlined to remove all bureaucratic hurdles in the process of admission.

(c) There should be short-duration courses on India's rich culture and tradition, history, folk arts, music, temple architecture and philosophy and these should be called "Study India Programmes".

(d) There should be single window system for admission of foreign students for creating a hassle-free environment.

(e) The present system is that the foreign scholars have to seek clearance from the Home Ministry for doing research on "sensitive topics", which should be done away with.

(f) The Central Government has to work out a system of helping foreign post-graduate students and research scholars from the University Grant Commission.

Q.26. If the major rivers of India are linked up by the year, 2012 as proposed by the NDA government, what would be the consequences?

Ans. The ambitious project of linkage of major rivers of India was mooted out by the President, A.P.J. Abdul Kalam in August, 2002 and endorsed by the Supreme Court of India through an interim order. Following the order of Apex court, the Vajpayee government considered to take up the project with all seriousness for linkage of all major rivers in the country by the year, 2012 at an expenditure of Rs. 560,000 crores. If this ambitious project is translated into reality, the following consequences are bound to come up which would not, of course, be beneficial for the country, as a whole:

(a) Diverting the courses of rivers would destabilise the Ganges and Brahmaputra river systems that carry over 60 per cent of India's water resources. If the Ganges is diverted near Patna, it would dry up the lower basin and lead to a drought like situation in West Bengal and the Kolkata port will have to pay a heavy price for the same,

(b) The project if implemented is bound to fail

because of the country's difficult topography. The Deccan plateau is nearly 2000 feet above the Gangetic plain and hence it will require substantial power to pump up water from north to south.

(c) In the process of linkage of the rivers thousands of villages will have to be evacuated and millions of people will be displaced.

(d) Realignment of rivers would lead to ecological disaster as it will disturb the natural flow of rivers and affect the ecosystem causing sedimentation and erosion. Apart from this, the base water level would be substantially lowered.

(e) Networking system of the major rivers would lead to large-scale wastage of water with only 40 per cent of the water meeting the requirement.

(f) Linkage of rivers will foment international discontent and outrage, as the sources of the major rivers are not from India. Pakistan shares the Indus, Bangladesh and Nepal share the Ganges and Bhutan, China and Bangladesh share the Brahmaputra. Therefore, in the event of networking of such rivers, these countries will be affected very much which will be antagonistic to international convention.

Q.27. In what way V.R.S. can be made ineffective for the purpose of solving unemployment problem amongst the educated unemployed adolescents seeking general category of employment?

Ans. Application of V.R.S. has no doubt precipitated unemployment problem in the country and added fuel to the fire especially when the educated youths are already groaning under the pangs of unemployment problem. This has obviously resulted in destabilising the social order, as the educated adolescents being frustrated for remaining unemployed for unnamed period of years have become obstinate and restless and this restlessness is the rhyme and reason of derailing social order.

Problem of unemployment exists mostly amongst the educated people after completing their academic education from colleges and universities. These educated adolescents are questing general category of employment in great majority of cases. In order, therefore, to ease unemployment problem among such candidates, retirement age of the working employees of such categories has to be slashed down to 55 years and accordingly V.R.S. should not be made applicable in their case, thus avoiding payment of extra amount for dispensing with their services under V.R.S. By this way, the new generation can conveniently expect to get berth in the Organisations against the vacancies created due to leaving of the employees on superannuation at 55.

As far as the other categories of employees are concerned, who are in managerial and technical position and also whose services are considered essential in accordance with the nature of job performed by them, superannuation age of such employees should continue to remain at 60 years, as the Organisations need such employees for effective running of the same for all times. The employees who would be elevated to the managerial position or the like by virtue of their outstanding calibre and performance in the discharge of their duties should be superannuated at 60 years.

Under the present situation of acute unemployment problem in the country there is no wrong to have two classifications of superannuation age—one 55 years and the other 60 years in the light of what has been discussed in the foregoing. If it could be adhered to strictly, unemployment problem amongst the educated adolescents, who could not further their education to qualify themselves technically or the like other than acquiring academic qualifications only, could be solved to a great extent which is the crying need of the day and also V.R.S. could be made ineffective and infructuous which is also of paramount importance in order to avoid payment of extra amount by the

Organisations for dispensing with the services of the employees under V.R.S.

It is, however, recommended that superannuation age at 55 years for the employees other than the special categories of employees, as discussed above, should be introduced initially for five years to gauge its practical applicability.

Q.28. What is the picture of rural India with regard to education, health and sanitation?

Ans. Notwithstanding customary rhetoric from successive governments, progress in rural India in the fields of education, health and sanitation has been abysmally poor. Surveys show that one in three children does not attend school. Even many of the children discontinue studies before completing primary education. The situation becomes more depressing when it is realised that the low average level of performance coexists with a great deal of disparity within the country. For instance, the literacy rate in Bihar and Rajasthan in the early Nineties was below 40 per cent which was significantly below the average figure for the category of "low human development" countries.

The highest infant mortality rate amongst states in India is rural Orissa where it is 120 per 1000 live births. Madhya Pradesh stands second with 111 deaths per 1000 live births.

As far as sanitation in rural areas is concerned, almost half the rural population does not have access to safe drinking water. Uttar Pradesh has roughly 25 hospital beds per million persons in the rural sector, while Kerala has as many as 1768 hospital beds per million persons in the rural sector.

Both education and health are "state subjects". Hence, it is the state governments which have to take the initiative in these areas for amelioration. Since all state governments are facing severe budgetary constraints, the task ahead does not seem to be cosy. It is, however, recommended that at this stage when there is the financial crunch being faced by the state governments, it is imperative to divert some expenditure from higher education to primary education. Similarly, preventive health care deserves far greater attention that it has received so far.

Q.29. How are the innocent and ignorant people of India beguiled in the name of religion?

Ans. God is a source through which one achieves peace of mind. Service to mankind is service to God. Adherence to religion no doubt regulates disciplined way of lives of the people, yet it is not the be all and end all. Success of things is not purely due to adherence to religion; it depends mainly on practicalities. From the practical point of view, it has been widely observed that things are not achieved even with full devotion to God in all the cases. The following examples will prove the facts:

(i) Yagyas and Pujas were performed at several places spending thousands of rupees praying for India's victory in the final world cup cricket. But, most unfortunately even after receiving Pujas, God was not kind enough to make Indian cricket team crowned with victory to win the world cup.

(ii) At Guwahati's Kamakhya temple, the seat of the tantrik cult in the country, on 13th June, 2003 a man tried to sacrifice his 18-month-old daughter by slitting her throat. His conception was that sacrificing his daughter would prompt the deity to bestow him with divine power. This ritual is nothing but an anathema.

(iii) For winning Gujarat election held in the month of November-December, 2002, the Congress party started their poll campaign by offering prayers at temples. But, contrary to this Bharatiya Janata Party sweeped the poll.

(iv) India is the only country in the world, where people are contributing lavishly towards subscriptions for performing religious rites and functions with pomp and grandeur, but with no bounties from God in return.

(v) Cases are plenty that Maharajas of a number of 'Ashrams' are making false predictions and the people believing in them are spending substantial amount of money as donations with the ultimate purpose of attaining their future prosperity, but in practice it is not translated into a reality in most of the cases.

(vi) Feng Shui is another artifice in the name of God to beguile the weak minded people to win prosperity in life.

(vii) Saints are abound who are impressing upon people to have faith in them, thus squeezing money from them with no practical benefit.

(viii) In the remote villages where the people are the staunch believers in God, the following are the instances how they are beguiled in the name of religion.

Patients needing medicines are given fake tablets on the first day with the advice to swallow after praying to God for curing their disease. But, there is no effect. On the second day another patients are given similar tablets with the advice to swallow after praying to Allah, but to no effect. On the third day the other patients are provided with real medicines with the advice to swallow after offering prayer to Jesus. This time the medicines work wonders. The awestruck villagers are then told that Gods and Allah are not as powerful as Jesus. This way the innocent and ignorant people of India are beguiled in the name of God.

The above are the concrete instances as to how the people are motivated towards God blindly. It is an admitted fact that God is omnipotent. The crux of the question is that for attaining success people themselves have to work hard and failures should not deject them. Man is the architect of his own fate. God helps those who help themselves. Dependence on God without doing work will not help the purpose. India is of course a religious country and the religion must be subservient to the deeds and actions of the people and then only the country can reach the goal of prosperity.

Q.30. What were the recommendations of the Justice, V.C. Malimath, former Supreme Court Judge, suggesting sweeping changes in the country's criminal laws (Criminal Procedure Code) in particular?

Ans. The Malimath Committee, which was originally constituted on 24th November, 2000, named after Justice V.C. Malimath, former Supreme Court Judge, suggested amendments to Section 125 of the Criminal Procedure Code among others which were submitted to the Union Home Ministry on April 21, 2003, for adoption. The changes were proposed for the first time in 150 years. The Malimath Committee recommended that from now on, criminal laws were to be reviewed every 15 years so that they were in tune with the changes of time. The following were the recommendations:

(i) The existing criminal justice system was inefficient and ineffective due to which people were losing confidence in the system. The Committee, therefore, recommended that evidence recorded on video and audio tapes before a police officer of the rank of a Superintendent of Police should be admitted as evidence in the court. This would convince the Magistrate that the confession of the person was not taken under threat and duress.

(ii) The Committee sought amendment to Section 25 of the Evidence Act to enable audio-video recordings of confessions before an officer of the rank of Superintendent of Police.

(iii) A women living with a man like his wife for a reasonably long period was entitled to the benefit of her maintenance by the man including her children, if any, as illegal wife and illegitimate children.

(iv) On the law for rape, the Committee prescribed that non-penile penetration should be construed to constitute an offence along with lines of rape. The Justice Malimath Committee, however, recommended that there should not be death penalty for rape, but life imprisonment, without commutation or remission.

(v) The Committee recommended that a "Serious Fraud Office" should be set up by an Act of Parliament with the creation of a body such as the Asset Recovery Agency to deal with economic crimes. The Serious Fraud Office should be given adequate power to investigate and launch prosecution into such cases with utmost speed.

(vi) The Malimath Committee recommended segregation of the investigating wing of the police from law and order functions. Also in order to cut off from political or other influences to ensure fair treatment to the investigating officers, the Committee recommended the formation of a National Security Commission.

(vii) A new police Act was recommended by the Committee to set up an "Apex Criminal Intelligence Bureau" that would help in collection, collation and dissemination of criminal intelligence.

(viii) The Committee recommended that offences of cruelty by a husband or his relatives on his wife should be bailable.

Q.31. What have you to say about the education policy of the government of India?

Ans. The existing education policy as per government's own statement has not fulfilled the purposes for which it was drawn up. It would, therefore, be in the fitness of things that the entire concept of education should be analysed afresh. What is needed most is that education should be conceived as part of developmental process of the country rather than regarded as part of social service. In this context, I emphasise the need for development of education on the lines of Mahatma Gandhi's Wardha Scheme of Basic Education under which the children undergoing training would learn their handiwork side by side, so that they could be trained in their own line through practical application. This system has the advantage of encouraging creativity amongst children, generation of new ideas and give them self-confidence in their field. I am not of course suggesting that the higher education based on research and development and computer technology should be discouraged. They should be there so that we do not lag behind in technological and scientific advancement. Keeping in view that India is an agro-based country and 75 per cent of the total population is living in rural India, the government has to take care of mass education combined with training in some rural technology so that the ruralites could earn money in the villages itself without thinking of flocking to the cities to earn their livelihood. While unemployment is of vast magnitude and it is extremely acute in the rural sector, the government should devote its utmost attention to develop the rural industry, particularly the agro-based industries, food processing industries, manufacturing industries such as soap and house construction with the available local resources.

Therefore, the entire education system should be restructured taking into account the pragmatic view of acute unemployment problem facing the country—both in the urban and rural areas.

Q.32. Is it correct that too much of holidays/leave enjoyed by the employees are recommended particularly when India is poised for all-round development?

Ans. When we turn our attention to the developed countries of the world, it is observed that the employees working in the Organisations—both government and private, are not entitled to enjoy too much of holidays/leave. They believe in the maxim, "Work is Workship" and this was the reason as to why such countries progressed by leaps and bounds on account of increased output of work and consequently the productivity due to longer working of the employees during the year.

Contrary to this, Indian employees working in the government establishments are enjoying holidays/leave for 201 days and work for only 164 days per year, as per the under-noted details:

(a)	Medical leave	...	20 days
(b)	Earned leave	...	30 days
(c)	Casual leave	...	8 days
(d)	Restricted holidays	...	2 days
(e)	Half Pay leave	...	20 days
(f)	National/Festival holidays	...	17 days
(g)	Holidays on Saturdays and Sundays	...	104 days
		Total:	201 days

Added to the 201 holidays for the government employees, there are also *bandhs*, strikes, pen-down agitations and several other factors of striking work. Nowhere in the world do the government employees have so much of leave.

By contrast to the above leave/holidays enjoyed by the government employees, the employees working in private organisations are enjoying holidays/leave for 176 days and work for 189 days per year.

It is pertinent to mention that most of the ministerial staff members working in government establishments do not generally put in full time in discharging their duties during their working hours. When this is the work culture and colossal waste of man hours the Utopian scheme as announced by the President of India to make India a prosperous country by the year, 2020 will be set at naught. India should take a lesson from Saudi Arabia, which sanctions only a two-and-a-half hour holiday on the death of the monarch.

Now, what is needed most at this hour of need is to

scale down holidays/leave for the employees working in organisations for increased output of work and consequently the productivity to hasten the country to the path of all-round development and prosperity. In this connexion, the union leaders have to play a pivotal role.

Q.33. What is the effect of V.R.S.?

Ans. Application of VRS is a pointer to the fact that the organisation has ceased to look up, for which it has been felt an absolute necessity to downsize the staff strength to arrest further financial debilitation in the organisation.

The adolescents in large number after passing the college examinations find the doors of employment virtually closed and in consequence they are very much down-hearted seeing practically no future for them and finding no other way out they have to become parasites on their parents who can also ill-afford to sustain their grown up and educated sons and daughters, as their fathers have been rendered unemployed due to premature retirement from service on VRS. When many industrial establishments are being closed down, application of VRS at the same time is another way of accentuating deterioration in the situation.

Since the employment scenario is becoming drowsy because of the above two reasons, the educated girls are also debarred from getting suitable partners for marriage and this results in heightening of the marriageable age of the girls and at times it poses a great problem to give the daughters in marriage at increased age in majority of the cases.

Another disquieting feature is that the bank interest rate has been slashed down to bare minimum and also is in the process of slashing down further. Therefore, the invested amount so received by way of VRS is attracting very negligible amount of interest which is hardly sufficient to defray the expenses with unemployed and unmarried sons and daughters in the families owing to high cost of living. In order, therefore, to meet up the family expenses the principal amount deposited with the bank on being retired prematurely from service due to VRS is gradually eroded from the balance and in consequence the middle class people are becoming impoverished with no other source of income.

When the negotiated marriage of the daughters are settled even at a later date, the VRS amount so received at the prime age of the employees is mostly spent in marriage as a result of which the financial condition of the families is debilitated again. If the services of the employees would not have been dispensed with on VRS, such awkward situation would not have cropped up.

Situation is destined to be more critical in future years to come with the growth of population and this will be a staggering blow to the process of development of the country. The immediate solution to the problem is to check growth of population which should be brought down to 1 per cent at the maximum at any cost by adopting stringent measures as in the case of China, taking into account that life span of human beings has increased. For this purpose, family planning programme has to be geared up especially amongst the village people who are still allergic to the control of growth of population because of their lack of education. There should also be rationalisation in the application of VRS which is the source of evil. It is, however, a happy augury that notwithstanding constraints being faced by India in number of cases, India has been marching forward steadily to achieve economic reforms in the not too distant future.

Q.34. The rate of absenteeism in employment in India is comparatively more than that of other developed and developing countries of the world. What are the reasons for the same and what steps are to be taken?

Ans. One of the biggest stumbling blocks facing Indian industries is absenteeism resorted to by the employees.

When the sales and profits are under tremendous pressure, increase in the productivity is the only answer to the problem, which is possible when the rate of absenteeism is curtailed. Economy of the countries like Britain, the United States of America and Japan, in particular is no doubt stimulating which has been made possible because the employees there work very long hours having fewer holidays. This has resulted in heightening of productivity.

The rate of absenteeism amongst the Indian employees is more because of the following reasons:

(a) Female participation in the workforce adds to the absenteeism because of their commitments to childcare and house-hold tasks. They have also to avail of maternity benefits.

(b) Availing of E.S.I., leave for longer days by influencing the E.S.I., doctors, results in absenteeism of the employees covered under E.S.I. scheme.

(c) It has become the experience that employees in the tropical countries indulge in absenteeism from work.

(d) Fraying of the bond between the employers and the employees means that staff have less loyalty towards their employers and hence they do not feel involved very much in the working and this tends them to remain absent from duties every now and then.

(e) Poor working condition at the work place leads to absenteeism by the employees.

(f) Strikes and *bundhs* are the reasons for absenteeism from work.

(g) Availing of too much of leave and holidays is the cause of absenteeism.

In order to remedy the above maladies, the steps are to be taken as follows:

(i) Amendment must be made in the Employees State Insurance Scheme so that the employees are not inclined to take more E.S.I. leave unnecessarily even if they are fit to work.

(ii) Congenial working atmosphere as also sweet employer-employee relations are to be maintained. Generous labour welfare schemes are to be introduced.

(iii) It should be considered to introduce attendance bonus to induce the employees to cut absenteeism.

(iv) There should be selective posts in which female employees are to be engaged so that their absenteeism from duty does not have much of serious impact and consequently affect productivity.

(v) Leave rules should be amended as also number of national/festival holidays are to be curtailed.

(vi) Strikes and bundhs are to be done away with, which in other ways means financial loss to the enterprises to the extent of crores of rupees.

For the purpose of successful implementation of the steps to be taken under serial Nos. (v) and (vi) above, it is of paramount necessity to take into confidence of the trade union leaders.

Q.35. India is a unity in diversity. How could it be explained?

Ans. India is a miniature world where heterogeneous people with different languages, religions, culture, dresses, food habits and ways of living have been dwelling in different states which are not akin to one another. Notwithstanding the above differences, India is one under the hegemony of federal government at the centre. Needless to emphasise unity in India will be strengthened further when there will be no wrangling between one state and the other and the people forget the barriers of provinces. We have only one identity that irrespective of all differences we are all Indians.

Dr. A.P.J. Abdul Kalam, President of India mentioned, "Whenever I look at the map of India I always feel that the railways have been able to network this vast country in such a manner that the whole country is united by these lines. It is a wonder of technology and human effort."

Since India is united in spite of heterogeneity, there is free movement of people throughout the length and breadth of the country in quest of employment and settling down for their living in different states amongst multitudinous people.

That India is united is also proved by the fact that the following fundamental rights have been guaranteed by the Constitution of India:

(i) Right to Equality,

(ii) Right to Freedom,

(iii) Right against Exploitation,

(iv) Right to Freedom of Religion,

(v) Right to Constitutional Remedies,

(vi) Cultural and Educational Right.

It is poignant to observe that certain states are not friendly in settling disputes amicably. This proves diversity in their attitude which is averse to unity of the country. The following examples will reveal the fact:

(i) Cauveri water dispute between Karnataka and Tamil Nadu, Narmada Bachao Andolan in respect of sharing of water between Madhya Pradesh and Gujarat as also non-supply of water through canal to Haryana by the Punjab government are the glaring examples of non-cooperation between states, which of course does not augur well for the unity of the country. There must be rational views in sorting out water disputes between states.

(ii) When Hindi is a national language of the country, people of the southern states like Tamil Nadu should not have any reservation to accept this language as the national language of the country. This speaks animosity towards the language which has been accepted by other states as the national language of India. This also goes against the unity of the country.

(iii) In order to preserve the unity of the country there should not have been agitation in the matter of bifurcation of Eastern Railway especially when the Railways are the main channel of communication throughout the length and breadth of the country.

When the great country like India is a unity in diversity, all the differences must die down as India has already projected itself homogeneous.

Q.36. What is the integrated action required to make India fully developed by the year, 2020?

Ans. It was the vision of the President, Dr. A.P.J. Abdul Kalam that India would be made a fully developed and prosperous country by the year, 2020. Apart from his vision, Shri Atal Bihari Vajpayee, the then Prime Minister of India also in his Independence Day address from the Red Fort on August 15, 2002 declared that India would become a developed nation by 2020.

In order to translate the vision of both President and Prime Minister into reality, the following five key areas have been identified for an integrated action:

(a) Infrastructure development including reliable and quality electric power for all parts of the country, which is vital for all core sectors.

(b) Information and communications technology—this is one of the core competencies, promoting education in remote areas and creating massive employment and national wealth through export earning.

(c) Agriculture and food processing with a target of 360 million tonnes of food and agricultural products in a year. Other areas of agriculture and agro-food processing will bring food security and prosperity to rural people and speed up economic growth.

(d) Critical technologies and strategic industries—the progress in nuclear, space and defence technologies will provide sustained growth and self-reliance for the nation and

(e) Education and health-care aimed at increasing the employment potential leading to social security and population control.

These five areas are closely interrelated and will lead to national, food and economic security.

Q.37. In what way the Bush administration realised that India is truly an effective ally and not Pakistan in the matter of combating terrorism?

Ans. The United States of America came to realise the impact and horror of terrorism only when there were the terrorist attacks on their own soil on 11th September, 2001 at New York and Washington *i.e.*, the attacks on World Trade Center and Pentagon. When these attacks were the handiwork of Al-Qaida of Osama-bin-Laden, duly supported by the Taliban government in Afghanistan, Bush administration embraced Pervez Musharraf of Pakistan as their best ally in the campaign against terrorism in preference to India in spite of its being the constant target of Pakistan sponsored terrorist attacks.

But as time passed and the Americans were unable to apprehend many terrorists under the leadership of Al-Qaida or the Taliban, they started taking a serious look at inputs coming from the Government of India. In time, the Bush administration realised that many of the harrowing tale of terrorism the Indians were telling the Federal Bureau of Investigation (FBI) and other agencies were indeed coming true. The Government of India has given the American government dossiers on how Pakistan has become a haven for terrorists. American government was also made aware of how 183 terrorist cells across India had been shattered by the BJP-led government apart from successfully putting an end to the exfiltration of subversives.

Bush administration has now realised that India has been far more successful than the United States of America in fighting terrorism by taking draconian measures and that the dossiers furnished by India are being taken for their real worth in the fight against terrorism.

In view of the above facts, it has been substantiated that India is actually a powerful ally and not Pakistan in the Bush administration whose role will be vital to India's fight against terrorism.

7

Industrial and Financial Topics

Q.1. In what way India was affected financially on account of American war on terrorism?

Ans. India has become a victim of terrorism for the last more than one decade. The terrorist outfits which have been operating in India are from the Organisations, such as Lashker-e-Toiba, Jaish-e-Mohammad and Al-Qaida originating from Afghanistan nurtured by erstwhile Taliban Government. All these organisations have become very much active in collusion with ISI supported by the Government of Pakistan. These terrorists have been continuing to get their constant training in occupied Kashmir (Azad Kashmir) with full backing from the Government of Pakistan. The hijacking of Indian Aircraft—IC: 814 from its flight from Kathmandu on 24th December, 1999 with the avowed intention of compelling Government of India to release three hard-core Kashmiri militants including Maulana Masood Azhar who was the architect of the formation of the terrorist organisation in the name of Jaish-e-Mohammad after his release from detention under Indian custody when the terms of the air pirates hijacking the Indian plane were met with by the Government of India, attack on Assembly House of Jammu & Kashmir on 1st October, 2001 and the dreadful attack on Indian Parliament which is the citadel of Indian democracy by the Pakistani sponsored terrorists on 13th December, 2001 are the glaring examples of the dreadful, heinous and nefarious acts of terrorists operating from Pakistan. United States of America was fully aware of that the hijacking of Indian Airline flight to Kandahar was the handiwork of Taliban and Pakistan.

India has been raising the issue of fighting terrorism with iron hand and sought the help of the U.S. Government in this direction; but the U.S.A. closed its eyes to the terrorist activities operating in India which were of little interest to them, as they were not affected in such terrorism going on in India. Instead of taking any concrete step to quell terrorism going on in Indian sub-continent they simply showed lip sympathy and urged India to have patience when India was bent upon taking drastic action against Pakistan sponsored terrorism after the attack on Indian Parliament. The U.S.A. probably thought that India and Jammu and Kashmir are far away and that they (U.S.A.) will be safe from the attack of terrorists on their soil. But, they should bear in mind that terrorism does not recognise any barrier and distance which was proved by the fact when the World Trade Center and Pentagon in New York and Washington respectively were attacked by the terrorists with the machination of Osama-bin-Laden of Al-Qaida from the soil of Afghanistan under Taliban Government.

United States of America than came to sense and realised that terrorism is a global menace and resolved to wage war against the Taliban Government of Afghanistan to catch hold of dreaded terrorist, Osama-bin-Laden—either dead or alive. The Anglo-American bombardment on Afghanistan began on 7th October, 2001 at 10.00 P.M. (Indian Standard Time) taking Pakistan's help in the hunt for Osama-bin-Laden despite its supporting Taliban Government and militancy in Jammu & Kashmir. The purpose of American war against Afghanistan was three-fold—firstly, to hasten the fall of Taliban Government, secondly to catch hold of Osama-bin-Laden and thirdly, to have a foothold in Pakistan-Afghanistan soil to exercise its hegemony in middle East. U.S. Government took the military Government of Parvez Musarraf into full confidence assuring all help to rejuvenate its moribund economy with the purpose of establishing their authority in this region.

Now, this war against Afghanistan by the U.S.A. had direct impact on Indian economy, which are as follows:

(i) Even after fall of Taliban Government in Afghanistan when Pakistan did not abate patronising militancy in Jammu and Kashmir and other parts of India but started mobilising troops on massive scale along the India-Pakistan borders, Indian government had also to prepare for possible war taking into account the belligerency of military Government of Pakistan. This consequently led to the heavy concentration of Indian troops with all sofisticated war equipment procured from all possible sources entailing huge amount of money which had a direct bearing on the economy of India.

(ii) The attack on the World Trade Center in New York came at a time when the economies of the world were passing through recession. U.S. slowdown in economy accentuated by its war expenses had a direct impact on Indian economy on three key areas—exports, foreign direct investment and institutional inflows.

(iii) Taking into account that the U.S. war against Afghanistan was likely to be prolonged to combat terrorism there would be no control over oil prices globally and accordingly India's oil import bill was destined to cripple Indian economy.

(iv) The U.S. is the single largest destination for India's software exports totalling over Rs. 28,000 crores. The U.S. expenses for fighting terrorism and war against Afghanistan had an impact on the software industry of India, as the exports of software to the U.S.A. had a serious set-back.

(v) Tourism industry was in the apprehension that the terrorist attack and the war against Afghanistan were to trigger 20/30 per cent decline in travel and tourism sectors.

Q.2. What are the reasons for the degeneration in industrialisation of the state of West Bengal?

Ans. When the British first came to India in the 17th century, Bengal was the first place where they came to trade and establish offices and factories. In the 18th century Bengal emerged as the British bridgehead. During the last three decades Bengal started falling the way behind the race of industrialisation. From the mid-Sixties when the Communist Party of India (Marxist) came to prominence in the political life of West Bengal, communists did everything possible to exterminate capitalists from the state. Not only this, they nurtured trade unionism very much unlike other states of India, which completely eroded the work culture of West Bengal. Both the blue collar and white collar sections of the employees were given the assurance that even if they neglected their duties at the cost of development of industries, their rights and wages would be protected as long as they remained within the folds of the Left. As a result, West Bengal has become a red desert as far as industrialisation of the State is concerned.

When Buddhadeb Bhattacharya became the Chief Minister of West Bengal he realised the utter folly of the attitudes the Left had pursued and also of the economic policies the previous Left Front Government nurtured. It is no doubt a happy augury that he is working overtime to change things and to create an atmosphere conducive to investment. But, at the same time, he is of course not oblivious of the fact that investors still harbour fear and suspicion towards a communist ruled state. Buddhadeb Bhattacharya is very much up and doing in dispelling the fear and suspicion from the minds of the investors to set their feet on the soil of West Bengal for setting up industries. Now, it is to be seen how far his sincere intention and efforts are crowned with success, when the industrialisation in the State has received a stumbling block during the last three decades.

Q.3. What are the ways and means to revitalise the industrial climate in West Bengal?

Ans. Presently, industrial climate in West Bengal is no doubt in doldrums. But, there are ways and means to revitalise the same in the state. They are:

(a) The employees have to change their attitude. Their notion that the Management has to mitigate their demands first and then the employees will concentrate their full devotion to work has to be shunned. What is required to maintain the congenial industrial climate is that firstly, the employees have to work with full devotion for attaining viability of the industrial establishments. They should bear in mind that their future in the organisation is directly chained with the prosperity of the Organisation. If it is attained, the legitimate demands of the employees will be automatically fulfilled by the Management. In this way, peace in the industrial establishment will be maintained.

(b) Militancy in Trade Unionism is to be done away with. Legitimate demands of the employees of Trade Unions are to be attained by way of peaceful negotiations with the Management and not by resorting to violence, coercion and threat.

(c) Work culture of the employees is to be improved upon. They should not refuge to do overtime work, when needed.

(d) Government should hold discussions time to time with the intending entrepreneurs to set up industries in the state by telling them that all facilities and cooperation would be extended to them by the Government for smooth running of the industries.

(e) Government should persuade foreign investors to set up their industries in the state and once such industries are set up, the government must assure the foreign investors that their industries will run smooth all through. With the setting up of large scale industries, ancillary industries will automatically spring up in and around such large scale industries.

(f) Labour Directorate should speed up settlement

of industrial disputes without affecting the interest of both the employees and the Management, when the disputes are referred to for adjudication.

(g) Chambers of Commerce and Industries must play a pivotal role to help setting up industries in the State.

(h) NRIs should be welcome. They should be persuaded to set up industries in the State assuring them of all the facilities.

(i) All infrastructural facilities, of which high tension uninterrupted electricity is very important, should be guaranteed to attract entrepreneurs.

(j) Wrangling among the shareholders should not be allowed to crop up at any time.

Q.4. What steps are suggested for rejuvenating the Indian economy with the commencement of Tenth Five-Year Plan starting from 2002 to 2007.

Ans. Global economic recession has no doubt affected the Indian economy also from attaining viability. Although the meeting of the National Development Council held on 1st September, 2001 at New Delhi approved the draft approach paper to the Tenth Five-Year Plan which envisages eight per cent annual growth in the next five years (2002-2007), multiple steps are also required to be taken to lend greater momentum to the economic reforms. These economic reforms to speed up development process are as follows:

(a) There is absolute need for downsizing the government.

(b) Reformation and rejuvenation of power sector to produce more electricity will be a step in the right direction to lure investors including the NRIs to set up industries.

(c) Increasing food production by re-orienting strategy is to be given importance.

(d) In order to attain viability in the economy there must be launching of labour reforms.

(e) There must be elimination of corruption and red tapism.

(f) Unnecessary and superfluous government expenditures are to be curtailed.

(g) Long term strategy has to be adopted to control floods and droughts.

(h) There is need to redouble efforts to contain population explosion.

(i) There should be removal of deficiencies in the judicial system.

(j) There should be greater centralisation for more devolution of financial and administrative powers to Panchayati Raj.

(k) Top most attention has to be paid for attaining viability in rural economy and infrastructure.

(1) Priority has to be given to programmes of road construction, port development, airport construction and also the sectors that could increase the demand for cement, steel and the capital goods.

(m) Voluntary Retirement Scheme, otherwise called the 'Exit Policy' or 'Golden Handshake' or 'Separation Scheme' is to be enforced in the case of unproductive/inefficient permanent employees who have already attained 50 years of age.

(n) Human Resource Development is to be given special priority for achieving 80 per cent literacy in order to create more gainful employment opportunities during the Tenth Plan period and by 2012 there must be reduction of poverty to 10 per cent.

Q.5. What was the health of India's economy in the beginning of 21st century?

Ans. From the beginning of 21st century, India's economy was of course going down and not up. Although tax collections, improvement in prices of industrial products and rise in non-food bank credit were hailed as a signal of revival of Indian economy, the fact was that the economy was not in good shape. This was true of all segments. The following were the multiple factors showing records of downward trend in Indian economy:

(i) Of the major financial institutions except for ICICI, Power Finance Corporation, National Bank for Agriculture and Rural Development and Infrastructure Development Finance Corporation, the others were in varying degrees of difficulty. The reason was that majority of the borrowers were finding it difficult to make enough money to compensate their borrowings.

(ii) Export growth decelerated whereas there was growth of imports which indicated that recession was continuing. The value of rupee was gradually declining in relation to US dollar despite the fact that the dollar also weakened.

(iii) Foreign institutional investment was at a low ebb and foreign direct investment in building new capacities was also almost at a standstill.

(iv) Industrial production was growing at the lowest rates in the last few years. This was for the reason that demand recession was spreading and a very large number of businesses were closed, closing or in acute trouble. Profit margins were badly squeezed for almost all products, many of which were cutting prices or giving away substantial amounts as gifts.

(v) Agricultural production was accelerating but stocks of food grains piled up for lack of proper distribution, as a result of which poor people were denied of having square meals a day.

(vi) Tourism sector was down, as was the business in hotels and restaurants which showed declining occupancy and tariffs, mainly because of Jammu and Kashmir tangle.

(vii) The financial sector was in great difficulty with many Stock Exchanges having closed down and even the biggest, the Mumbai Stock Exchange, showing scant business.

(viii) The advertising industry was facing extreme recession, as a result of which lay-offs were uncheckable in growth. This was compounded by the fact that manufactured products were in decline as retail and wholesale trade had not been fairing well.

(ix) With many units/organisations closing down necessitating the use of large-scale voluntary retirement schemes as also the general slackening in the economy, the overall employment situation was grim.

(x) The retired and the pensioners were facing hardship on account of decline in interest rates on saving instruments.

(xi) There was downward curve for numerous textile mills in the country, especially in the Punjab-Haryana belt. From March, 1999 to January, 2002, 100 mills were closed down in the country and about 50,000 workers lost their jobs. This downward trend in the textile mills was mainly due to competition from China, Korea and Nepal.

(xii) Repayment of colossal foreign debts combined with unavoidable and emergent expenditure on procurement of sophisticated defence equipment as a means to arm the country fully against the external threats time and again put financial stress to a great extent.

(xiii) Evacuation of foreign nationals, the set-back to foreign orders on domestic Companies, fall in foreign investments, colossal extra expenditures by Government, the rise in oil prices, lack of any action on the inefficient and wasteful food procurement and public distribution system, all combined to make the Indian economy even more difficult.

In every country of the world there is upheaval in state economy and India should not be taken as an exception. Even some of the already financially viable countries of the world were facing degeneration in their economy which got a chain reaction affecting India also. The bright feature was the apparent acceleration of the government's disinvestment programme which would hopefully rid the country out of the economic sluggishness in due course of time. It is certain that the Indian economy will not go downhill in the future years to come.

Q.6. What were the aims and objectives of the Tenth Five Year Plan (2002-2007), as decided in the meeting on 5th October, 2002 of the Planning Commission chaired by the then Prime Minister, Shri Atal Behari Vajpayee?

Ans. The Tenth Five Year Plan has public sector outlay of Rs. 15,92,300 crores, out of which the central plan has an outlay of Rs. 9,21,291 crores and the rest of the amount has been split among the states and Union territories.

It was an ambitious and tremendous economic growth oriented plan aimed at achieving 7.92% growth rate target. The Prime Minister pinned hope that it would not pose any problem to achieve this target if there were concerted efforts on all directions within the framework of Tenth Five Year Plan.

The aims and objectives of the Plan, which targeted achievement of not only 7.92% economic growth but also other reforms, were as follows:

(a) The Plan aimed at ensuring 5 years of compulsory elementary education for all children which would attain literacy rate from 65 per cent to 75 per cent.

(b) It aimed to reduce poverty level to 21 per cent mark from the pre-level of Tenth Plan of 26 per cent and create 50 million jobs.

(c) The Plan sought to double per capita income in 10 years.

(d) Since economic growth was not the only objective of the Tenth Five Year Plan, it was felt necessary to harness the benefits of growth to improve the quality of life of the people.

(e) There would be more expenditure in social sector, power, rural roads and irrigation.

(f) The Plan sought to reform ailing financial institutions.

(g) There would be annual increase in Foreign Direct Investment (FDI) inflows to around $7.5 billion.

(h) It would seek reforms in the agricultural sector by streamlining trade and commerce and amendment in the Essential Commodities Act as well as the Agriculture Produce Marketing Act.

(i) The Plan aimed at attaining 26.8 per cent domestic savings rate of Gross Domestic Product (GDP) *i.e.,* more than 3.5 per cent higher than before and also a high investment rate of 28.4 per cent.

Q.7. What were the probable reasons for which the Indian economy was affected?

Ans. There was affliction in the resurrected Indian economy. The huge foreign exchange reserve was also of no avail in checking the deterioration in the economic health of the country. The probable reasons for the same were not far to seek which were as follows:

(a) The world situation, with the US economy getting into slump affected Indian economy,

(b) The recourse to reckless borrowings from the financial institutions of the world in the last few years to finance non-plan expenditure and the repayment of the same by instalments together with interests told upon the Indian economy,

(c) Substantial increase in the salary/wages of the government employees due to adherence to Fifth Pay Commission report, potentially difficult situation of the financial institutions of the country and the rise in the outlay on both defence and internal security afflicted the economy,

(d) Vagaries of nature by way of flood and drought dwindled agricultural production,

(e) Looming danger of a war on Iraq leading to stoppage of supply of oil from them and consequently the rise in price of the same as also a dip in the remittances from the workers working in Iraq reflected adversely on Indian economy,

(f) There was the pressure on government expenditure and the consequential compulsion to borrow more,

(g) The bailout of the Unit Trust of India, Industrial Development Bank of India and Industrial Finance Corporation of India caused adverse effect on Indian economy,

(h) Theft of electricity aggregating about Rupees Twenty Five Thousand crores per year told upon the economy,

(i) Taking into account the sub-continental size, India is inhabited by more than 100 crores of people. Since many of such people, who are already able bodied, are parasites quality of life has dwindled affecting the economy,

(j) Reduction in the interest rates had an impact on the realisation of loans advanced by the banks to the entrepreneurs in many cases,

(k) Foreign investment did not seem to be adding new capacities,

(l) Most state transport undertakings run at a loss and there is no sign of their being privatised, though governments are not able to better the transport system for the loss sustained,

(m) Capital formation both in private and public sectors was poor, because savings were not growing as in the past years,

(n) Payment of compensation for lump sum amount to the victims of train accidents and others—both killed and wounded.

All these factors combinedly had obviously an impact on Indian economy. But, still then the Government of India is bent upon resurrecting the economy by successful implementation of Tenth Five Year Plan.

Q.8. What is the impact out of lowering of bank interest?

Ans. Lowering of bank interest is the outcome of messy economy of the country, which otherwise indicates that country's economic condition is in the retrograde step. Reducing the bank interest means that the deposits of the people in general will not be accelerated to the extent it is desired. Withdrawals of amount by the depositors from bank lead to reduced balance in the bank account, as the money is not multiplied reasonably owing to reduced interest rate. In the absence of sufficient balance kept in the bank accounts in majority of the cases, country's economy does not definitely show promising trend.

The first step to attain viability in the economy of the country is to reduce extravagant expenditures on all fronts instead of exerting pressure to the countrymen by the government for generating additional funds by increasing/levying extra taxes, which in turn will further weaken the financial status of the people with the result that their purchasing capacity will continue to dwindle and the economy of the country will be reversed further. Not only this, increased taxes and/or levying additional taxes will clandestinely lead to generation of black money in the country, as the tax payers will take recourse to tax evasion and this unaccounted money is a bane for the specific reason that such money cannot be utilised for development of the country with the result that the economy of the country will be degenerating further.

Under the circumstances, what is needed most is that the government has to cut down extravagant expenses on all fronts instead of reducing the bank interest rate, so as to lure the depositors to keep more money in the banks and this way the viability in the economy will be heightened and the inflation will be controlled.

Q.9. What are the factors which tend to the rise in the income of the middle class people?

Ans. Middle class income grows after the economy grows. When the after-tax income of the middle class people increases at a faster rate than the cost of living and also when their savings earn healthy returns, the middle class people look to the brighter aspect of their economic regeneration. There are number of factors leading to the rise in the income of the middle class people, which are summed up as follows:

(i) When there is the growth of employment potentiality in the country, the middle class people benefit immensely by way of getting employment, thereby paving the way of earning for their uninterrupted and comfortable living, since the middle class people form the substantial percentage of total population of the country.

(ii) The redeeming feature is the likely upturn in GDP growth which of course comes from agriculture. Although this is not exactly the middle class' cup of tea, yet there could be more jobs in services—restaurants, fashion shops and the new glamour industry and the middle class people will reap the harvest of benefits for themselves.

(iii) The middle class people will derive benefit financially with the growth of economy which will be possible when the country will not be caught in violent communal conflicts.

(iv) If the optimism pervades amongst the industrialists it will tend to industrial growth which otherwise means the rise in the income of the middle class people. Rise in exports of India-made goods stimulates industrial growth.

(v) If there is the normal rainfall in the country, economy is destined to grow and the middle class income rises.

(vi) The large central and state fiscal deficits cause concern. The government will have to trim some subsidies, which mostly benefit the middle class people.

(vii) The impact of cost of living should be less than the rise in incomes.

(viii) The major factor is taxes. When the subsidy burden dwindles, taxes go down. The government should, therefore, think of working out tax reforms for the benefit of the middle class people in particular.

(ix) If the middle class people can think of return of their savings, they will get maximum financial benefit when they will tend to deposit more money due to increased rate of interest in banks.

(x) The government allowed small investors to trade in government securities (G-secs) thereby providing them with an alternative market for investments. The advantages of investing in government securities are—the securities are highly liquid which can be sold at any time, secondly there is a regular flow of income in the form of half yearly interest payments and thirdly there is an additional income-tax benefit of Rs. 3000/- under Section 80-L which is over and above the limit of Rs 9,000/-

These are the principal factors by which the middle class people could think of rise in their income.

Q.10. What were the major steps taken by the government for attaining higher economic growth in India?

Ans. The following were the main positive steps taken by the government of India ensuring steady growth in the Indian economy:

(a) The announcement made by the then Prime Minister, Shri Atal Bihari Vajpayee on 9th January, 2003 at a gathering of 1500 people of Indian origin at Pragati Maidan that the Government of India considered favourably for granting dual citizenship to the people of Indian origin (NRIs) which initially applied to seven countries: the United States of America, the European Union, Canada, the United Kingdom, Australia, New Zealand and Singapore, was a step in the right direction for attaining steady economic growth in the country. While the NRIs who are considered as the economic giants, having Indian citizenship also, would tend to invest hefty amount in setting up large scale industries in India, this would hasten industrialisation of the country in a bigger way side by side with the industrialisation under the Tenth Five Year Plan (2002-2007) having public sector outlay of Rs 15,92,000 crores, achieving minimum 7.9% economic growth rate target. Therefore, the contribution of the NRIs also would be a step forward in higher economic growth in India.

(b) Notwithstanding the vagaries of nature the overall growth in the agricultural sector started becoming reasonably satisfactory mainly because of the manufacturing sector performing quite creditably. This gave rise to a large degree of optimism about the future performance of the economy.

(c) When the NDA government came to power in the year, 1998, India had hardly foreign exchange reserves even to pay for a few weeks imports. The step taken towards current account convertibility resulted in capital inflows from abroad which increased dramatically and the figure of foreign exchange reserves exceeded seventy billion dollars upto the year, 2002. This was no doubt a very happy augury for rejuvenation of Indian economy.

(d) Disinvestment of public sector organisations was a step in the right direction to attain viability in Indian economy, though the process brought some unemployment problem initially. It would be prudent on the part of the government not to divest the oil sector organisations including other profitable undertakings.

(e) The step taken by the government to allow the Indian currency to be freely exchanged in international currency market was a welcome decision. Convertible rupee was viewed as a symbol of the strength of the Indian economy, as the Indian economy would completely integrate with the world economy.

(f) The government imposed quantitative restrictions on the amount an Indian tourist could take out of the country. The purpose of this ceiling was to restrict the capital flight from the country.

(g) Foreign investors were willing to invest more in India when the government assured them that the risks associated with their investments were minimal.

(h) During the currency of Tenth Five Year Plan (2002-2007) government's commitment to provide employment to as many as one crore persons in a year *i.e.*, five crores people during the entire plan period was a very good sign of rejuvenation of Indian economy.

Q.11. Under what circumstances privatisation of State Owned Enterprises (SOEs) has been felt a necessity and what advantages would be accrued out of it?

Ans. Privatisation means transferring assets from the state to the private sector instead of passing them from one arm of the government to another arm. The trend for privatisation of State Owned Enterprises (SOEs) is being observed in developed and developing economies. More than 8500 SOEs were already privatised in over 80 countries during 1980-92. In recent years the countries which have already sold or announced the policy of sale of State Owned Enterprises are Argentina, Bangladesh, Brazil, Britain, Germany, France, Italy, Japan, Mexico, Nigeria, Spain, Thailand, Turkey and India. Apart from the above countries, the communist countries such as—former USSR, China, East European countries and Cuba have also embarked upon a policy of privatisation.

It has been observed that the performance of State Owned Enterprises have been by and large far from satisfactory. They have often put large burdens on public budgets and external debt. Heavy financial burden, growing public discontent on account of inefficiency, indifferent and irresponsible attitude towards the customer needs, corruption, favouritism and rapid expansion of bureaucracy tightening the public budget and causing problem in labour relations within the public sector organisations are the main reasons for the growing interest in privatisation of SOEs. All these reasons combinedly have made the public sector financially weak in most of the cases.

The following advantages and benefits would be derived by the government of India after privatising the Public Sector Undertakings:

(a) Relieving the financial burden and trimming the size of the administrative machinery,

(b) Improving the efficiency and productivity of economic activities and facilitation of economic growth,

(c) Reducing the size and presence of the public sector,

(d) Helping meet national development policy targets,

(e) Reducing the size of bureaucracy,

(f) Enabling the government to mop up funds,

(g) Enabling the government to concentrate more on the essential state functions,

(h) Accelerating the space of economic development as it would attract substantial resources from the private sector for development,

(i) Ensuring better management of the privatised enterprises and consequently the economy of the country would go on surging,

(j) The sale proceeds so received from the privatisation of the SOEs could be utilised by the government in the following manner:

   (i) The amount be earmarked for revitalisation of economic ills of the country,

   (ii) The substantial sum of Rs. 10,000/- crores raised under the voluntary disclosure of income scheme, was squandered in paying increased salaries to the government employees in pursuance of the directive of the Fifth Pay Commission despite pious intention of using the money for infrastructure development of the country. Under the circumstances, this should be done in the sale proceeds arising out of the disinvestment of Public Sector Undertakings.

Q.12. While the disinvestment policy of the government of India is welcome, what were the points of opposition for disinvestment of HPCL and BPCL, as decided by the government?

Ans. It was a happy augury that the Indian economy particularly the industrial sector was gradually inching its way out of stagnation on account of pursuing disinvestment policy by the government of India, because fabulous amount of money was being generated out of the sale of the public sector undertakings to the private sector entrepreneurs.

But especially in respect of disinvestment of HPCL and BPCL, the following oppositions were advanced giving all justifications not to disinvest the same.

RSS Spokesman, Mr. M.G. Vaidya expressed apprehension about the impact of privatisation of the oil sector on the country's economy and security. He demanded that oil should be deemed an area of "strategic" importance on a par with railway and defence production. He further contended that the strategic sector was one where the government alone should have a role to play like Railway and defence production.

Mr. George Fernandes, NDA Convener and the then Defence Minister was against the oil sector disinvestment. He raised the point that disinvestment of oil companies could harm the country's strategic interest, because it was linked to country's security. He also expressed fears that the disinvestment of strategic oil sector would create private monopolies and have adverse implications for national security. He further argued that handing over entities created with the wealth of the people would further enrich the already rich. He not only made it very clear that he was against strategic sales, but also advocated that the government should first sell loss-making units.

Mr. M.M. Joshi, the then Human Resource Development Minister opined that the disinvestment policy on oil sector should be reviewed keeping in mind the energy security issue. Mr. Joshi referred to some multinationals' reluctance to release oil when the government wanted it during 1965 and 1971 wars. He also pointed out that since agriculture was dependent on oil-based energy, it was unwise to hand over the oil sector to private hands.

Mr. Ram Naik, the then Petroleum Minister argued that Bharat Petroleum Corporation Ltd. and Hindustan Petroleum Corporation Ltd. should not be handed over to the private companies through strategic sales, keeping in mind the experience when foreign oil companies refused to assist the government in its war requirement, forcing Indira Gandhi to nationalise them.

In an apparent reference to the war clouds hovering over Iraq, the Congress Spokesman, Mr. S. Jaipal Reddy said in the party's Plennary Session at Bangalore that the Vajpayee government should not sell public assets in such a vital sector and sale of such assets would be nothing but a betrayal of the country's interest.

Attorney General, Soli Sorabjee in his opinion elicited on 20-1-2003 allowed denationalisation of Hindustan Petroleum Corporation Ltd. (ESSO) and Bharat Petroleum Corporation Ltd. (Burmah Shell) without parliamentary approval. Sorabee's advice was that there was no need to repeal the Acts of Parliament under which both the Companies were taken over by the government in the 1970s.

Notwithstanding steep opposition, the Cabinet Committee of the Vajpayee government gave green signal to privatise HPCL and BPCL on 27th January, 2003.

The Cabinet Committee decided to offload 5 per cent of HPCL equity to its employees while the government would retain 12 per cent. As far as BPCL is concerned, the meeting decided to sell 35.2 per cent equity through a combination of an Indian public offer and issue of depository shares in the global market. The company employees would get 5 per cent of the equity and the government would retain 26 per cent. To make the HPCL sale offer more attractive, the centre decided that the bidder should provide a Bank Guarantee of Rs. 2,000 crores.

Q.13. Hefty amount of money has been concentrating in the hands of few. What are the probable reasons for the same?

Ans. Lust for acquiring money by hook and crook has become persistently the order of the day. A section of the people has acquired riches in two different ways—one by honest means, by virtue of their intellectual superiority, as well as education and the others are amassing riches by dishonourable means and sucking people's blood. This is the reason how some are living in ivory towers and the others in ramshackle dwelling houses and shanties. This inequality has rendered the economically downtrodden to lead a life of curse and this presents a disquiet between the Haves and the Have-nots, which is unbecoming for a country like India having the largest democracy in the world.

Dishonest way of acquiring wealth is more pernicious for health of economy than the way of earning by upright means. This was probably among others the rhyme and reason as to why the country could not enjoy fully the fruits of sound economy even after more than fifty years of independence. Riches earned through dishonest means by a section of the people is a hidden money which cannot be put to circulation and the country's progress stumbles. So has happened in the case of India which must be an indisputable reason.

The subsidy spent by the government, which according to the budget for 2002-2003 was more than Rs. 39,000 crores, did not percolate to the people living below poverty line, constituting 26% of the total population of India. It was estimated that barely 10% of the subsidy could reach the poor and the lion's share of the subsidy constituting 90% of the same was eaten up fraudulently by the disgruntled people and this way the government money is being pocketed and concentrated in the hands of few.

Misuse of government money is another factor of concentration of the same in the hands of the few. Digestion of this money is due to the absence of decentralisation of expenses by the government.

Undurable construction with sub-standard materials without looking to the interest of the people for long time use of the same contribute another important factor of concentration of unaccounted wealth in the hands of the disgruntled builders.

As is observed there is mushroom growth of the promoters all over India building dwelling houses. Although they are providing employment to the bulk of the people engaged in house construction, these promoters are constantly running after money and thus there is huge concentration of riches in their hands.

Sudden and abrupt artificial increases in the prices of commodities have led to the concentration of money in the hands of the traders.

Party politics have made certain section of the people wealthy, thus concentrating fabulous money in their hands.

Q.14. Under what circumstances the government of West Bengal continued to face acute financial debilitation?

Ans. The following are the reasons for facing acute financial debilitation by the government of West Bengal:

(i) On account of adherence to the Fifth Pay Commission's recommendation, there has been staggering salary bills of the state government employees including the teachers and non-teaching staff.

(ii) The government has to make massive interest

payments as west Bengal owes more than Rs. 70,000 crores to the centre.

(iii) West Bengal's achievement in generating massive investment in the small savings scheme had turned into a "liability" because of Central policies.

(iv) Food Corporation of India discriminated against small peasants of the state while favouring the powerful farm lobby of the north.

(v) Jute industry is in crisis following the loss of market to cheaper Bangladeshi products. This has led to the sickness of thirty-two of the 63 jute mills in the state.

(vi) With the return of investors in the iron and steel as well as ferroalloy sector in west Bengal, the problem is faced with the inter-state tariff barriers from the states like Andhra Pradesh and Chhatisgarh as these states have imposed 10 per cent entry tax on the iron and steel products from West Bengal and other states.

Q.15. What were the objectives of Essential Services Maintenance Act and when was it introduced and lapsed and under what circumstances why could it not be revived?

Ans. The Union Government felt that strikes and other agitations in industries associated with essential services were one of the principal reasons for the economic crisis of the country. It was, therefore, felt an extreme necessity to introduce Essential Services Maintenance Act (ESMA). The objectives of ESMA were to ban strikes, go-slows, lockouts and layoffs and make each a cognisable offence in industries considered essential services. ESMA laid stress on maintenance of essential services and authorised prohibition of the commencement of strike without reference to arbitration and also for continuance of uninterrupted production essential for national security and defence as well as the economy of the country. ESMA was introduced by the Indira Gandhi government in the year, 1981 which lapsed in 1990.

The National Front Government, then in power, could not revive ESMA after it was lapsed following steep opposition from the left parties. Between January and October, 1990, the Union Government had sought the views of the state governments on whether ESMA should be revived and 12 state governments such as Assam, Andhra Pradesh, Bihar, Goa, Karnataka, Maharashtra, Mizoram, Nagaland, Rajasthan, Orissa, Sikkim and Tripura had suggested that ESMA be given an extension. But, only three states—West Bengal, Kerala and Tamil Nadu had expressed strong opposition to it. Apart from these three states, all the Trade Unions in the country also vehemently opposed reintroduction of ESMA and made it clear that they would stage demonstration outside the Parliament if the government was bent upon extending ESMA. Such being the circumstances, ESMA could not be reintroduced by the Union Government.

Q.16. What are the labour problems faced by industrial establishments and the solution thereof?

Ans. Cosy employee-employer relations are the determinant factor for trouble-free running of industrial establishments. Constitution of India has of course guaranteed right to trade unionism, but it should not be construed that the Management of industrial establishment has to be coerced upon to yield to the pressure of the representatives of the labour union to accept their unreasonable demands by virtue of their right to trade unionism. This policy is beyond inkling of doubt detrimental to the interest of smooth running of the industrial establishment.

When India is determined to forge ahead to become a developed nation, maintenance of industrial production is of paramount necessity. Generation of employment potentiality breeds out of optimum production necessitating expansion of industrial capacity which becomes a retrograde step when the industrial establishments are threatened with strikes and lockouts. Solution to the unemployment problem to a considerable extent on account of trouble-free running of the establishment, leads to standardisation of living of the people. Being thrown out of employment on account of closure of establishments, it is distressing that such unemployed persons have to shuttle from door to door begging for financial assistance to make both ends meet. This is nothing but a social degeneration. This obviously is the result of closure of the establishments owing to militant attitude of the representatives of the labour union.

It has to be admitted by all and sundry that the entrepreneurs never long for that their establishments are closed down entailing colossal financial loss arising out of militancy of the union people. While the attitude of militancy has to be eschewed it is also at the same time absolutely necessary that the Management finds its ways not to breed discontent in the minds of the employees by their benevolent approach to problems.

The employees must bear in mind that maintenance of production by them by diligent discharge of their duties has to be ensured in the interest of their own growth with the growth of the organisation, which depends upon the propensity of the employees, as capital, plant and machinery are not be all and end all for an establishment. Therefore, in order to blur problems in the industrial establishments it is always recommended that both the Management and its employees have to create congenial atmosphere by pursuing a policy of give and take, that is, it is to be borne in mind that it should be a two-way traffic between the employers and the employees. In this case, the government has to make necessary changes/ amendments in the labour legislation dispelling aggravation of unemployment problem in the country.

Another pertinent point is that in the interest of rapid industrialisation, it is very important that the employees' Union has to ensure smooth running of the establishments without resorting to militancy, so that the Management does not find any pretext to declare lock-outs of their establishments. It is an admitted fact that militancy in some of the labour unions is the reason for closing down of many industries in some states and that prospective entrepreneurs are shy to set up their industrial establishments although infrastructural facilities are plenty in certain states.

Q.17. In what way India could think of ranking amongst the world's leading super-powers in respect of industrialisation of the country?

Ans. Defying the constraints and bottlenecks, India can surely march forward to rank amongst the world's leading super-powers in respect of industrialisation of the country, if the entrepreneurs have dreams like Dhirubhai Ambani to build industrial empire in the country. Dhirubhai Ambani's belief in the potential of the Indian markets and the capabilities of the Indian people, was unwavering. His confidence in the growth potential of the Indian economy was unshakable. He was convinced that India would one day rank amongst the world's leading economic super-powers. His dream was translated into reality in building his own industrial empire from scratch. It is the Indian industrialists who have to reorient industrial structure of the country for attaining economic liberalisation of the people of India in general. Dhirubhai Ambani has left a legacy which the Indian industrialists have to mimic.

It is important to note that although there is labour union in his giant industries, yet they have never grown militant which paved the way for expansion of Reliance Industries to the zenith, as a result of which the employees working there have been relishing the fruits of economic liberalisation, which is the need of the day. It is, therefore, of paramount necessity that the labour unions of other establishments should follow the principles of unionism of Japan, as to how they have been behaving with the industrialists with soft attitude and this was the most important factor as to why Japan expanded rapidly in the field of industrialisation of the country, thereby standardising the economy of the people of Japan.

What is needed most in 21st century is to build industrial empire in India for which birth of hundreds of Dhirubhai Ambani is the crux of the question for following his ideals for making India amongst the world's leading super-powers in respect of industrialisation of India and to achieve this the labour unions have to play a vital role.

Q.18. In what way small scale industries are important for a country like India?

Ans. Side by side with the large scale industries, small scale industries assume tremendous importance in attaining viability of economy especially for India where more than 70% of the total population of the country dwell in villages, whose needs are to be mitigated with the products of small scale industries, in particular. Small scale industries in India have rosy future which will shape the economy at a faster rate. Network of small scale industries is of paramount necessity especially when the government of India has been divesting public sector units and in the process of their divestment unemployment problem is no doubt aggravating, which can be eased largely if more small scale industries are set up. SSIs will absorb sizeable number of unemployed youths of non-urban/semi-urban areas, which in consequence reduce migration of these youths to the cities in quest of employment and the city dwellers will heave a sigh of relief being free from overcrowding of people.

In an agro-based country like India rural development is the true replica of financial soundness which the small scale industries can only provide. Therefore, top-most attention has to be given by the government of India in setting up large number of SSIs throughout the length and breadth of the country in order to uplift the lot of the village people in particular from the financial morbidity and then only the Indian economy will have a boost.

The picture of small scale industries in India was as under:

As in the year, 2002 there were 35,00,000 SSI units in the country producing over 8,000 items and providing direct employment to over 2 crore persons. While the average growth rate of small scale industries sector during the last three years was 7.4% as compared to 4.7% for the overall industrial sector, its contribution to GDP was 6.86%. Over the last three years upto the year, 2002 there was the increase in employment to the extent of 21 lakhs.

From the above statistics it transpires that there is great importance of small scale industries in the country and hence the Ministry of Small Scale Industries, government of India has to lay special emphasis to the spread of SSIs in large number in the country as part of rapid development of India by adopting the following comprehensive policies, as announced by the then Prime Minister of India, Shri Atal Bihari Vajpayee:

(a) Enhance competitiveness both domestically and globally through increased fiscal and credit support,

(b) Better infrastructural and marketing facilities and

(c) Incentives for technological upgradation.

Q.19. What are the factors which govern a state's economic performance?

Ans. Economic performance of a state depends upon the following factors:

(i) The measure of economic growth of a state is the State Domestic Product (SDP). It represents the total value of goods and services produced in a state in a year.

(ii) There is another indicator which is the tax to SDP—an indicator of the state's ability to raise resources. The higher the SDP, the higher is the tax collected.

(iii) Initiative to promote agro-industries is another measure of economic growth of a state.

(iv) Land reform is an important factor which gives a push to agricultural products. Growth of agriculture helps ameliorate the financial status of the agriculturists.

(v) Per capita income or income of each citizen in a year is a factor which determines the economic performance of a state.

(vi) Economic performance is also reflected in a commensurate growth in other areas like employment and consumption of various goods and services.

(vii) In order to ensure economic growth of a state there must be large fresh investment or technical improvement.

All-India level of economic growth is worked out on the basis of the performance of individual states taking into account the above factors, in particular.

Q.20. What were the different Industrial Policy Resolutions adopted by the Government of India in different years?

Ans. Time to time Government of India adopted Industrial Policy Resolutions in successive different years, salient features of which are as under:

(i) *Industrial Policy Resolution,* 1948

Industrial Policy Resolution of 1948 envisaged that the state has to play an active roll in the development of industries with absolute monopoly in the case of (a) manufacture of arms and ammunitions, (b) production and control of atomic energy, (c) ownership and control of railway transport, (d) coal, iron and steel, (e) aircraft manufacture, (f) ship building and (g) manufacture of telephone, telegraph and wireless apparatus. The rest of the industrial field was left open to the private enterprise.

(ii) *Industrial Policy Resolution,* 1956

The Industrial Policy Resolution, 1956 made the industrial policy of the Government of India more socialist oriented and widened the scope of public sector. It decided that the state would assume a predominant and direct responsibility for setting up new industrial undertakings and for developing transport facilities. It would also undertake state trading on an increasing scale. Also the Industrial Policy Resolution of 1956 reiterated government's determination to provide all possible assistance for the development of small and cottage industries in consideration of the fact that such industries generate large-scale employment. This policy was designed to enable the Government of India to gain a dominant position in the industrial sector of the country.

(iii) *Industrial Policy Resolution,* 1980

The main objective of this Industrial Resolution was to optimise utilisation of the installed capacity of plants and machinery, maximise production, achieve higher employment generation, narrow down the regional imbalance through development of industrially backward areas and strengthen agricultural base by setting up agro-based industries.

(iv) *Industrial Policy Resolution,* 1991

The Government of India made major changes in the industrial policy by invoking Industrial Policy Resolution, 1991, the salient features of which were as follows:

(a) Liberalisation of foreign investment and technological participation,

(b) Scrapping of the MRTP regulation pertaining to concentration of economic power,

(c) Delicensing with certain exceptions,

(d) Redefining of the role of the public sector,

(e) Maintaining a sustained growth in productivity and gainful employment and

(f) Attaining international competitiveness.

Q.21. Is it worthwhile that lowering of bank interest rate will rejuvenate the moribund economy of the country?

Ans. By intermittent lowering of bank interest rates as announced by the Reserve Bank of India time to time, it seems that the RBI is all set to make the financial scenario in the country gradually look like an international one. When we look to the already developed and fast developing countries of the world, it is observed that with the lowering of bank interest rates their economy looked up. Lowering of bank interest rates seems reasonable on certain arguments.

Reduced rate of interest, as is understood, stimulates private investment and stimulating private investment is of course injecting fresh blood into our moribund economy. Apart from private investment low rate of interest also encourages private consumption. When the rate of interest is low, consumers are tempted to hire-purchase durables against easy instalment payments. Low rate of interest will also tempt the educated young entrepreneurs to take loans from banks for setting up their small enterprises generating employment which has now become acute in the country, and the country will move towards betterment. While making repayment of such amount, they will also not be required to pay high rate of interest.

Although the middle class people having bank deposits and the employees retired under VRS will be debarred from getting reasonable rate of interest against the principal amount deposited by them in banks, which they received in lump-sum due to dispensation of their services on VRS, yet the overall economy of the country will get a boost on account of the above reasons. Also even after lowering of bank interest rate deposits in banks will not be affected because the VRS amounts are plenty which are deposited mostly in banks.

There is of course no denying the fact that lowering of bank interest rate with the hope of rejuvenating the moribund economy of the country is a text-book theory. It will, therefore, be in the fitness of things that we should watch the situation for a couple of years or so and gauge the impact it creates on the overall economy for a country like India.

8

Political Topics

Q.1. Dr. A.P.J. Abdul Kalam is a scientist having no political background in his career. But still then under what considerations his candidature for the apex position of the President of India were taken into account?

Ans. Knowing fully well of his non-affiliation with any political activity, Dr. A.P.J. Abdul Kalam's interaction with the media in the Press Conference held at New Delhi on 19th June, 2002 reinforced his desire to serve as an apolitical, independent and non-partisan President.

The ruling National Democratic Alliance with the subsequent support of Congress party came up with the name of Dr. A.P.J. (Avul Pakir Jainulabdeen) Abdul Kalam as its nominee for the post of President of India. The considerations for his nomination as President of India cropped up on the following counts:

(a) The largest party in the Opposition discovered that the Bharat Ratna scientist had huge acceptability all over the country, especially among the middle-class. A net-poll showed 79 per cent would vote for Kalam in a direct electoral contest. There is a strong link between middle-class ambition and national security and that Kalam's name evokes a sense of success and security.

(b) Top scientists and policy makers who have known Dr. Kalam and have worked with him, say he is well equipped to handle the new assignment. It was opined by K. Kasturirangan, Chairman of the Indian Space Research Organisation where

Dr. Kalam had worked for several years that he is a problem solver. He has experienced the realities of life that a majority of Indians have experienced and thus understand and communicate with people at all levels.

(c) In recent years, Dr. Kalam has turned his focus on national, social and economic development issues, culminating in a call to the country to work towards acquiring a developed nation status by the year, 2020. It will be an inspiration to the rest of the country to have a President with this dream.

(d) Political parties have reasons to eulogise his candidature of President of India. He is an outstanding performer in his own field and it is confidently nurtured that he would be a President par excellence.

(e) In a troubled polity like India, President should be above controversies. He should also combine a sense of restraint. Dr. Kalam definitely fulfils these objectives in his capacity as President of India.

(f) Those who know Dr. Kalam from close quarters predict that he is likely to be pro-active in nation, building issues such as development. He will not meddle in political controversies and will not be inclined to take political sides. He may be inexperienced from the political point of view, but he is not unaware of the political cross-currents, as he had worked under six Prime Ministers in the past.

Q.2. Is there any possibility of converging between CPI (M) and CPI?

Ans. At the outset it can be construed that converging between Communist Party of India (Marxist) and Communist Party of India seems to be remote in the near future. There is a saying that when two brothers are engaged in quarrelling with each other, the breach seems to be irreparable. So is the case with CPI (M) and CPI. The split in the Indian Communist movement in 1964 resulted in the birth of two separate Communist parties in the name of CPI (M) and CPI. Although Mr. A.B. Bardhan, General Secretary of CPI advocated the case of uniting the two Communist parties in view of the changes in the programmes of CPI (M), Mr. Harkishen Singh Surjit, General Secretary of CPI (M) threw cold water on the proposal of Mr. A.B. Bardhan. Mr. Surjit categorically mentioned that the differences persisting between these two political parties are not the things of the past. He blamed the CPI of conspiring to break the unity of CPI (M) by colluding with Congress party and hence reconciliation with CPI on this count was not a possibility. CPI (M) is still a large cadre based party. Under the circumstances, unification of CPI (M) and CPI is not foreseen in the immediate future unless otherwise some drastic upheavals take place in Indian politics in future.

Q.3. What is the relation between RSS and BJP? Can BJP survive without the support of RSS?

Ans. Basically, BJP (Bharatiya Janata Party) pays respects to the ideologies of their mother Organisation, RSS (Rashtriya Swayamsevak Sangh). The question has arisen whether BJP can survive without the support of RSS. It is to be seen whether the issues like abrogation of Article 370 and cow slaughter which BJP had before 1998 have now any relevance or not for their prospects. Moreso, the BJP has to see whether it will be able to fulfil the dream of RSS about making India a Hindu Rashtra.

After the year, 1998 it has been observed that there have been changes in the actions of BJP as a political party. This party has come to power and formed a coalition government with heterogeneous political parties with different ideologies, in the name of NDA (National Democratic Alliance). Under the circumstances, is it possible on the part of BJP to strictly follow the ideologies of RSS alone for governing the country? The answer must be in the negative. The welcome of the erstwhile BJP President, Mr. Bangaru Laxman to the Muslims of India who are the largest minority community of this country and his desire that the party should be proactive in bringing the minorities into its fold is well-timed real politic. Time has testified that under the governance of BJP this party is not at all anti-Muslim riot inciter.

Moreover, there are some more Muslim enrolments in the NDA government. The then Home Minister (later Deputy Prime Minister), Shri L.K. Advani already declared that ideology had nothing to do with governance of the country. BJP now seems to be increasingly turning a politely deaf ear to the RSS exhortations. BJP is also tactfully distancing from the RSS on account of governance of the country in the name of NDA, which cannot be communal. Fulfilling the desire of RSS by BJP to project India as a Hindu Rashtra is not a possibility. Although BJP respects the ideologies of their mother Organisation, RSS, yet this party can now of course survive without the support of RSS.

Q.4. In a democratic country what is the role to play of opposition party?

Ans. Abraham Lincoln said, "Democracy means government of the people, by the people and for the people". Based on this theory democracy works successfully under two systems—either multi-party system or bi-party system. In the United States of America and Great Britain there are two-party system. In other democratic countries of the world there are multi-party system of government.

Democracy is a representative system of Government and the political parties act as the cohesion between the electorate and the government. In democratic form of government the electorates give their verdict in the ballot box to which political party they want to handover to rule the country and depending upon their verdict the party which has succeeded in getting two-thirds majority forms the government and the second highest political party remains in the opposition.

The political party not forming the government has great role to play in the politics of a democratic country. The tasks of this party are to straighten the follies and loopholes of the ruling party as also suggest ways and means for good governance bearing in mind that they are the representatives of the electorate. Therefore, there must be close interaction between the ruling party and the opposition party in running the government in the best way for development and progress of the country. For existence of opposition party, which has to check and to keep a constant watch on the day to day affairs of the ruling party, it (the ruling party) has naturally to follow the constitutional norms for any decision taken. In a democratic country the opposition has to come forward with healthy and constructive criticism always for the mistakes and loopholes of the ruling party and not condemn the party government in their partisan interest. Then only the governance of the country moves in the right direction.

It is often observed that in many cases, in connivance with other political parties the opposition party tries to discredit the government in arrogant and vociferous manner and brings no confidence motion against the government with the object of bringing down it. Such action of the opposition party does not display glorious norms and tradition of democracy.

Q.5. On a subject of debate in Indian Parliament how do the elected representatives of the people behave in the true democratic spirit?

Ans. Indian Parliament—as it is called Lok Sabha or the House of Commons or the House of Representatives, represents the country's highest preservation of dignity. The dignity of Parliament is reflected of course in the way the members of Parliament preserve and uphold parliamentary etiquette and protocol. The subject the members of Parliament choose and the wit and learning that mark their speeches add to the dignity of Parliament. In the bye-gone days there were a few good orators like Shyamaprosad Mukherjee, Hiren

Mukherjee and Jawaharlal Nehru whose speeches in Parliament were memorable for substance and rhetoric. But the memories of such speeches are now extinct.

As ill luck would have it, the proceedings of today in the Parliament can hardly be described as debate. It is more in the nature of mud-slinging and the atmosphere of the Lok Sabha is made to resemble that of a village pond around which women assemble to squabble. What is worse is that the lead comes from the treasury benches. The abuse of the dignity of Parliament as is observed today is a sure sign of the fragility of the democratic ethos in India. The Indian democracy is the largest in the world and the whole world has to learn as to how Indian democracy works. But, the way some of the members of Parliament who are the pillars of democracy act today is not of course a healthy sign of upholding the true spirit of democracy. It is a humiliation to the democratic ethos of India. Violence, vilification, tumultuous uproar and lawlessness mark the day when the proceedings of Parliament are in a state of being in progress. At times when the situation goes out of control the Speaker of the Lok Sabha has had to adjourn the session of debate intermittently at the cost of huge expenses and the Indian Parliament becomes the laughing stock in the eyes of the nation and the world.

What is needed most is upholding of true democratic spirit in India by maintaining the civilised polity for which the Members of Parliament have to eschew collectively the path of recrimination. This is the only way how Indian democracy will be placed in high esteem in the comity of nation—nay the whole world.

Q.6. Is it always possible to maintain fixed tenure of five years of Parliament and State Legislature in the present state of democratic set-up of India?

Ans. It is always recommended that once the government is formed either at the centre or the states, it should continue for a period of five years till next election is held. This will ensure better democratic functioning and to deliver good governance in the country. Government for a period of five years has distinct advantages. A stable government can conveniently undertake developmental activities for the rapid all-round prosperity of the country as also foreign investments will be forthcoming which is of paramount importance. The foreign investors can gauge the policy of the government which is stable, in the matter of investments. A government which is vacillant and instable loses the confidence of the foreign investors and the country's development is impaired. In earlier years in Indian democracy when there were no multiplicity of political parties, the installation of government after election was stable, as the government was formed without conglomeration of heterogeneous political parties with different ideologies and policies and in fact with the stable government the country marched forward for development at a quicker space especially in the quarter century of independence.

What is observed today even after completion of Ninth-Five-year Plan, the country's development has not been spectacular. The onus of responsibility lies with the instable government formed with different political parties. The government which is put under absolute stress and strains with internal squabbles is intercepted in undertaking the development process of the country. Almost all the opposition political parties of India today are vociferous and clamourous at the lapses committed on any occasion by the ruling government instead of suggesting ways and means to correct the lapses. The intention is nothing but either to weaken or pull down the government by demanding forced resignation of senior ministers for the purpose of partisan interest.

Fixed tenure of five years of Parliament and State Legislatures is not possible in the present state of democratic set-up of India. The then Prime Minister, Sri Atal Bihari Vajpayee's remarks about a fixed term for the Lok Sabha and the State Legislatures at the Golden Jubilee Celebrations of the Election Commission of India in New Delhi on January 17,

2001 justifying that frequent and unscheduled elections impaired the quality of governance, stirred up critical response from different political parties. The contentions of the political leaders who are averse to fixed term for the Lok Sabha and State Legislatures for uninterrupted five years governance of the country are as follows:

(a) When the government formed with conglomeration of heterogeneous political parties is reduced to minority on account of withdrawing support by some of the parties, how could the government be allowed to rule even after it lost majority?

(b) How could the Prime Minister who is defeated in a no-confidence motion run the country if the term of his office is fixed for five years?

(c) Taking cognizance of the country's past experiences in minority government and the inability of various political combinations to muster ruling majorities, a fixed term for the Lok Sabha would be impracticable.

(d) As soon as a no-confidence motion is moved against Prime Minister/Chief Minister, a simultaneous vote of confidence for an alternative PM/CM should be moved so that there is continuity in government and the Legislatures without going for fresh election. This practice is also followed by many European countries.

In view of the facts and circumstances as are observed in Indian politics of today where multifarious political parties are there, the concept of uninterrupted five-year term for Lok Sabha and State Legislatures cannot be guaranteed, even if the country's progress stumbles. Even the President of India in his address on the eve of Republic Day celebration on 26th January, 2001 opposed the concept of fixed term for Parliament.

Q.7. What are the Indo-Afghan relations after the installation of interim government in Afghanistan under the Chairmanship of Hamid Karzai?

Ans. Basically, the foreign policies of a government are the yardstick on which depends upon the establishment of relations with a country. Therefore, before analysing the Indo-Afghan relations it is prudent to discuss the foreign policies of Afghanistan initiated after installation of interim government in Afghanistan under the chairmanship of Hamid Karzai. The priorities of foreign policies of the interim government are as follows:

(a) Afghan government has to establish credibility and effectiveness in the eyes of the major powers of the world led by the United States of America.

(b) To obtain maximum amount of economic and developmental assistance as speedily as possible to stabilise the war ravaged Afghanistan and to restore civil administration in Afghanistan.

(c) To establish contacts with immediate geographical neighbours to seek their cooperation in the above process.

(d) To restore Afghanistan's identity as a moderate Islamic country within the community of Islamic states.

(e) To interact with governments which have a direct interest in Afghanistan's stability and development.

Hamid Karzai, Chairman of the interim government of Afghanistan visited India on 26th and 27th February, 2002. Naturally, question arose whether his visit was of political significance or whether it laid down foundation for an entirely new and positive edifice of Indo-Afghan relations. There was criticism and concern in some circles in India that despite the support which India gave to the campaign against the Taliban and promptitude with which India extended developmental assistance to Afghanistan, Karzai did not give sufficient attention to India. One important point to mention here is that Hamid Karzai was critical of India for her support to the Soviet backed Babrak Karmal government in Afghanistan, as he was part of the Afghan struggle against that government. But, with the change of situation now, his resentment does not seem to linger in his policies towards India.

The following actions which India has taken towards Afghanistan are indications that there will be positive revival of Indo-Afghan relations:

(a) India pledged a hundred million dollars of assistance to Afghanistan at the Tokyo Conference in January, 2002.

(b) India played an important role in Afghanistan's reconstruction and re-stabilisation.

(c) India resisted revival of religious extremism and terrorism in Afghanistan.

(d) India ensured a proper security environment for certain categories of defence supplies and some training facilities for Afghan administration and security personnel in India.

(e) Indian government planned to develop Chabhahar port in South-eastern Iran and build a 200-km long road connecting Chabhahar to Kabul in order to expedite transportation of Indian goods to the Afghan government.

(f) India delivered to Afghan government forty thousand tonnes of high-protein biscuits meant for Afghan school children.

It is, therefore, a happy augury that Indo-Afghan relations are going to be cemented in the years ahead based on the visit of Hamid Karzai to New Delhi on 26th and 27th February, 2002 as also the subsequent visits of Afghan Defence Minister, Deputy Defence Minister and Interior Minister to India when matters concerning Indo-Afghan cooperation was discussed at length leading to signing of Agreements on various issues.

Q.8. Some politicians are of the view that creation of more states is a solution to the problems and aims at development of India as a whole. How far is it correct?

Ans. With the creation of three new states in November, 2000 total states in India are now 28 in number. These new states are Chhatisgarh, Jharkhand and Uttaranchal created out of the states such as Madhya Pradesh,

Bihar and Uttar Pradesh respectively. Government has opined that the new states were created in response to the aspirations and wishes of the people for attaining viability and contributing to greater socio-economic development. There is also demand for creation of more new states like Telengana in Andhra Pradesh, Vidharba in Maharashtra, Bodoland in Assam and Gorkhaland in West Bengal. If the creation of small states goes on continuing, India will be fragmented into many petty states with emergence of more new political parties. Emergence of more political parties means that there cannot be any single political party in India winning 2/3rds majority in the election for the purpose of forming government at the centre by a single party and accordingly government will be formed with conglomeration of different political parties with different ideologies and policies which does not augur well for governance of the country in the manner it is desired. Formation of such government at the centre will be weak which will retard progress of the country.

Now, it is a subject of debate as to whether the new states which are created will serve the purpose for which they were created. Analyses in true perspective will reveal that axing of states to form another states is a sheer squandering of money in the Government Exchequer and the development of these states will no doubt be affected. All these states will require appointment of Governors, Chief Ministers, Council of Ministers and State Secretaries, entailing colossal amount of money necessitating payment of handsome salaries to them as also their upkeep by way of maintaining fleet of motor cars, ministerial/residential bungalows/houses, travelling, telephones etc. etc. Also all required personnel of top hierarchy including IAS and IPS officers and State Services personnel have to be deployed for the new states. Moreover, development of the new state capitals by way of civil construction and other basic amenities will drain out state Exchequer. Apart from this, several crores of rupees will be spent to build the basic infrastructure for these states. This will retard progress and development of the new states for some years ahead.

There is no guarantee that creation of new small states will be conducive to better the lot of the people especially in the neglected regions. There are many small states in India such as Kerala, Assam, Weat Bengal, Tripura, Manipur, Meghalaya, Nagaland and the like and each one of these states is plagued with its own distinctive multifarious problems. Development and progress of these states have been retarded due to continued militancy and periodical strikes and bundhs. Creation of new small states is no solution, but the development of the states already in existence is the crying need of the hour. What is needed most is the dynamic leadership in every state that alone can create congenial atmosphere where the people can enjoy basic needs and facilities to show their maximum potentiality. All these show that it is immaterial whether a state is small or big; what is required is a will to govern with all sincerity. Lust for power for becoming Chief Ministers of new states should not be the criterion. Every penny meant for development of states should percolate the lower level instead of pocketing money by the politicians and bureaucrats. Creation of new states will only add to the financial crunch and multiply problems.

Q.9. What are the fundamental rights guaranteed under the Constitution of India?

Ans. The fundamental rights guaranteed by the Constitution of India are classified under the following heads:

(a) *Right to Equality*

It guarantees to all Indian citizens equality before law as also equal protection of law. It blurs discrimination between citizens on ground of religion, race, caste, sex and place of birth. The Constitution guarantees equal opportunities to all citizens as far as public employment is concerned excepting in the case that some posts may be reserved for backward classes. It also abolishes untouchability.

(b) *Right to Freedom*

Article 19 of the Constitution guarantees the following freedoms:

(i) Freedom of speech and expression,

(ii) Freedom to assemble peacefully and without arms,

(iii) Freedom to form associations and unions,

(iv) Freedom of movement throughout India,

(v) Freedom to reside and settle down in any part of India and

(vi) Freedom to practise any profession or to carry on any occupation, trade or business.

These freedoms are of course subject to reasonable restrictions that may be curbed by the state in the interests of the sovereignty and integrity of India, security of the state, friendly relations with foreign states, public order, decency or morality or any other restrictions in the interest of the general public.

(c) *Right against Exploitation*

The right bans traffic in human being, begar or any other form of forced labour. Employment of children below the age of 14 years in any factory or mine or other risky occupations is also prevented by law.

(d) *Right to Freedom of Religion*

All citizens of India have been guaranteed freedom to profess, practise and propagate any religion. Every religious group has also the right to own, acquire and administer property for religious purposes.

(e) *Right to Constitutional Remedies*

It guarantees the right to move the Apex Court for the enforcement of Fundamental Rights. This right can, however, be abrogated during the operation of promulgation of emergency by the President.

(f) *Cultural and Education Right*

This right guarantees to the minorities the right of conserving their language, script and culture, to receive education and administer educational institutions of their choice.

Q.10. Under what circumstances Emergency can be proclaimed in the country.

Ans. Three types of Emergency are promulgated in the country in times of grave national peril as per the provisions of the Constitution of India which are (a) National Emergency, (b) Constitutional Emergency and (c) Financial Emergency. Under the following circumstances three types of Emergency are declared:

(a) *National Emergency* (*Article: 352*)

When the President of India is fully satisfied that the country is facing great danger to its security either from external aggression or armed insurrection or internal disturbance or there is likelihood of the imminent dangers of the above threats, he can declare National Emergency in the country under Article 352. Declaration of Emergency by the President is of course subject to prior approval of the Parliament voting separately both in Lok Sabha and Rajya Sabha. As per the Constitution there is no specific time limit of continuance of such type of Emergency. When there is promulgation of this Emergency people's rights are abrogated and they do not have the right to move the court of law for enforcement of their basic rights as citizens of India.

(b) *Constitutional Emergency* (Article: 356)

On the recommendation of the Governor of a State if the President is satisfied that the government of a particular state cannot function in conformity with the Constitution, he can proclaim Constitutional Emergency at his own for a maximum period of two months without approval of the Parliament, On account of proclamation of this Emergency the President assumes himself all functions of the state dissolving the State Legislature and dismissing the State Council of Ministers. With the approval of Parliament proclamation of this Emergency will be for one year at a stretch which can be extended every year but not for more than three years and that too with due approval of Parliament.

(c) *Financial Emergency* (Article: 360)

The President can proclaim financial Emergency if he is satisfied that there is threat to financial stability or credit of the country either wholly or partly. In this case, he can issue directive to any state government to observe financial propriety strictly. He may also issue orders to reduce salaries and allowances of the employees working for the state and union governments including those of the judges of Apex Court and High Courts. He may also ask the state governments to submit before him all money bills for his concurrence after they are passed by the State Legislature. Proclamation of Financial Emergency will expire after two months unless approved by Parliament. This Emergency can be extended by one year at a stretch but not for more than three years.

Q.11. In what way the nationalistic spirit amongst the Indians could be heightened?

Ans. Nationalistic spirit amongst the Indians is very important. The spirit of rallying round the government by the people in times of weal and woe gives an impetus to overcome any hurdle and danger facing the country especially in times of threat or attack by foreign power which was displayed unitedly by all the Indians at the time of Chinese aggression in the year, 1962. India was liberated from the British rule after prolonged struggle and now the people are enjoying the laurels of freedom. This independence has to be upheld at any price and the onus of responsibility in this respect lies with all the citizens of India by upholding nationalistic spirit. The strength of the government increases manifold when the citizens of the country are behind the government for any action taken by the government in the best interest of the country, and the foreign powers will think twice to undertake any misadventure against the country looking to its solidarity and toughness of the people of the country.

Here lies the nationalistic spirit of the people. Although there is no wanting in the nationalistic spirit of the citizens of India, still there is absolute need to heighten it to the maximum for speedy prosperity of the country. The following gestures are suggested to inculcate the spirit of nationalism amongst the Indians in a bigger way:

(a) National flag symbolises country's esteem. Showing respect to the National flag is the inherent obligation of the countrymen as a mark of nationalistic spirit. Respect to the National flag must be exhibited by throwing away the stubs of sigarettes/bidis by the passers-by at the time when the National flag is being hoisted—what to talk of others assembling at the place of hoisting the flag.

(b) When the national anthem is played people must stand up as a mark of respect.

(c) There must be close cooperation amongst all people—high or low and all wranglings must be forgotten and buried. Also the people are to be courteous in their behaviour. Sense of nationalism must flow in the blood of the people.

(d) Armed forces are the country's defence. Their valour as well as morale is to be rejuvenated by extending moral support to them by the countrymen at times of peril of the country when there is incursion by foreign forces.

(e) Majority of the countrymen are to think of two morsels of food by the sweat of their brow, because of economic disparity between the rich and the poor. Nationalistic spirit is enkindled when the people feel cosy from economic embarrassment. Government should, therefore, redress them from economic pangs by adopting pragmatic economic policies for alleviating the distress of the poor.

(f) Some section of the people working in Organisations of strategic importance should not give vent to/pass on documents/information clandestinely to the foreign agencies the strategem of the Government of India in respect of defence deal and its vital installations which are strictly confidential, thus jeopardising the country's interests. This will tell upon the patriotic spirit of the people in general. In order, therefore, to generate nationalistic spirit it is of utmost necessity that a section of persons should desist from such fraudulent act.

Q.12. What were the probable reasons leading to the assassination of Abdul Gani Lone, the senior leader of the separatist All-Parties Hurriyat Conference on 21st May, 2002?

Ans. The assassination of Abdul Gani Lone has no doubt been hatched by deep rooted conspiracy aimed at scuttling the saner voice of the Kashmiri people and its leadership. On the afternoon of 21st May, 2002, when Abdul Gani Lone was about to get in his car after attending a rally at the martyr's graveyard of the Kashmir Mirwaiz, Moulavi Mohammad Farooq on his 12th death anniversary, he was shot at his chest by two unidentified gunmen wearing police uniform.

Following are the probable reasons for the assassination of Abdul Gani Lone:

(1) On his way to the U.S. in the month of April, 2002 for treatment of his heart ailment, Abdul Gani Lone had attended a conference at Dubai along with Omar Farooq and the former Prime Minister of Pak-occupied Kashmir, Sardar Abdul Quyoom Khan. After the consultations in the conference, Lone went on record to say that foreign militants, were no longer welcome in the state of Jammu and Kashmir and that guns could not solve the Kashmir problem. Lone had come out against *jihad* as a means of achieving political goal. His statements asking the foreign militants to leave Kashmir was seen as a dangerous step by the I.S.I.

(2) The fear of free and fair Assembly election in Jammu and Kashmir was also another factor that went against Lone. Militant groups in Jammu and Kashmir were all along dread against holding Assembly elections by the Government of India. They were scared that Lone might even participate in the ensuing Assembly election amid signs that the Hurriyat Leader was trying to revive his party, the People's Conference and if it was achieved the activities of the terrorists duly supported by the I.S.I, would be curbed and their design would be foiled to undermine the hopes of the Kashmiri people for free and fair election in Jammu and Kashmir thus upsetting Pakistan's stratagem.

These were the probable reasons for the assassination of Abdul Gani Lone and the plan to kill him was hatched at a meeting of the Islamic Jehadi Council in Pakistan-occupied Kashmir just 10 days before the murder. This meeting was also attended by ISI officers in Muzaffarabad.

Q.13. What is all about Poll Reforms Ordinance?

Ans. The Supreme Court of India on 2nd May, 2002 directed the Government and the Election Commission to bring in a series of reforms to the Representation of People's Act, of which three guidelines became contentious:

(i) A candidate would have to declare his criminal record while filing his nomination for contesting election,

(ii) He would have to declare his assets and liabilities, including those of his spouse and dependants,

(iii) He would have to make his educational qualifications public.

In the event of not implementing the directives of the Apex Court, the President, Dr. A.P.J. Abdul Kalam asked the government what the legal implications of these directives were and why they were not to be implemented.

As per the suggestion of the Attorney General, Soli J. Sorabjee and the desire of the President, the Union Cabinet passed a Bill to amend the Representation of People's Act, which were as follows:

The Lok Sabha passed the Bill on 17th December, 2002 stipulating that an elected candidate in the Parliament and Assembly has to declare his assets and liabilities before the Speaker or the Presiding Officer of the House concerned.

A candidate contesting for a Parliament or Assembly seat will have to disclose whether he is accused of any offence punishable with imprisonment for two years or more in a pending case in which charges have been framed.

The Supreme Court declared the amended electoral reforms of the Government of India as "unconstitutional" which negated the Court's 2nd May, 2002 verdict. The Apex Court emphasised that it was mandatory for the candidates to disclose their criminal antecedents, assets and liabilities as also educational qualifications in the nominal paper.

The Apex Court, therefore, pronounced separate but concurring judgements as follows on 13th March, 2003:

(i) Whether he is convicted/acquitted/discharged of any criminal offence in the past, if any, whether he is punished with imprisonment or fine,

(ii) Prior to six months of filing the nomination, whether he or she is accused in any pending case of any offence punishable with imprisonment for two years or more, and in which charge is framed or cognisance is taken by the court of law.

(iii) The assets (movable, immovable, bank balances etc.) and of his/her spouse and that of dependants,

(iv) Liabilities, particularly whether there are any overdues of any public financial institutions or government dues,

(v) Furnishing the candidate's educational qualifications in the nomination paper.

After pronouncing the judgement, Justice Shah said that the judgement was aimed at cleansing the democracy of unwanted elements and give the country a competent legislature. Unless the government attempts to circumvent the judgement, each candidate would have to furnish on affidavit as many as five types of information while filing his/her nomination. The adherence to order of Supreme Court is in the interest of displaying India as a prestigious democratic country of the world. The judgement of the Apex Court is also very important in the sense that the electorate will be in a position to know that they would be going to caste their votes in favour of genuine candidates who would be representing them from Indian Parliament. Also the legislature cannot declare that the law declared by the Supreme Court is not binding.

Q.14. What are the impediments facing the government to undertake speedy developmental activities of the country although the country is endowed with plenty of resources?

Ans. India attained 55 years of independence on 15th August, 2002. As many as 9th Five-year Plan was already completed with no abatement in the unemployment problem in the country. India has attained "Green Revolution" but still then there are starvation deaths in the country. With the lapse of years there has been the birth of multifarious political parties which are contesting the elections for getting maximum seats in the Parliament. But, not a single political party is emerging out to get absolute majority to form government of its own and the result is that conglomeration of different political parties with different ideologies and policies is the way out for formation of government at the centre. This results in installation of government practically on weak foundation.

For such type of government the Prime Minister has

to be very much meticulous to exercise his wit, mental acumen and political sagacity to bind the heterogeneous political parties in one fold in the face of threats by any of the political parties to quit the Alliance Government for any dissension. The opposition party and the other political parties not joining the Alliance Government come forward with scathing criticism against the ruling all-party Government for the lapses committed and go on demanding resignations of the ministers every now and then in the matter of their involvement in corruptions and scams and the like which have become a regular feature in the Government. Under such circumstances, the ruling Alliance Government has to be very much nimble in tackling the situation to save the Government from possible disintegration—what to talk of looking after the development of the country giving priority to it.

The country has become the hot-bed of uneasiness and disquiet everywhere. I.S.I. has become rampant determining to aggrandise their nefarious activities. Cross-border terrorism in Jammu and Kashmir has been let loose with no abatement. Belicosity of Pakistan in bedeviling the relation with India has resulted in preparation for war at the cost of development of the country. ULFA activities in North-Eastern region are uncheckable in their growth. Vilification against the individual ministers has become common. Tumultuous uproar and lawlessness in Parliament has marred the proceedings. It is more in the nature of mud-slinging. The abuse of the dignity of Parliaments as observed today is a sure sign of the fragility of the democratic ethos in India.

For all these situations the Government is not finding plain sailing and their road of progress is full of unbreakable rubbles. They have to remain busy althrough in its attempt to bring normalcy in the situation. To all intents and purposes, it has posed a direct challenge to the Government to divert its attention for speedy development of the country pregnant with plenty of resources, although 55 years is sufficiently a long time for development on all fronts. It is noteworthy to mention that during the regimes of Jawaharlal Nehru and Indira Gandhi the wheel of development of the country moved faster than what it is now. The plausible reason for the same was that India during their Prime Ministership was not fraught with the invincible problems like the above and particularly when it was a one party government with no political wrangling and turmoil and the world as a whole was more or less peaceful.

Q.15. How could it be justified that Parvez Musharraf, President of Pakistan lacks political sagacity by his actions and deeds with special reference to Kashmir issue?

Ans. The assertions of Parvez Musharraf and his actions and deeds prove that he is devoid of political sagacity, as per the analyses of the points, as enumerated below:

(i) Parvez Musharraf, who became the darling of the West after joining the U.S.-led coalition against terrorism, exposed himself both to the outside world and to the people of Pakistan by deciding to hold a referendum in the country to formalise his presidentship. The stage-managed elections made it clear to the people of Pakistan that Musharraf was no better than the politicians in Pakistan.

(ii) The elections in Jammu & Kashmir which the U.S. and the other world powers supported made Musharraf jittery as he feared that this could lead to the isolation of Pakistan on Kashmir issue. Islamabad said that elections in the state of Jammu and Kashmir could not be a substitute to the Kashmir's demand for a plebiscite. If the election in Kashmir was no substitute to the demand for plebiscite, would the October, 2002 election in Pakistan be a substitute for democracy in Pakistan?

(iii) Parvez Musharraf asserted that elections in Jammu and Kashmir would not be credible if there was no free participation of other political parties. If this contention of Parvez Musharraf was correct, would the exclusion of former Prime Ministers, Nawaz Sharif and Benazir Bhutto and other important political leaders in the polls in Pakistan give it credibility?

(iv) The Pakistani establishment often said that the earlier elections in Jammu and Kashmir were rigged. If claim of the President of Pakistan was correct that the elections in Pakistan for formalising his Presidentship were free and fair, was not the counting of the votes rigged?

(v) Parvez Musharraf argues that a low voter turn out in the Kashmir valley means that the people reject India. But, does the low voter turn out in Pakistan in the elections for formalising Parvez Musharraf as President of Pakistan for the next five years also mean that the people of Pakistan have rejected Musharraf?

(vi) Parvez Musharraf attempted to ridicule India's failure to grant greater autonomy to the Kashmiris despite provisions in the Constitution. But, have not the constitutional amendments in Pakistan led to the curtailment of its Parliament's autonomy and marginalising the role of the Prime Minister?

The above assertions, deeds and actions of Parvez Musharraf are the justifications that he is the biggest violator of democracy and democratic traditions in Pakistan and, therefore, he has no right to meddle in the matter of Jammu and Kashmir, which testify his lack of political will and sagacity.

Q.16. What is distressing is that Pakistan has been continuously daring to resort to proxy war and treating India a weak country even threatening to strike militarily with nuclear bomb. Under the circumstances, what should be the policies and actions of India to counteract the belicosity of Pakistan to stand with prestige and honour?

Ans. It is an undisputed fact that the strength of India is much greater than that of Pakistan in all respects such as, size of the country, number of population, education of the people, science and technology, economic sovereignty and military power.

In Pakistan there is fragile democracy even though civilian governments are formed with two-thirds majority. It represents long-standing tussle between military and parliamentary rule that has characterised government in Pakistan since independence in 1947. Since there have been number of bloodless coup in Pakistan, overthrowing the democratically elected governments, the military rulers have practically no other business but mainly to nurture military strength and adventurism. This tendency of the military governments in Pakistan has tended to divert attention in its first priority to equip the country militarily even at the cost of economic development of the country. This is the reason as to why the people of Pakistan have not still tested the economic liberalisation and prosperity.

The only objective of Pakistan is to ascend to the position of military power to have a sway over the big country—India and, therefore, they are ruthlessly and frantically exploring other countries for procuring military hardware and arsenal for land, air and sea. Although they met with failures in all the wars with India in the past, they seem to be bent upon obliterating the blot of their discomfiture in wars and are, therefore, harnessing themselves to find opportunity to come out triumphant over India militarily at the opportune moment, which will of course be a distant dream for them. In order, therefore, to bolster their morale to undertake any misadventure on India, the military government of Pakistan have chosen the path of undermining the strength of India, when they could find that the Government of India could not put in any resolute hindrances to the following acts:

(i) 7,00,000 lakh of Indian army deployed along the Line of Control in Jammu and Kashmir cannot even check the infiltration of terrorist outfit across the border.

(ii) Defenceless Kashmiri people are living at the mercy of ruthless militants whom the government of India seem powerless to fight.

(iii) Ghastly terrorist attack on Jammu & Kashmir Assembly House on 1st October, 2001.

(iv) Audacious terrorist attack on Indian Parliament on 13th December, 2001 which was a major attack on Indian democracy.

(v) Militants' attacks on Jammu bound Himachal bus near Vijaypur on the Jammu-Pathankot highway and the army residential quarters at Kaluchak near Jammu in disguise of Indian army on 14th May, 2002.

(vi) The Agents of the Inter-Services Intelligence of Pakistan have spread all over India to collect vital and secret information for passing over to the government of Pakistan at the nose of the Intelligence Branch of Government of India.

Under the circumstances, the policies and actions of the Government of India to counteract the belicosity of Pakistan undermining the real strength of India should be as follows to stand with prestige and honour:

(i) Diplomatically, Pakistan has to be cowed down by mobilising the world powers. This will be advantageous for India especially for the reason that no democratic country of the world puts in high esteem the military government of any country.

(ii) India has to redouble its endeavour to sweeten relations on perennial basis with all the G-8 nations of the world namely, the United States of America, Great Britain, France, Germany, Canada, Russia, Japan and Italy as also other countries especially China burying the old hatchet.

(iii) With the support of all these countries India

should endeavour to become one of the permanent members of United Nations Organisation.

(iv) India must be resolute to deal with the terrorists so that they do not dare to sneak into Indian territory of Jammu and Kashmir.

(v) The activities of I.S.I. operating in India have to be completely routed by gearing the Intelligence Branch of the Government of India.

(vi) Human Resource Development is to be given special priority for achieving 80 per cent literacy in order to create more gainful employment opportunities during the 10th Plan period ending in 2007 and by 2012 there must be reduction of poverty to 10 per cent.

(vii) India must be made a welfare state latest by 2015 and not by 2020, as envisaged by the President of India, Dr. A.P.J. Abdul Kalam.

(viii) India should go on continuing to develop militarily side by side with economic development by launching family planning programme strictly to reduce growth of population, because mushroom growth of population is the hurdle for economic development.

(ix) Unnecessary and superfluous Govt. expenditures are to be curtailed.

(x) Efforts should continue that Pakistan is declared as a terrorist country, as it is probable that Pakistan still supports Osama bin Laden and the Al-Qaida clandestinely.

By all these actions India will no doubt command suzerainty over Pakistan as a powerful country in South East Asia and Pakistan in turn will cease to vilify and underestimate the strength of India in future years to come.

Q.17. What is the political and strategic significance arising out of the arms agreement between India and the United States of America?

Ans. The arms agreement signed between India and the United States of America is of immense political and strategic significance. Under this Agreement, the US will supply India with eight AN/TPQ-37 Firefinders, which is a long-range weapon-locating radar system. The deal is worth about $146 million. There are important features of the sale which merit attention. The Kargil War Review Committee had identified weapon-locating radars as an absolute necessity for ensuring the country's security and to help prevent future incursion by Pakistan. The US Firefinder will be able to detect and pinpoint the location of the enemy's weapons. The Firefinder is light in weight, small and highly mobile. It is also capable of detecting weapon projectiles launched at any angle. Pakistan already has deployed AN/TPQ-36 Firefinder radar but it is not equipped with communications equipment of the same level of sophistication as the ones supplied to India.

This is the first arms deal signed between India and the US in over a decade. The Defence Security Corporation Agency of India has termed this defence deal as historic and epoch making. What is most important is the Pentagon's argument that the sale of AN/TPQ-37 would help the national security interests of the US by helping to improve the security of India, political stability as also economic progress in South Asia. More significantly, the sale reflects the growing convergence of strategic interests between India and the United States of America which also cements defence cooperation between these two countries. This is also vitally important to confront the belicosity of Pakistani attitude towards India. This arms deal with the US will further substantiate India's suzerainty over Pakistan in the matter of military strength, so that Pakistan thinks twice to undertake any military misadventure against India in future. Out of this arms deal, Indian and US air force have chalked out an agenda for joint training and cooperation and it is in the interests of both the countries to ensure that this cooperation is further solidified in future years to come.

Q.18. How are the Indo-U.S. relations?

Ans. Formulation/change of foreign policy of any Government depends upon the change of world political scenario. In the past there was no incident which soured the Indo-U.S. relations. After the attack on the World Trade Center and the Pentagon on 11th September, 2001 and war against Afghanistan, there has been a perceptible change in the formulation of foreign policy of the United States of America towards South Asian countries. The U.S. has now made a major contribution to forging new political, economic and technological ties between India and the U.S. As a first step to better relations, the US Government has lifted the sanctions imposed against India after detonation of atom bomb by India. The disclosure that the United States of America has advised Pakistan to hand over the 20 terrorists wanted for trial in India is the latest instance of Washinton's understanding of India's security concerns. This new development in American policy has been in evidence since the Kargil conflict, when Washington's supportive stance came as a pleasant surprise to New Delhi. There are some indications that in the Bush administration's perception a relatively strong India would better serve the cause of maintaining peace and stability in Asia. India's economic growth is undoubtedly the major reason for India's heightened profile in the U.S. India has come to acquire a distinctly higher profile in Washington during the last decade. The change in U.S. perceptions towards India is explained by the following facts:

(1) The termination of the strategic alliance with Pakistan removed the principal impediment to closure ties with India.

(2) Washington is no longer prepared to turn a blind eye to Pakistan's clandestine acquisition of nuclear and missile technology from China and North Korea.

(3) The steady decline of the Pakistan economy and the serious law and order situation contributed to declining American interest in that country.

(4) India's economic reforms since 1992 drew attention of the U.S. Government as a potential partner in trade and investment.

(5) Liberalisation and simplification of regulations for foreign investors stimulated American interest in the Indian economy.

(6) The past few decades have for the first time witnessed emigration of Indian professionals to the U.S. on a substantial scale.

(7) India has an obvious stake in the success of current U.S. moves to exterminate terrorism in Afghanistan and Pakistan. India and the United States are planning military cooperation in select areas in the immediate future which has become important in the context of the war on terrorism.

(8) The Bush administration appears to show some understanding of the compulsions behind India's modest nuclear weapon programme.

(9) The hurdle has been cleared for scrapping restrictions on Indo-U.S. cooperation in space and nuclear energy following a 35-minute meeting between the then Prime Minister, Atal Behari Vajpayee and President, George W. Bush on 12th September, 2002 at New York when Shri Vajpayee went to attend the 57th UN General Assembly. The restrictions which were in force even before India's nuclear tests in 1998 were tightened by the Bill Clinton administration after India declared itself a nuclear weapons state.

The above facts are transparent evidences that India and the U.S. have made a promising start to establishing a new partnership, but it will require sustained efforts by both sides to build up truly durable ties.

Q.19. How are the Sino-Indian relations after the terrorist attack on World Trade Center and Pentagon on 11th September, 2001?

Ans. It is admittedly recognised that Sino-Indian relations deteriorated after the Chinese invasion to India in

1962. All cooperations between these two countries came to a stand-still since then.

The U.S. led attack on Afghanistan to suppress international terrorism has changed the South Asian policies of China in the context of the challenge which the U.S. has posed to Chinese influence in the area by the U.S.'s planned long-term strategic presence in South Asian countries. There is U.S. military presence now in Pakistan at Peshawar, Abbotabad and at the ports of Pasni, Gwadar and Karachi. This has complicated China's naval presence in the Port of Gwadar. Apart from this, the U.S. Central Command's physical presence in Uzbekistan, Kyrgyzstan and Afghanistan has also become a matter of great concern for China. Although China has close political and strategic involvement with Pakistan, yet she has now felt the absolute necessity that the controversies which afflicted Sino-Indian relations in the aftermath of India's nuclear weapon tests in 1998 have to be set aside to get bilateral relations back on track.

The visit of the Chinese Prime Minister, Zhu Rongji to India early in January, 2002 has got tremendous importance at a point of time when India's relations with Pakistan were in a state of high tension. This clearly indicates China's desire to have an even-handed and impartial relationship with India. The discussions between the Chinese and Indian leaders have emphasized the revival of continuity in Sino-Indian relations which began with the visit of the former President of India, K.R. Narayanan to China. As a step forward to cement the bond of relationship between India and China, the following significant bilateral agreements were signed with China during Rongji's visit to India in early January, 2002:

(a) Resumption of direct civil aviation contact between Beijing and New Delhi,

(b) Cooperation in the fields of tourism, space, science and technology,

(c) Cooperation in countering terrorism through the

creation of a Sino-Indian joint and comprehensive disarmament,

(d) Agreement on working towards a just and fair economic order and potential for bilateral technical cooperation.

Rongji's visit to India at a time of sub-continental crisis and his statements indicate that possibilities of Sino-Indian cooperation exists in the wake of US presence in the area for directing next targets on North Korea, Iraq and Iran.

As a gesture of goodwill China has also offered India as follows:

(a) China offered Exchange Defence Training Facilities: As a gesture of goodwill China has offered for the first time training facilities for senior Indian military officers at the National Defence University in Beijing on a reciprocal basis with Chinese military officers to be trained at National Defence College in New Delhi.

(b) China has invited Indian Companies to set up Units in SEZs (Special Economic Zones). Apart from this, China's Economic Development Bureau also invited Indian Companies to set up units including joint ventures in power, telecom, construction, pharma and petro-chemical sectors.

(c) Indo-China Border Talks: At the 13th meeting of Sino-Indian Joint working Group held in Beijing on 2nd August, 2001, India and China agreed to hold the next round of Experts Group on delineation of line of Actual Control by the end of the year, 2001.

All these developments and changes arising out of the US led campaign against international terrorism, China and India have no doubt come closer in establishing cordial relations on sound footing.

Q.20. How is the relation between the Arab countries and India?

Ans. During the last one decade or so the relation between the Arab countries and India was not of course very much cosy. The following reasons were responsible for the same:

(i) The fallout of the destruction of the Babri Masjid was not taken as a good omen by the Muslim countries.

(ii) Sporadic communal violence over the last three and a half years and on the top of it Gujarat violence affected the Muslims of India.

(iii) When the Arab countries are depricating Israel for its continued attacks and occupation of part of territory of Palestine, denying its liberation movement, India's relations with Israel at the same time in the context of expansion of Indo-Israeli political, economic and defence cooperation have not been taken in good taste by the Arab countries.

(iv) When the US government was contemplating to attack Iraq to put an end to the Saddam Hussein government and when the Arab countries were all united to protest against this naked design of the USA, India's leaning towards the US government in the matter of fighting international terrorism was not supportive by the Arab countries.

India evaluates very much maintenance of perennial relations with all the Arab countries of the Gulf and West Asia for a number of reasons. The first fortnight of August, 2002 witnessed an interesting initiative by the Government of India to restore warmth and expand cooperation with all the Arab countries for the following reasons:

(a) Nearly 15 per cent of India's citizens are Muslims. They have spiritual, emotional and cultural affinities with the people of the Arab countries.

(b) India has a long historical connection with the Arab countries, stretching from Algeria and Morocco to the countries of the Gulf over nearly a period of 1200 years.

(c) India's culture and languages have been immensely influenced by the interaction with the Arabs.

(d) Arab countries form an important segment of the membership of the United Nations. Hence, their support is very important to Indian matters which are discussed there.

(e) The support of the Arab countries are essentially needed by India for the cause of Kashmir.

(f) Between 60 to 70 per cent of India's energy resources imports come from the Arab countries.

(g) Large number of skilled and unskilled Indian population employed in various Arab countries are a major source of foreign exchange earnings for India.

(h) Continuing cooperation with Arab countries has growth potential in India in terms of energy, investments and transfer of technologies, goods and services.

In view of the above, India has felt an imperative need to improve relations with the Arab countries. In this connexion, the most important event was the visit of the Deputy Prime Minister and Foreign Minister of Syria to India from 12th to 14th August, 2002 with whom the matters concerning regional security environment, the West Asian crisis, India's regional concerns, its worries about cross border terrorism and Pakistan's India policies were discussed in detail. Along with Egypt and Saudi Arabia, Syria is the most influential country in the region and a key player for forging on the Palestine issue.

The second significant factor in the initiation of improving relations with the Arab countries was the hosting of a tea reception by the then Foreign Minister, Yashwant Sinha for all the Arab Ambassadors and heads of diplomatic missions in New Delhi in the first week of August, 2002. In this tea reception Mr. Sinha briefed the Ambassadors about the current state of Indo-US relations, circumstances under which relations with

Israel is being maintained in the sphere of political, economic and defence cooperation, the initiation for normal governance in Jammu and Kashmir, India's concerns regarding cross-border terrorism sponsored by Pakistan, India's reservation and opposition to the planned invasion of the USA on Iraq and India's support for the fulfilment of the legitimate aspirations of the Palestinian people.

The current initiative taken by the Government of India will no doubt yield positive result and the Arab countries would come to a rational and practical understanding with India in the matter of maintaining cosy relations for all the future years to come.

Q.21. Is it correct to say that Kashmiri Muslims are gradually converging with India?

Ans. Pakistani sponsored militancy and terrorism unleashed in Kashmir valley has caused terror and the lives of the people living there have become most unsafe. During this period thousands of innocent human lives have perished in the hands of the Pakistani sponsored militants and terrorists. The militancy has also led to the prolonged closure of University and Medical and Engineering Colleges sine-die. As a result, Kashmiri students have been compelled to seek admission in other Indian Universities as also Medical and Engineering colleges. Also, after the outbreak of violence and resurrection in 1990 when tourists and traders stopped coming to the valley, Kashmiri manufacturers found no other way but to start doing business by opening shops and restaurants in different parts of India. Kashmiris have now very clearly understood that their future prosperity rests with India and not with Pakistan. India is a secular country. Hindus and Muslims are living in peace and amity. India is also the second highest Muslim populated country in the world, forming about 15 per cent of the total population of India. In the year, 1971 Pakistani authorities conducted stream roller military operation in the then East Pakistan to suppress the voice of the people, for which Gen. Parvez Musharraf tendered apology to the people of Bangladesh during his visit there in the month of June, 2002. The adverse effect is that the Kashmiris have naturally shifted their leaning from Pakistan. All these factors have now led to the converging of the Kashmiri Muslims with India and that they would be well accommodated with India and not with economically moribund Pakistan and so there was no question of separating Jammu & Kashmir from India. The 2002 Assembly elections in Jammu & Kashmir was also a welcome development.

Q.22. Why did the U.S.A. consider Pakistan as their best ally in war against Afghanistan to crush Taliban Government and apprehend Osama bin Laden of al-Qaida, although it is a known fact that Pakistan Government supported althrough these Organisations surreptitiously?

Ans. In the war against Afghanistan practically three powers were in direct action *i.e.*, the U.S.A., Great Britain and Northern Alliance to fight against the Taliban Government and apprehend Osama bin Laden who master-minded the attack on World Trade Center, New York and Pentagon in Washington on 11th September, 2001. It is no hidden to the world that Pakistan is the hotbed of terrorist movement. Militants of al-Qaida have been receiving training from the soil of Pakistan occupied Kashmir, duly supported by the Government of Pakistan.

When India repeatedly appealed to the U.S.A. to crush the terrorist outfit *i.e.*, al-Qaida group also in Pakistan occupied Kashmir simultaneously when the war against Afghanistan was continuing with the object of crushing Taliban Government supporting the terrorist outfit, al-Qaida and apprehending Osama bin Laden, the U.S. Government categorically told that their principal object was directed against Afghanistan only.

When terrorism is a world-wide menace and particularly when the U.S. Government has vowed to eliminate terrorism operating world-wide to make the world a place for peaceful living for the humanity, as committed by the U.S. President, W. Bush, the inaction of the U.S. Government to quell terrorism operating in Pakistan occupied Kashmir is a clear manifestation to appease Pakistan who has been fomenting cross border terrorism against India.

The U.S. Government needs Pakistan very much under its suzerainty with the sole object of making foot-hold on the soil of Pakistan to have sway over middle East so that it would be easy for the U.S. Government to make another likely strike against Iraq to hasten fall of Saddam Hussein government. The U.S. Government has lauded Parvez Musharraf, President of Pakistan for rendering help to them for striking U.S. military operation against Afghanistan and assured to waive debt in terms of millions of dollar to help Pakistan come out of financial stringency. In return Parvez Musharraf was also feeling complacent that with the support of the U.S.A. it would be able to take the entire Jammu & Kashmir which is no doubt an illusion and a distant dream on the part of Pakistan, as India has now taken a very tough stand as far as Jammu & Kashmir is concerned. Therefore, the surreptitious policy of the U.S. Government on Middle East has revealed the fact when they openly lauded Pakistan in the war against Afghanistan although the role of Pakistan in the war was not significant. This was the probable reason as to why the U.S. Government considered Pakistan as their best ally in the war against Afghanistan.

Q.23. How was the Indo-Pakistan relation after Parvez Musharraf took over the rein of Pakistan?

Ans. General Parvez Musharraf is a military man. History tells that there was no rapprochement in the relation between the civilian government and the military government. From the actions and activities of Parvez Musharraf it was brought to light that basically he harboured anti-India policy. Belicosity towards India was his life blood being a military personnel. Although he was one of the global coalition partners to suppress terrorism, he nurtured hostile policy towards India by supporting and fomenting cross-border terrorism in India.

That Parvez Musharraf always wanted to put India on the tenterhooks of restlessness for his policy of unleashing terrorism in India was proved by the following major and serious acts of terrorism:

(a) Ghastly terrorist attack on the Assembly House of Jammu & Kashmir at Strinagar on 1st October, 2001.

(b) Audacious terrorist attack on Indian Parliament by the Pakistani sponsored terrorists on 13th December, 2001.

(c) Militants' attacks on Jammu bound Himachal bus near Vijaypur on the Jammu-Pathankot highway and the army residential quarters at Kaluchak near Jammu in disguise of Indian army on 14th May, 2002, killing more than 30 bus passengers, army personnel and their wives and children. Surprisingly, this attack coincided with the visit of Ms. Christina Rocca, U.S. Assistant Secretary of State for South Asia, who was sent to India and Pakistan by Bush Administration to de-escalate tension prevailing between India and Pakistan. But, as ill luck would have it her mission for de-escalation of tension in the region has not yielded any result by this terrorist attack.

(d) Terrorist attack on the Swaminarayan temple at Gandhinagar (Gujarat) on 24th September, 2002, in which at least 27 devotees were killed. This terrorist attack also coincided with the visit of Ms. Christina Rocca, U.S. Assistant Secretary of State for South Asia.

It is very clear from the above evidences of unleashing terrorism in India that the promises made by the President of Pakistan, Mr. Parvez Musharraf in his January, 12, 2002 speech, which included a commitment to stop sponsoring terrorism in Kashmir, did not translate into a reality.

India is a peace loving country which has no tendency of territorial aggrandisement. Indo-Pakistan relation started worsening after Gen. Parvez Musharraf took over the reins of Pakistan as President and also after the failure of Agra summit. During the civilian governments of Pakistan under the Premiership of Mrs. Benazir Bhutto and Nawaz Sharrif, the relation between India and Pakistan was not as bad as that during the Musharraf regime.

Gen. Musharraf was the architect of Kargil war without any provocation from India during the Premiership of Nawaz Sharrif. Mr. Musharraf even clandestinely planned use of nuclear bomb against India during this war when Pakistani troops started retreating by the fury of counter attack by the gallant Indian army. But his stratagem was not successful when the war was to be halted at the intervention of the then U.S. President, Mr. Bill Clinton.

A summit was arranged by the Indian Government at Agra to discuss all issues including Kashmir with Gen. Parvez Musharraf. But for his stubborn attitude at the Summit all disputes between India and Pakistan could not be discussed and resolved and the Agra Summit ended in fiasco. Agra is a place which symbolises love and affection at the instance of the Taj Mahal and with this purpose in view the Government of India earmarked Agra as the ideal venue for such a Summit. President Musharraf did not even feel it worthwhile to stay back at Agra at least for the night but hastened to leave for Islamabad even at the dead of night itself when nothing tangible came out of the Agra Summit which concluded in the night. His immediate leaving for Islamabad was not at all necessitated for his presence there at the dead of night. This was another instance that he did not want to be cosy with India. Since then evidences show that Indo-Pakistan relations started rupturing fast and the tension in the South Asian region continued to mount up due to incalcitrant attitude of the military Government of Pakistan under Gen. Parvez Musharraf and India had to guard its borders with Pakistan by deploying army in massive scale which is an instance for the first time in the history of Indo-Pakistan relations. Not only this, all communications—rail, bus and air were snapped between these two countries. There has been downsizing of the High Commissions Offices of both the countries as also Indian and Pakistan planes are not using air space of each other's country for overseas flights.

Gen. Musharraf had also nullified the Simla Agreement and Lahore Declaration which were the instruments of initiating talks between India and Pakistan to normalise relations between these two countries by resolving peacefully all the disputes across the table. This shows his another step to toughen relations with India.

Who knows what more are stored in the womb of future at the instance of incalcitrant Pakistani attitude towards India under President Parvez Musharraf until India stands firm to retaliate suitably.

Q.24. Pakistan has been telling although that what is happening in Jammu & Kashmir is a liberation movement. How far is the contention of Pakistan true?

Ans. One of the stumbling blocks on the road to the rapid progress of India is Pakistan's consistent and continuing anti-India policy, beginning with its refusal to accept the constitutionally validated and democratically endorsed accession of Jammu & Kashmir to India.

For a long time, the rulers in Islamabad relied on military confrontation with India, as exemplified by the wars they waged in 1948, 1965, 1971 and finally in Kargil in 1999 to settle the Jammu & Kashmir issue militarily. When they could not achieve through open military aggression, the anti-India forces in Pakistan decided to foment cross-border terrorism and religious extremism as the principal means to instigate separatism in India. They also failed miserably in their nefarious and evil design in Punjab. They could not dent Hindu-Sikh unity there. The terrorist attack by Lashker-e-Toiba and Jaish-e-Mohammad with the collusion of

I.S.I. nurtured by Pakistan on Indian Parliament on 13th December, 2001 has shown beyond inkling of doubt that the Anti-India forces in Pakistan are prepared to inflict any havoc on the soil of India. Although India has become a victim of cross-border terrorism and proxy war for the past two decades and has lost tens of thousands of innocent men, women and children as also security forces in Jammu & Kashmir, the outrage of 13th December, 2001 has breached the limit of India's endurance.

Not only Pakistan with the help of the terrorist outfits of Lashker-e-Toiba and Jaish-e-Mohammad fomented terrorist activities in Jammu & Kashmir but also they became an ally of the Taliban Government in Afghanistan for transporting Afghan militants especially of al-Qaida group to Pakistan occupied Jammu & Kashmir for training to bolster terrorist attacks on the state. Terrorist attack on the Jammu & Kashmir Assembly on 1st October, 2001 was a pointer to their nefarious activity. When terrorist attach on Jammu & Kashmir are on its peak, there is practically no liberation movement in Jammu & Kashmir under the aegis of Jammu and Kashmir Liberation Front. All these stratagems adopted to heighten terrorism in Jammu & Kashmir whole-heartedly supported by Pakistan cannot be called liberation movement. Liberation movement is something different which should be actually in the form of Quit India Movement launched by Mahatma Gandhi in August, 1942. But the so-called movement in Jammu & Kashmir is not akin to such movement. In this connexion, it is noteworthy to mention here that Kashmiri people as a whole have not at all revolted against the Indian Government to show that they are fighting for liberation of the state of Jammu & Kashmir.

In view of the above facts and circumstances, there is in fact no liberation movement in Jammu & Kashmir as claimed by Pakistani rulers, but terrorism so that India is cowed down to cede Jammu & Kashmir to Pakistan being unable to contain wild terrorism fueled by Pakistan.

Q.25. What is Pakistan's policy under Gen. Parvez Musharraf towards India on Kashmir issue?

Ans. The policy that Pakistan has been pursuing towards India on Kashmir issue is not maintainable as it is based on supporting terrorism and militancy. Other than this there is no policy. The definite policy of Pakistan towards India on Kashmir issue would be governed to a large extent by its negotiations with the U.S. Government. It is a fact that Parvez Musharraf will have to depend heavily on the U.S. for his survival. If Musharraf is badly needed by the U.S. he will try to push and negotiate for the policies he has always followed. If he is not needed, then he will listen to the U.S. By constantly criticising Benazir Bhutto and Nawaz Shariff, he will project himself as one who did not compromise on Kashmir. It is a worthy point to note that no military government in Pakistan has been able to achieve a breakthrough in relations with a civilian government in India. It is likely that the internal problems of Pakistan would push Gen. Musharraf to change his attitude towards India to some extent. But since Gen. Musharraf has basically anti-India policy on Kashmir issue he may not have the will for radical change of policy towards India, unless otherwise pressurised by the U.S. government in the context of growing bilateral relations between U.S. and India. Although India is opposed to direct third party interference in the matter of solution to Kashmir issue, Pakistan's stand on Kashmir is most likely to be flexible when U.S. will come forward to pressurise Pakistan to concede in the best interest of maintaining peace and stability in South Asia and it is a step forward when India is on the threshold of entering into a new phase of relations with U.S. government.

Q.26. Why is there tussle between India and Pakistan on Kashmir issue and what is India's position in the matter of Kashmir?

And. During the British rule of Indian Sub-continent the state of Jammu & Kashmir was a princely state outside the purview of the suzerainty of British Government as in the case of other French colonies in India. At the time of exit of the British rule from India, the question of merging of Jammu & Kashmir with the new born state, Pakistan did not arise at all, as it was an Independent state, although majority of the people of Jammu & Kashmir were Muslims. The rein of the state of Jammu & Kashmir vested exclusively under its King and the people of the state were not instrumental in deciding their will as per the constitution of independent state of Jammu & Kashmir. Jammu & Kashmir came to India legally and constitutionally because Maharaja Hari Singh signed the instrument of accession in favour of India in 1947 and the people of Jammu & Kashmir did not resent to this verdict of their King, as it was not at all a whimsical and surreptitious decision on the part of the Maharaja. Such being the circumstances, Pakistan must not have any say in the matter.

In this context, it is important to mention here that the infamous Laiq Ali had persuaded the Nizam of Hyderabad to sign the instrument of accession in favour of Pakistan. But, when the emotions and sentiments of the people of the territory veered overwhelmingly in another direction, the instrument of accession in favour of Pakistan did not come to play and hence Hyderabad could not become an inalienable part of Pakistan notwithstanding the Laiq Ali Coup. Viewed in this light the inalienability of Jammu & Kashmir is an illusory concept.

Jammu & Kashmir has its tremendous territorial and strategic importance and Pakistan, as it thinks, can ill afford to part with it and so is bent upon taking possession of the state by hook or crook though they have no locus standi over Jammu & Kashmir from the legality point of view. Their tactical efforts to get Jammu & Kashmir are aimed at the following:

(a) The blood of the Kashmiri Muslims is flowing in the veins of the Pakistanis, as they say, which is absurd, unrealistic and ridiculous.

(b) They waged wars with India on Kashmir issue and could not succeed winning over the territory militarily.

(c) They occupied a part of Jammu & Kashmir militarily in 1948 which is still in their possession and surprisingly they gifted a part of occupied Kashmir measuring more than 5,000 sqare kms. to China with the very clear intention of cementing the bond of relations for all the years to come and making direct link geographically with that country for transportation of war equipment and arsenals in particular for making Pakistan strong militarily with the avowed intention of counteracting India with all military might in the event of war with India on Kashmir issue.

(d) Pakistan has been fomenting cross-border terrorism killing thousands of innocent Kashmiris. They have now adopted stratagem to draw the world attention that what has been happening in Kashmir is not terrorism but liberation movement for Kashmir.

India's Position on Kashmir

(a) Jammu & Kashmir is an integral part of India since 1947 in view of the instrument of accession and hence there is no question of self-determination for the people of Kashmir.

(b) Kashmir came to India because Maharaja Hari Singh signed the instrument of accession in favour of India in 1947 and the people of Kashmir were not instrumental in the matter of deciding their will.

(c) Pakistan is the proven aggressor in Kashmir and it is only with the grace of India that it continues to occupy that part of the Indian state of Jammu & Kashmir which is on the other side of the line of control. Now, the task with India is to get back the occupied portion of Kashmir. India is now sticking to the principle that unless the occupied part of Jammu & Kashmir including the one gifted to China is handed over to India, no discussion on Kashmir issue would take place.

(d) The Simla Agreement signed in 1977 made it clear that the outstanding issues including Kashmir are to be resolved only through bilateral parleys between India and Pakistan and no third party could be involved in the matter of such negotiations.

(e) Although East Pakistan was a Muslim dominated state, it cut asunder from the control of West Pakistan and emerged as a sovereign state in the year, 1971 in the name of Bangladesh. This clearly testifies that the Muslim dominated state is not the criterion that Jammu & Kashmir should belong to Pakistan on this count, as was the contention of the Pakistani ruler that the blood of Kashmiri Muslims was flowing in the veins of the Pakistanis.

Q.27. How far is it true that the Muslims and the other minority communities of India have been persecuted as alleged by Parvez Musharraf, President of Pakistan, during the course of his speech in the 57th U.N. General Assembly at New York on 12th September, 2002, citing instance of Gujarat riot in February, 2002, thus spoiling the secular fabric of India during the regime of NDA Government headed by Bharatiya Janata Party?

Ans. Shri Atal Behari Vajpayee, the then Prime Minister of India, gave a fitting reply to this allegation of Gen. Musharraf, in the U.N. General Assembly on 13th September, 2002. Shri Vajpayee assured that the Gujarat riot should be seen as an exception and not the rule. He recalled some of the steps taken in the wake of the Gujarat violence to ensure that they do not happen in future, including punitive measures against those guilty of sparking the riots. The BJP government has the real intention to ensure safety and security of the religious minorities in India. India is a multi-religious state ever since partition in 1947 and the minority communities are fully adjusted with the culture and traditions of India as one nation. Constitution of India guarantees equal rights to all citizens irrespective of caste, creed and religion. Muslims, Christians and other minority communities have been living in juxtaposition with the Hindus with prestige, honour and without fear. Shri Vajpayee reminded the world leaders that with 150 million, India is the second largest Muslim populated country in the world, more than in Pakistan. Had there been any injustice and persecution to the Muslims of India, their number would have been much lesser than this. If Musharraf was so touchy about the minorities issue, what about the selective massacres of Christians and sectarian violence in Pakistan? At least in India, people are not attacked while they are praying in temples, mosques and gurdwaras. Gujarat killings were, therefore, an aberration and the BJP Government at the centre was strongly rooted in the secular tradition of the country.

Q.28. Is it possible to wipe out terrorism operating from Pakistan under military government headed by Gen. Parvez Musharraf?

Ans. India had been urging the U.S. to look for democratic alternatives to Parvez Musharraf in Pakistan saying it could be more effective in the global war against terror. All the world leaders were unanimous in their opinion that volatile situation was created in Jammu and Kashmir on account of Pakistan sponsored terrorism. Military government is just opposite to democratic form of government, dictatorship and belicosity being their life-blood and hence no military government of any country can be tough to deal with terrorism, rather they would go on supporting terrorism at heart, as their basic policy is to bleed the neighbouring country in particular. Military government will never dismantle terrorist infrastructure in their soil. Otherwise, infiltration of the terrorists across the line of control of Jammu & Kashmir would have been halted. Since the military government in Pakistan under Parvez Musharraf was lax in dealing with terrorism, the epi-centre of the al-Qaida was shifted to Pakistan from Afghanistan since the ouster of the Taliban. Though the Taliban and the al-Qaida continued to hold some pockets in Afghanistan, most of their activities were transferred to safer havens in Pakistan. The arrests of Ramzi Bin al-Shaibah and Khaled Sheikh Mohamed—two senior members of the al-Qaida's military wing—and the other activists, from Karachi who were in close collusion with Osama bin Laden master-minding the attack on World Trade Center in New York on 11th September, 2001, indicated how deep the alQaida penetrated inside Pakistan.

Gen. Musharraf has been telling althrough that they would not allow the terrorists to use the soil of Pakistan; but in fact nothing tangible has been done so far to root them out by dismantling their infrastructures on the soil of Pakistan. From the actions of military government of Pakistan, it was proved that having belicosity in their mind, they would always try to keep India to be tortured by suspense and anxiety by unleashing terrorism in Jammu & Kashmir and other parts of India. Therefore, it would not be possible to stamp out terrorism operating from Pakistan under military government notwithstanding pressure from the West especially the United States of America to rid Pakistan from terrorist's activities.

Q.29. What was the conviction of George W. Bush, U.S. President towards India expressed by him within 10 days of the end of the 57th UN General Meeting for maintaining close Indo-U.S. friendship?

Ans. It was the established conviction expressed by George W. Bush, U.S. President after holding parleys with Shri Atal Behari Vajpayee, the then Prime Minister of India, within 10 days after the end of the 57th UN General meeting at New York, that nothing would stand in the way of cementing Indo-U.S. relations despite India's nuclear and missile programmes as also earlier slow pace of India's economic reforms.

These factors were of the past for which U.S. was of course dilly-dallying to maintain relations with India hitherto, but with the changed world situation the U.S.

government started with a view of India as a growing world power with a steady space of India's economic reforms with which U.S. had common strategic interests, as expressed by U.S. President, George W. Bush. This unequivocal statement of intent on future relations with India was significant because these two countries were on the threshold of unprecedented cooperation.

Bush asserted that the U.S. undertook a transformation in its bilateral relationship with India based on a conviction that U.S. interests required a strong relationship with India. In references to India, Bush also made the point that U.S. and India were the two largest democracies of the world committed to political freedom. In addition, India was moving towards greater economic freedom as well. He also reiterated that U.S. had a common interest in the free flow of commerce, including through the vital sea lanes of the Indian ocean. Finally, U.S. shared an interest in fighting terrorism and in creating a strategically stable Asia. Through a strong partnership with India, U.S. can shape a dynamic future.

Q.30. What was the importance of Jammu & Kashmir election of 2002?

Ans. Two-nation theory applied only to the partitioning of British India and accordingly India was partitioned in 1947 and there was the birth of a new state in the name of Pakistan. Jammu & Kashmir was a princely state and hence two-nation theory did not apply in the case of the state. India's position was that Maharaja Hari Singh of Jammu & Kashmir signed the Instrument of Accession to India and by virtue of this accession Jammu & Kashmir legally and constitutionally became the part of Indian territory to which Pakistan was not amenable to accept. Pakistan had been telling that the blood of Kashmiri Muslims forming bulk of the total population of the state was flowing in the veins of Pakistani Muslims and hence the Kashmiris could not remain under Indian subjugation.

Assembly elections of 2002 proved otherwise. Through

ballot boxes the people of Jammu & Kashmir gave their mandate that they overwhelmingly participated in the democratic process in the state. In the first, second, third and fourth phases of elections in Jammu and Kashmir, the percentage of voting was 47%, 42%, 41% and 46% respectively, which would have been much more higher than this, had there not been repeated terrorists attacks during the elections with the tacit support of Pakistan to disrupt elections. This proved once again that the Kashmiris convulged with India and not with Pakistan and that their safety, security and prosperity were with India only. Needless to emphasise, the Jammu and Kashmir elections of 2002 once again placed India in most advantageous position to prove to the world powers that the people of Jammu and Kashmir had no attachment with Pakistan, as claimed by them.

The foreign observers who were in Jammu and Kashmir to see for themselves the election process there, were very happy with the transparency of the elections in the state. Under the circumstances, Pakistan had nothing to do with the governance of Indian-state of Jammu and Kashmir, because this was a matter already sorted out through elections by the people of the state. Moreover, participation of the people of the state in the elections in large number negated Pakistan's claim for plebiscite in Jammu & Kashmir, for which they had been clamouring for a pretty long time.

Jammu & Kashmir elections, 2002 was a clear testimony that the state was not at all a problem to be settled with Pakistan for its being an integral part of India, but India was always willing to enter into parleys with Pakistan to settle other bilateral issues that existed between the two countries.

The economy of Jammu & Kashmir was wrecked because of years of proxy wars waged against the state by Pakistan. With the substantial number of the electorates casting votes for maintaining democratic process in the state under the Government of India, defying Pakistan's all-out attempts to set at naught the election process, the tasks before the democratically elected Government in Jammu & Kashmir immediately after 2002 election were to revitalise the economy and complete other jobs of prime importance for the prosperity and well-being of the Kashmiris, which were as follows:

(a) To work out a political arrangement with the regions of Jammu and Ladakh to end their alienation from the administration,

(b) To reinstate the faith of the people in the administration,

(c) To initiate economic reconstruction and salvage,

(d) Priority to be given to projects which have the high employment generation potential,

(e) Expeditious completion of the Jammu & Udhampur rail link and also study the feasibility of Udhampur-Srinagar rail,

(f) Laying of petroleum products pipeline from Jammu and Srinagar,

(g) Development of Manali-Leh highway as a major artery and the rehabilitation of schools and hospitals.

Q.31. Why did Pakistan resort to attacking India through terrorism?

Ans. Ever since the birth of Pakistan they became inimical to India on Kashmir issue for their not having reconciled with the Instrument of Accession of Jammu & Kashmir to India by Maharaja Hari Singh. Jammu and Kashmir was a princely state and hence it was not within the purview of partition of the Indian Sub-continent with the exit of the Britishers. There were as many as four military confrontations with India on the issue of Jammu & Kashmir, but in all the wars Pakistan suffered discomfiture at the hands of the Indian mighty military force. Since they felt that such defeats were a derogation to them, they became frantic to amass sophisticated military hardware from whatever source they could at the cost of their economic development to take on India if they could win war at least once. Since they could not balance with Indian military strength, they in fact were thinking twice seriously to wage war again with India militarily in order to express their self-contentment of superiority over India from the military point of view.

Pakistan then embarked upon a stratagem of fomenting terrorism to weaken India instead of entering into misadventure of direct war which meant loss of their armed forces as well as rockets, tanks, war planes, etc. entailing crores of rupees which they ill-afforded looking to their already moribund financial condition.

Pakistan occupied Jammu and Kashmir was the hot-bed of the Pakistani trained terrorists. In order to strengthen and bolster their activities, the Government of Pakistan entered into alliance with the erstwhile Taliban Government of Afghanistan who were in collusion with the terrorist outfit, al-Qaida of Osama-Bin-Laden. The terrorists belonging to Jaish-e-Mohammad and Hizbul Mujahideen patronised by Pakistan and the al-Qaida combinedly started sneaking into Jammu and Kashmir to wreck in the state. They not only remained confined within the state of Jammu and Kashmir but also spread other parts of India with the purpose of killing innocent people and striking assets and properties of India after getting secret information from the ISI who were active in India, with the help of remote controlled bombs and grenades. This way of undeclared war of terrorist attacks on India saved Pakistan financially and also avoided loss of their armed forces and also rockets, tanks, war planes, etc.

Pakistan thought that India would get tired by this war of terrorism and would give up Jammu and Kashmir for handing over to them, But, this stratagem of terrorist war devised by Pakistan would not last long when the Kashmiri people gave a fitting reply through assembly elections of 2002 by rejecting violence and showing their faith in Indian democracy. India also got the exclusive opportunity to tell the world that they (India) represented a credible expression of the people's will and the international community would accept that.

When India had taken the wishes of the Kashmiri people into account through elections and with the mounting of pressure exerted on Pakistan by the world community, Pakistan would come to sense and end cross-border terrorism, which would be another victory for India.

Q.32. What was the speech delivered by the Shiv Sena chief, Bal Thackeray at Mumbai on the day of Dussehra, the 15th October, 2002 and what was the furore arising out of his speech?

Ans. Shiv Sena Chief, Shri Bal Thackeray delivered the following speeches at an annual gathering of Shiv Sainiks in Shivaji Park, Mumbai, on the day of Dussehra, the 15th October, 2002:

(i) "Those Muslims who have objections when Pakistani flags are burnt in this country should not remain here and after partition, we have every right to call ourselves a Hindu nation."

(ii) "If I were to be given charge of the army I would flush out the unwanted elements within the Muslim community in one day."

Apart from the above speeches, Shri Thackeray called for the formation of Hindu suicide squads to fight Islamic terrorism.

The Shiv Sena Chief clarified that his Dussehra speech was not at all targeted at minorities. He was only talking about pro-Pakistan Muslims. He also clarified that he accepted the Muslims as citizens of this country, though he strongly felt that they too have to see themselves as citizens of India. The Sena Chief further added that he had not made any objectionable statements against Indian Muslims.

In defiance of the clarifications made by Shri Bal Thackeray, Maharashtra police purported that in his address to the Shiv Sena cadre he had allegedly incited communal violence in India and charged him under Sections 153 and 153-A of the Indian Penal Code and accordingly a case was registered against him at the Shivaji Park Police station under the said Sections. While Section 153 deals with offences of wantonly giving provocation with intent to cause riot, 153-A is for promoting enmity between different groups on grounds of religion, race, language, place of birth, etc. The conviction under Section 153-A is three years' imprisonment.

With regard to the case against Shri Bal Thackeray the Union Law Ministry had put a note to the Central Government stating that "alleged" crime of Shiv Sena Chief, Bal Thackeray was not a punitive offence and accordingly advised the Home Ministry not to precipitate the matter as a move against Thackeray would spark communal violence. The note further stated that the letter of law should not be followed in the matter and the spirit of law was against arresting Thackeray as the charges made out under the Indian Penal Code could not be carried out. But, still then if the Maharashtra state government decided to go ahead with Thackeray's arrest, the centre would have nothing to do about it, as law and order is a state subject.

Q.33. What are the fruits of Indian democracy?

Ans. The citizens of India have an exultant sense of credit and gratification as well as boasting that India is the largest democratic country in the world being placed in high estimation in the comity of nations. In true sense, the Indian citizens in fact can never expect more than this ostentation. Now, the analyses will reveal the outcome of such democracy:

(i) There is no denying the fact that in a country of multifarious political parties the citizens are obviously supporting different parties with different characters and ideologies. Supporting different parties by different sections of people gives birth to hatred and recrimination amongst the people and instances are plenty that this leads to political clashes at party level which culminates in the fleeing of the people from their native areas, murders and burning of their houses by opponent parties with the sole purpose of establishing stronghold and suzerainty of one political party in the area. It also happens that even after living in a democratic country and society many people, although they are supporting at heart a particular political party, yet feign that they are exhibiting their support to the other party mainly with the purpose either to escape wrath and fury of the opponent party or to get inner information and stratagem of that party clandestinely for their partisan interest.

(ii) During elections—either general election or state election, clashes are frequently taking place to silence the voices of the election campaigners and even eliminate candidates either by kidnapping or otherwise with the purpose of annulling neck-to-neck fight between two rival political parties.

(iii) With emergence of new states which are now 28 in number, multifarious political parties have sprung up which are all taking part in elections to win as many seats as possible. As per Constitution of the democratic country like India, unless otherwise amended, there cannot be taboo in the creation of separate political parties which are even increasing when new parties are formed in the event of rupturing the relation with the coalition government by any important political leader. With such multifarious political parties, the days of one party rule have dimmed, which does not augur well from the solidarity and stability point of view of the government in Indian democracy.

(iv) The government which is formed with conglomeration of heterogeneous political parties, passes through tough situations as there is always apprehension that the government may crumble without clinging to power for a full term of five years for reduced number below 2/3rds majority on account of deserting MPs/MLAs, when there is any dissension of opinion or disagreement with the policies of the government, of two or three or more political parties with the major political party of the coalition government.

(v) As is observed in Indian politics, there is lust for power. In the case of Indian democracy, when the coalition government is formed with either magic number or with thin majority, the opposition party with combination of other political parties not forming part of the coalition government and also by persuading some dissident MPs/MLAs of the coalition government are on the tip-toe of toppling the government.

(vi) In Indian democratic system no political party in majority of the cases can form government immediately after election because of absence of clear majority, although the electorates have exercised their franchise with the purpose of having good governance. The result is that the government is run either by caretaker Prime Minister or Chief Minister, or in the event of refusing by any Chief Minister of the defeated party to act as caretaker Chief Minister till the coalition government is formed, Governor's rule is imposed in the state. The main hurdle for prospect of installation of coalition government is that neither of the major parties can come to terms and compromise with the conditions set forth by both the parties in the matter of deciding to head the coalition government, as had happened in the case of Jammu & Kashmir after 2002 assembly election.

When the fruits and replica of Indian democracy are

like the above, rapid progress and development of India pose a problem, as such government is always busy in setting things for itself. Though India is progressing, which ought to have been rapid, had there not been wrangling among the political parties and also there would not have any tendency to topple coalition government. It, therefore, needs change in the system of Indian democracy for the sake of good of the country.

Q.34. What was the point of dispute in the matter of holding election in Gujarat beyond the scheduled six months time from the date of last sitting of Assembly arising out of the Chief Election Commission's directive to defer election in the state in the aftermath of Gujarat riot and what were the Supreme Court's interpretations in the matter?

Ans. The Chief Election Commissioner, Mr. J.M. Lyngdoh after visiting riot stricken areas of Gujarat rejected on 16th August, 2002 the BJP's demand for holding early polls there latest by the 1st week of October, 2002, saying that the situation in riot stricken Gujarat was still not congenial for holding election early and that he recommended imposition of President's Rule under Article 356 of the Constitution. He further suggested holding of election in the state in the month of November-December, 2002 *i.e.*, after six months of gap between the two sittings in the assembly.

In this connexion, the BJP said that Mr. Lyngdoh went beyond his propriety as Chief Election Commissioner by deferring election in Gujarat and infringing the Indian Constitution. In this connexion, the BJP contended that:

(a) As per Article 174 of the Constitution, the gap between the two sittings in Assembly should not exceed six months and accordingly election in Gujarat was to be held in the first week of October, 2002 since the Gujarat House had last met on 6th April, 2002.

(b) Article 324 of the Constitution authorised the Chief

Election Commission exclusive jurisdiction on conducting elections and accordingly under the circumstances whether Article 174 could be read in isolation.

(c) Another point as raised by the BJP was that—could the Election Commission ask for imposition of Article 356 or create situation that the centre was compelled to impose Article 356 in Gujarat?

Now, the question was that if the Article 174 was to be flouted in the matter of holding election in Gujarat within six months from the last date of sitting of Assembly there would be a "Constitutional crisis" in the state and this crisis could be solved only by bringing the state under central rule. But, in this case, another pertinent and moot question cropped up, "How could a BJP-led government at the centre dismiss one of its own state governments? And would Narendra Modi sign his death warrant and give up being a caretaker Chief Minister?"

An extra-ordinary meeting of the Cabinet to which Solicitor General, Shri Harish Salve and Additional Solicitor General, Shri Kirit Raval were invited, discussed the far-reaching implications of the poll panel's order and decided to invoke the President's power to consult the Apex Court under Article 143. Accordingly, on 18th August, 2002, the Cabinet decided to make a Presidential reference to seek the Supreme Court's opinion on the constitutional questions arising out of the Chief Election Commission's rejection of the BJP's demand for early polls in Gujarat.

Solicitor General, Shri Harish Salve opined that as per section 174 of the Constitution if election could not be held within six months of dissolving the State Assembly, it was not necessary that the Governor's rule in that state was to be imposed. He also told that after dissolving the Assembly, the Chief Minister could also go on continuing till election is held.

The Supreme Court of India after studying the pros

and cons of the complications gave its judgement on 28th October, 2002 on the above, as follows:

The Supreme Court held that the power to decide the poll schedule was within the "exclusive domain" of the Election Commission and neither Parliament nor an Assembly could interfere with this right. This meant that Centre's contention under Article 174 that elections had to be held in Gujarat within six months of the last sitting of the House stood dismissed. The Court further held that there was no time limit for holding election after premature dissolution of the House as in Gujarat.

Citing Article 174 of the Constitution, the Centre and the Gujarat Government had contended that election was to be held within six months from the last date of sitting of Assembly. Rejecting this argument, the Supreme Court said that in view of the scheme of the Constitution and Representation of Peoples Act, the election should be held within six months for constituting legislative Assembly from the date of dissolution of the Legislative Assembly and not within six months of last sitting of the Assembly.

The Court, however, rejected the EC's argument that President's rule should be imposed, if elections were not held within six months of dissolution of the House.

Q.35. In what different angles China had been undermining India from the time of Nehru regime and how its perception towards India started changing subsequently?

Ans. Being attracted by the bounties and fabulous resources, India was subjected to the subjugation of several foreign invaders before the Britishers finally set their feet on the soil of India, who governed the country for about 200 years and the country's resources were virtually exhausted by such external aggressions and foreign domination. Obviously, the partition of India in 1947 with the exit of the British rule left India in a state of deprivation.

Both China and India are neighbours and big countries. China's resources were not decayed as in the case of

India due to the obvious reasons as enumerated above and hence India had to start from scratch from the very inception of partition. Therefore, there was a good deal of contrast between China and India at the initial stage and naturally China claimed herself a superior country in relation to India when she was partitioned. Evidences were plenty that China underestimated India on the following counts:

(a) When Jawaharlal Nehru, the then Prime Minister of India tried to show India's leadership of the non-aligned movement at the 1955 Bandung Conference, the Chinese leaders, instead of appreciating Nehru's approach towards non-aligned movement, tried to scuttle his approach, as the Chinese leaders were not amenable that India being an infant country should be a fore-runner in such movement and accordingly Nehru appeared arrogant to Chinese leaders.

(b) China supported the insurgency in India's North-east and promoted disaffection against India among the Himalayan people.

(c) China supplied nuclear missiles to Pakistan and built naval power bases in the Bay of Bengal and also off Pakistan's coastline. The purpose of the same was to put pressure on India.

(d) When India was engaged in liberation war for emergence of Bangladesh in the year, 1971 and compelled the 95,000 Pakistani soldiers to surrender to the Indian army, China sided with Pakistan.

(e) China attacked the North-eastern parts of India in 1962 without any provocation. This war confirmed China's sense of superiority and its belief that Indians lacked staying power in military and diplomatic affairs.

(f) Beijing was of the opinion that the Indian economic reforms were at least ten years behind the Chinese. They also did not like basically Vajpayee regime, because it was a coalition among different parties, not all of which believe in socialism.

India is no doubt emerging as a great power marching towards rapid advancement. Western powers were also keen eyeing towards India occupying as one of the big powers in the not too distant future. Many countries were also backing India to become one of the permanent members of the United Nations Organisations. India's role in the comity of nations was also hailed by the foreign powers. Its relations with big powers of the world were cordial. Economic reforms undertaken by India were destined to achieve economic liberalisation for the Indians in general. India is also a big military power. The persuasive power of Agnis could even reach important Chinese targets. India is also a nuclear power. Such military capability helped to focus the attention of Chinese generals and politicians on the realities of India.

Such strides of India had naturally created a dent in Chinese leadership changing their attitude towards India. They were subsequently interested in arranging for a summit which required sustained military, economic, cultural and diplomatic engagement that called for patience and discipline.

Q.36. How is the bilateral relation between India and its neighbouring countries?

Ans. India occupies an important position as compared to its neighbouring countries, especially the SAARC countries on account of its territorial size, scientific studies, technology, military and economic strengths. India's relations with its neighbours leaving aside Pakistan are not deteriorating. Of course there are certain issues to be settled with some of the neighbouring countries. Bellicose attitude of Pakistan towards India has posed regional stability and security which needs steps to streamline by India with the help of regional cooperation with its neighbouring countries. The visits of Parvez Musharraf to Nepal, Bangladesh and Sri Lanka in the second quarter of

2002 were not basically good-will visits to establish cosy relations but to utilise these relations to generate negative pressures on India. But, unfortunately, for Pakistan his visits to these countries were not a fruition. The threat of terrorism in the region sponsored by Pakistan is a burning question. In the interest of maintaining peace and tranquility in the region, the neighbouring countries have to come forward to join hands with India to combat terrorism by not entertaining the same to operate from their countries and India in turn have also to settle all the disputes prevailing with the neighbouring countries to which India has committed to settle as a testimony of its viable foreign policy towards its neighbours.

The disputes with the neighbouring countries which India pledged to settle were as follows:

(a) *Disputes with Nepal*: India has territorial disputes with regard to Kalapani issue. India also assured the Nepalese government about India's continuing help to overcome the violence and destabilisation generated by Maoist rebellion. India sought the assistance of Nepal in controlling Pakistan-sponsored terrorism originating in Nepalese territory and permeating the Indo-Nepal border.

(b) *Disputes with Sri Lanka*: India has disputes about free access for Indian fishermen at Kachchativu island. The Sri Lankan government continued to seek India's endorsement of the peace initiative with Liberation Tigers of Tamil Eelem, but more importantly Sri Lanka desired India to desist from giving support for the LTTE's separatist activities from Tamil Nadu.

(c) *Disputes with Bangladesh*: Anti-Indian terrorists have bases in Bangladesh. For better relation with India, Bangladesh government has to dismantle the terrorist bases from their soil, as requested by India. India's main disappointment stemmed from Bangladesh not even being willing to act against militants arrested there. Dhaka released several of them instead of handing them over to India, though Delhi had repeatedly sought their repatriation. The issues of illegal migration of Bangladeshis to India and the treatment of Hindu minority exist on which there was difference of opinion between India and Bangladesh. There are border enclaves which have to be exchanged between India and Bangladesh. Apart from this, maritime boundary with Bangladesh is awaiting settlement. While India would welcome the supply of natural gas from Bangladesh, India would resort to other options respecting Bangladesh's sensitivities. India promised relaxation of import duties on Bangladesh exports to India.

(d) *Maldives*: Maldives is important to India because of its strategic location in the Indian ocean. The country's security relations with India have had a special significance since 1988 when the Indian military crushed an attempted coup in the islands in 1988 by the Sri Lankan militants.

As far as Bhutan is concerned no problem is faced with India.

Although the disputes as enumerated above exist with the neighbouring countries, which are not at all knotty to solve, India has been placed in high esteem which augurs well for existence of cordial relations with the neighbouring countries. In the economic sphere, India's neighbours wish India to give more trade concessions to their exports to redress the imbalances in trade which they have with India. Nepal and Bhutan desire India to take active interest in resolving their bilateral disputes about the Nepalese expelled from Bhutan. All the neighbours of India being the Asian countries have reposed faith on India to solve any problem of theirs which might emanate in future in view of India's territorial size, military and economic strengths, scientific studies and technology. In this connexion, it is worthwhile to mention that India's military interference helped a new state in the name of Bangladesh to emerge as a sovereign state in the year, 1971.

Q.37. How is the relation between India and Iran?

Ans. There is nothing inimical in the relation between India and Iran. The relation between these two countries was cemented after the visit of the President of Iran, Rafsanjani to India in the year, 1995. India had extended invitation to the Iranian President, Syed Mohammed Khatami to be the 26th January, 2003 Republic Day Chief Guest. This Indian invitation to Khatami showed India's acknowledgement of Teheran's re-emergence as a major world player. India and Iran, along with Russia, were the main backers of Afghanistan's Northern Alliance, when it was the only group left to resist the Taliban regime in Afghanistan. New Delhi and Teheran pledged to work together on the projects that would help rebuild the war-ravaged Afghanistan.

The Prime Minister, Sri Atal Behari Vajpayee's successful visit to Iran in April, 2001 had led to the "Teheran Declaration" that built the structure of the two countries' political and economic ties. Khatami's visit further strengthened the ties between New Delhi and Teheran. India preferred to consolidate ties because it wanted to get an influential Islamic country as an important partner of New Delhi.

Both the countries' economic relation is tied to the energy sector. Iran, the largest producer of natural gas, was an obvious choice for India's growing energy needs. Both the countries already signed an agreement on supply of Iranian gas to India through a proposed pipeline—whether overland, pass through Pakistan or through sub-sea level.

Iran along with Iraq and North Korea were described by the US as the "axis of evils". India's close economic relation with Teheran raised eyebrows in Washington. Still then, India's invitation to Khatami clearly indicated that New Delhi did not compromise on issues where its interests could be hampered, in spite of India's improved ties with Washington.

Q.38. The NDA Government led by Bharatiya Janata Party opined that the Kashmir problem could have been solved once and for all in the year, 1971 itself. How?

Ans. Pakistan annexed a part of Jammu and Kashmir in the year, 1948. Since then it was shown in their territory as an extended part of Pakistan treating it as Azad Kashmir.

At the distress call of Sheikh Mujibur Rahman, Indira Gandhi, the then Prime Minister of India, sent massive troops to East Pakistan to suppress the 95,000 Pakistani soldiers, who massacred innumerable number of East Pakistani people to throttle their voice for emergence of a new state in the name of Bangladesh. Ultimately, all the Pakistani soldiers could not withstand the Indian military might and surrendered to them and a new state in the name of Bangladesh was created in the year, 1971, thus renouncing the suzerainty of Pakistan.

These 95,000 Pakistani soldiers were then transported to India and interned for three months. When the question of returning back these soldiers to Pakistan came up, it was the propitious opportunity on the part of the then Congress government under the leadership of Indira Gandhi to set condition to the government of Pakistan to cede the conquered part of Jammu and Kashmir to India in exchange of the release of their 95,000 troops which was not unfortunately done. Otherwise, the Kashmir problem would have been solved once and for all in the year, 1971 itself disclaiming possession of the part of Jammu & Kashmir by Pakistan occupied by them in the year, 1948.

Q.39. What were the factors responsible for the sweeping victory of Bharatiya Janata Party in the Assembly election held in Gujarat on 12th December, 2002?

Ans. In the mid-Seventies, the anti-Emergency emotions among the people of India paved the way for the Janata Party to come to power. In 1984 the sympathy wave following the assassination of Indira Gandhi helped Rajiv Gandhi immensely to become the next Prime Minister. The demolition of the disputed structure in

Ayodha in the early Nineties translated into reality the Bharatiya Janata Party's dreams of ruling the country. These incidents established that the issues of importance were crucial determinants of the fate of political parties in elections. The outcome of the Gujarat election held on 12th December, 2002 was nothing but an addition to the lists of events.

The Hindutva card played in the context of Godhra proved the magic wand for Narendra Modi as well as the BJP. Gujarat rewarded Modi with a flood of support for his brand of 'Hindutva'. Gaurav Yatra rally organised by Narendra Modi on the day of Sardar Patel's death anniversary was also significant in the matter of attaining sweeping victory in Gujarat election. The strongest endorsement of Modi's agenda came from Godhra, where the S-6 coach of the Sabarmati Express was burnt with 58 Kar Sevaks returning from Ayodha. Godhra was the constituency where the Muslim vote was most likely to count which was practically of no avail.

The most unfortunate part of event was that nobody from the Muslim community condemned the Godhra incident which only showed how the country started showing inclination towards the end of secularism, which India has been nurturing from the very inception of partition. All Muslims in the state were being targeted because some of them were reportedly involved in the incident that had sparked off Godhra. Going by the same logic, every Hindu had to repent for the barbarous crimes of his community after the burning of the Sabarmati Express in Godhra and for the demolition of the Babri Masjid. The Ulemas and Islamic clerics appealed to their Muslim brethren to vote for the congress in the Gujarat assembly election. These religious leaders formed the only voice of the riot-affected community in the absence of any credible independent Muslim political leadership.

It is once again replicated that Hindutva was BJP's winning card in Gujarat election. It was a victory for Gujarat's pride, for Gujarat's self-respect. Narendra Modi argued that without the BJP returning to power, the state would have become a hotbed of terrorism and, perhaps, another Kashmir. With repeated references to Parvez Musharraf of Pakistan and question of a choice between him and the Pakistani leader, he successfully created apprehension among the electorate. These ploys were enough to ensure that the people of Gujarat elected BJP to come to power. Narendra Modi already went on record to declare that his government would work towards "appeasement of none and justice to all".

Q.40. Is the Gujarat victory for the BJP in the Assembly election held on 12th December, 2002, a first step towards the creation of India a Hindu Rashtra?

Ans. Bharatiya Janata Party's smashing victory in Gujarat in the Assembly election held on 12th December, 2002 was to all intents and purposes based on the fact that the Hindutva card played a significant role in the context of Godhra incident. Sangh Parivar hailed the Gujarat victory as a first step towards the creation of India as a Hindu Rashtra. That the Gujarat development was to have far-reaching repercussions on the character of national politics was pretty clear. After the victory in Gujarat Assembly election RSS (Rashtriya Swayamsevak Sangh) and the Vishwa Hindu Parishad started forcing the BJP to push Hindutva and Swadeshi on top of the NDA agenda. They also wanted that Vajpayee government should give national politics a pronounced saffron complexion. Shri Vajpayee might not have been successful in this endeavour all the time, but at least this was the thrust of his policy. He was although very clear on his insistence that Hindutva could never become an election issue. On being under duress by the Sangh Parivar and on his own insistence Shri Vajpayee was in fact at a crossroad.

The Gujarat victory made many people wonder how secure were the secular foundations of Indian society. In one case, the very division of the sub-continent on communal lines was a fatal blow to the secular ideal. The two-nation theory already rebutted by history was not solely the work of the colonialists. It was also a result of the failure of the Congress to mobilize the Muslim intelligentsia and youth in Hindu majority provinces. The bitter truth was that the British did not create the communal divide. They merely exploited what was already there to prevent the nationalist movement from fully mobilizing the Muslim community in the struggle for Independence.

Whatever the degree of success or failure of the secular ideal, a highly pluralist society such as India's cannot survive without finding more effective means of peaceful co-existence. While the Gujarat experiment of Hindutva card had yielded rich political dividends to the BJP in the context of Godhra incident, it would mar the peaceful co-existence to the detriment of both internal peace and economic growth of the country, if it was practised in other states of India. Furthermore, by alienating the minority communities it would provide a new incentive to Pakistan-based terrorist groups to extend their proxy war against the Indian state to new areas, in addition, the Muslim population in the country is still as large as in Pakistan and India is the second largest Muslim populated country in the world, first being Indonesia, together with a substantial presence of other religious minorities in the country. The then Prime Minister, Atal Bihari Vajpayee reiterated on 31st December, 2002 his government's commitment to the principle of secularism and clarified that Hindutva was an inclusivist concept which affirmed that "India belongs to all, and all belongs to India. It means that all Indians have equal rights and equal responsibilities". India is a unity in diversity. Hindutva is a parochial concept for a country like India. Under the circumstances, turning India into a Hindu Rashtra is altogether ruled out.

Q.41. What is India's nuclear weapons policy?

Ans. India first tested its nuclear weapons in 1974, when Indira Gandhi was the Prime Minister. Military aspect of this testing was shrouded in secrecy and ambiguity. But it was only in the year, 1998, during the Premiership of Atal Bihari Vajpayee, that New Delhi openly admitted having possessed nuclear weapons after testing five devices.

On 4th January, 2003 India announced formation of Nuclear Command Authority four years after declaring to the world that India was a nuclear power. The Nuclear Command Authority, responsible for the management of the country's nuclear weapons, will have two-tiered structure: (i) The political council at the apex will be chaired by the Prime Minister and will be the sole body which can authorise the use of nuclear weapons. The political council will have almost all the members of the Cabinet Committee *i.e.*, the Home Minister, the Defence Minister, the Finance Minister and the Foreign Minister would be part of it. The National Security Adviser and the Cabinet Secretary will also be in the political council, which will take the final decision on whether India should retaliate in the event of a nuclear attack, (ii) The political council will be aided by the executive council which will be chaired by the National Security Adviser. The Commander-in-chief of the Strategic Forces Command (SFC), the three chiefs of services and the Cabinet Secretary will be the other members. The Commander-in-chief of the SFC will be guarding India's nuclear assets.

Apart from the said two-tiered structure, a separate Strategic Forces Command has also been formed. This will be the military authority in operational charge of nuclear weapons and delivery systems.

The nuclear weapons doctrines adopted by India are as follows:

(i) India would embark upon a policy of no-first-use of nuclear weapons unless first attacked by nuclear weapons on Indian territory or on Indian forces anywhere.

(ii) In case of an attack by biological or chemical weapons, India retains the option of retaliating with nuclear weapons.

(iii) Nuclear retaliation to a first strike will be massive and designed to inflict unacceptable damage.

(iv) Nuclear retaliatory attacks can only be authorised by the Prime Minister through the Nuclear Command Authority *i.e.*, the nuclear button will be with the Prime Minister.

(v) India will not use nuclear weapons against non-nuclear weapons states.

(vi) India will have strict control on export of nuclear and missile related materials as also technologies to other countries.

(vii) India will observe moratorium on nuclear tests.

(viii) India will put in alternate Command Structure to retaliate in the event of wiping out the political leadership by nuclear attack from other countries.

Formation of Nuclear Command/Authority is a clear testimony on the part of New Delhi to establish itself as a responsible nation as a nuclear weapons state and reassure the world that its nuclear weapons are in safe hands. The nuclear weapons policy of India is also a clear signal to Pakistan and the terrorist outfits operating from its soil that attacks will be fatal for Islamabad.

Apart from India, only Russia and China have a no-first-use nuclear posture. The U.S. and its European allies—Britain and France insist on first strike. So does Pakistan.

Q.42. Under what circumstances Pakistan has to be declared a terrorist country?

Ans. There is ample and adequate proof that Pakistan has to be branded and declared a terrorist country. No other country in the world excepting Pakistan has been fomenting terrorism in full form.

Militancy/terrorism is the life-blood of Pakistan which was the outcome of the installation of the successive military governments headed by Field Marshall Ayub Khan, General Yahya Khan, General Zia-ul-Huq and finally General Parvez Musharraf who overthrew the democratically elected Nawaz Shariff government in a bloodless coup in 1999. As a result of the military governments ruling the country for half of the period ever since there was the birth of Pakistan on 14th August, 1947, the terrorist outfits such as Jais-e-Mohammad, Lashkar-e-Toiba, Hizbul Mujahideen and Al-Qaida have sprung up with the full-fledged patronage and support of Pakistan government. If there would have been no military governments in Pakistan, the terrorist outfits could not have most probably raised their ugly heads wrecking major havoc and destruction in India time to time. The Al-Qaida, the dreaded terrorist outfit of Osama-bin-Laden was shifted to Pakistan from Afghanistan since the ouster of the Taliban government from there and this was obviously on account of the patronage extended by the military government of Parvez Musharraf.

It is alleged that there is an unholy nexus between the Pakistan government and the al-Qaida which was substantiated by the report of the Pakistani Auditor General that the Al-Qaida has been utilising lakhs of dollars gifted by the non-resident Pakistanis in various relief funds of the Pakistan government. The Auditor General of Pakistan himself indicated that the money has been misused by various terrorist organisations operating on Pakistani soil, including the Al-Qaida, which is a matter of serious consternation to the entire world.

Another most important aspect of the Auditor General's report was that over 20,000 blank passports were found missing from various Pakistan embassies and High Commissions. This clearly indicates that the Pakistan government and the I.S.I. have been trying to systematise and spread terrorist activities throughout the world.

When it has come to light with the flagrant proof that Pakistan government has been directly and openly fomenting the terrorist outfits operating on their soil, there must not be any further delay that Pakistan has to be declared a terrorist country and all financial assistance is suspended from the donor countries—the sooner the better.

Q.43. In what way the continent of Asia is averse to peace and stability?

Ans. The United States of America evinced interest to leverage its intensifying partnership with India to cope with the instability in Asia. Speaking at the 5th Asian Security Conference on 27th January, 2003 hosted by the Institute of Defence Studies and Analyses, New Delhi, the U.S. Ambassador to India, Mr. Blackwill highlighted the threats in Asia. The theme of the Conference was "Asian Security and China in the period, 2000-2010". That the continent of Asia is pregnant with instability and is not a peaceful continent is substantiated by the following facts and circumstances:

(a) The Asian continent is the most threatening source of global terrorism. Emanating from Asia itself al-Qaida wrought havoc to World Trade Center and Pentagon on 11th September, 2001. Similarly, Indian Parliament attack on 13th December, 2001, which itself was an attack on the largest democracy in the world, was perpetrated from Pakistan which is the safe haven for conglomeration of all terrorist outfits including Al-Qaida from Afghanistan.

(b) Asia contains the most severe international territorial disputes and non-democratic rivalries over the right to rule.

(c) Many of the countries of Asia field large militaries and possess the ability to develop, acquire, use or export weapons of mass destruction.

(d) Iraq and North Korea have posed terror to the world community for their having in possession of weapons of mass destruction.

(e) Irresponsible and reckless governments in some Asian countries have provided fertile grounds for breeding terrorism.

Maintaining a stable Asia in these combustible

circumstances is the paramount goal of the Indo-U.S. relationship.

Q.44. What was the settlement arrived at among the Centre, the Assam government and the BODO Liberation Tigers (BLT) on 10th February, 2003?

Ans. After hectic and prolonged discussions, the Centre, the Assam government and the BODO Liberation Tigers (BLT) signed a tripartite agreement on 10th February, 2003 paving the way for creation of a Bodoland Territorial Council (BTC). The signing of the Memorandum of Settlement (MOS) would bring to an end a decade-long problem in the North-East and the people of Assam would heave a sigh of relief having perennial peace in the land.

In accordance with the Memorandum of Settlement, the following were decided:

(a) As many as 3082 villages would be included in the BTC which would be divided into four districts after the reorganisation of the existing districts of Assam. Under the MoS, it was also decided to set up a committee with one representative each from the centre, the Assam Government and BLT, to decide on the inclusion of 95 more villages and areas under the BTC.

(b) Bodoland Territorial Council would have 30 seats reserved for the tribals and five for non-tribals. Five seats would be open to representatives of all communities while six members would be nominated by the Assam government.

(c) The subject of law and order of the Bodoland Territorial Council would remain the presence of the state government. An officer of the rank of inspector general of police would be in charge of law-enforcement in the areas administered by the new Council.

(d) As far as the financial assistance is concerned, the central government would grant Rs. 100 crores annually to the BTC over the next five years. The funds would be routed through the state government.

(e) The BODO language would be considered to be included in the Eighth Schedule of the Constitution.

(f) The boundary demarcation of BTC would be subject to clearance of the delimitation Commission.

(g) A centrally-funded Central institute of Technology would be set up in the BTC area to impart technological and vocational discipline. It would be subsequently upgraded to a centrally-funded state university.

After formation of the autonomous Bodoland Territorial Council, it would have the following control:

(i) The BTC will have almost complete superintendence and even law-making power on the use of land.

(ii) Management of any forest other than reserved forest. This will empower the BTC to even sanction contracts for wood related industries.

(iii) Use of any canal or water course for the purpose of agriculture.

(iv) Power to regulate the practice of jhum or other forms of shifting cultivation.

(v) Establishment of village and town committees to which BTC would relegate or sanction powers.

(vi) All matters relating to village and town administration, creating and maintaining village and town police force, public health and sanitation.

(vii) Appointment of chiefs or headmen for villages and towns.

(viii) Power to decide on inheritance of property.

(ix) Conducting marriage and divorce.

(x) All other social customs.

By virtue of the above Memorandum of Settlement, it

could be construed that for the first time in the decade-long history of armed struggle of the BODO tribals in Assam, the Central Government gave constitutional recognition to a virtual BODO homeland in the North-Eastern state. This required an amendment to the Sixth Schedule of the Constitution.

Q.45. Is democracy successful in India?

Ans. Definition of democracy, as propounded by Abraham Lincoln, is government of the people, for the people and by the people. India with more than 100 crores of people is the largest democratic country of the world. Government is formed with the verdict of the people. The chief architect of the democratic set-up of India was Pandit Jawaharlal Nehru. Elections to the Assemblies and the Parliament have not only proved the merit of the Indian people, but also upheld the virtue of Indian democracy. The Chinese aggression and the Indo-Pakistan wars have no doubt hit the country economically and politically, but they have left it a better and unified nation, democratically resolved to fight out its problems. The world has to learn from the democratic set-up of India as to how democracy functions in a country like India where heterogeneous types of people with different culture, language, literature, traditions and religion live.

Now, the question has cropped up whether democracy in India is successful or not. Lust for power, parochial aims and sectarianism are often eating up the vitals of our democratic institutions which only a healthy education system spread in every nook and corner of the country can stave off. In a number of states anomalies in the conduct of elections are observed which are—on the day of election the electorate are intimidated and threatened, large scale proxy vote is there, there is booth jamming and snatching of ballot boxes, the electorate are intercepted to come out of their houses to cast their votes in favour of the party of their choice, casting of multiple votes by a single voter as also there is malpractice in the preparation of voters list and the like. This way of election does not augur well for a prospective party to win the election. When this is the replica of the election in India in some states, how could it be said that election is conducted in free and fair means? In such election, true verdict of the electorate is never gauged. Therefore, in the name of democracy such way of conducting election does not of course represent true democracy of the country when the electorate are instrumental in the hands of the politicians.

Under the circumstances, the Election Commission must devise ways and means to conduct elections in free and fair means so that the verdict of the people from the realistic point of view is reflected in the ballot boxes and in this way democracy in India will be successful in the true sense of the term. Moreover, spread of education in the remote villages is of paramount necessity for creating awareness of political consciousness amongst the village people so that they are not beguiled by the political parties during election campaign which would debar the people to cast their votes wrongly to a party.

Q.46. How is the relation between India and Japan?

Ans. Close relation with any country depends upon their foreign policy. The foreign policy of Japan has been guided by the establishment of a net-work of bilateral and multi-lateral relations with all the countries in the world with special reference to the countries in Asia with the objective of attaining stability and security in the region.

Japan has always been an important factor in India's external relations, especially since the mid-Sixties in the 20th century. Japan showed keen interest in India's persistent development consolidating its position as one of the dominating powers in Asia as also the role taken by India on many international issues. In consideration of these facts Japan considered it worthwhile to maintain close bilateral relations with India and the substance of this relationship was, of course, economic and technological. Japan has been a major donor of developmental aid to India. Japan was also very prompt in sending assistance in tiding over the crisis like the Gujarat earthquake in 2000.

As ill luck would have it, there was some misunderstanding between Japan and India about India's nuclear weapons tests conducted in 1998 in consequence of which there was ephemeral rupture in the bilateral ties between these two countries. This led to suspension of economic aid to India. It was a happy augury that things changed towards betterment after the visit of Jaswant Singh, the then Minister of External Affairs to Japan in the year, 2002 and subsequent visit of the Foreign Minister of Japan, Yoriko Kawaguchi to India between 7th and 9th January, 2003. That India's relations with Japan have now been fortified are based on the following facts:

(a) Where there was no change in the basic policies of India and Japan on non-proliferation issues, it was significant that during Kawaguchi's discussions, it was agreed that India and Japan would give primary attention to developing bilateral economic and technological cooperation and in forging political understanding to deal with the fundamental issues affecting security.

(b) There was agreement on sustaining, consolidating and increasing Indo-Japanese economic cooperation in terms of shipping, ports, roads, bridges and transportation.

(c) Kawaguchi exchanged views with Indian leaders on developments related to negotiations to resolve the ethnic problem in Sri Lanka.

(d) India also shared Japan's concerns in the matters of North Korea's threats to revive its missile and nuclear capacities, the security and strategic controversies related to Taiwan and the complex relations with China.

(e) There was complete agreement on strengthening the United Nations on working together to counter international terrorism and on the importance of strengthening the principles of democracy, good governance, human rights and international politics.

(f) India was supportive of Japan providing economic assistance to Sri Lanka, including its Tamil regions.

Thus, Jaswant Singh's visit to Japan in 2002 and Kawaguchi's visit to India in January, 2003 signalled the end of some distances which had developed between 1998 and 1999 because of India's nuclear tests, and Indo-Japanese relation was again back on track.

Q.47. Shahi Imam of Jama Masjid, Delhi, Maulana Syed Ahmed Bukhari appealed to the Muslims on 9th March, 2003 to form a separate national party in India. What have you to comment on the same?

Ans. The purpose of Shahi Imam's call to the Muslims of India for formation of a separate national party was to protect the interests of the Muslim community and stop supporting, in his words, the "so-called" secular parties of India, including the Congress on the plea of Gujarat riot in which hundreds of Muslims were killed and also it was the Congress party which triggered the Ayodhya controversy, as they opened locks, performed Shilanyas and Babri Masjid was demolished during their regime.

Needless to elucidate, the interests of the Muslim community who are the citizens of India have not been impaired even the least. The following analyses will reveal the fact:

(a) The reason for the outbreak of Gujarat riot was the burning of the Sabarmati Express which led to the killing of 58 Karsevaks returning from Ayodhya. If the Karsevaks travelling in the said train would have been allowed safe return to Gujarat, the question of outbreak of riot would have been annulled.

(b) As far as performing Shilanyas at Ayodhya is concerned, the relics of temple were found before the pre-demolition period by Geological Survey of India and Tojo Vikas International Pvt. Ltd., a Delhi based Canadian Company, adjacent to the Babri Masjid at Ayodhya. It was then conjectured that Babar built Babri Masjid on the site after demolishing the temple. This in fact led to the downing of the Babri Masjid for building Ram temple in its place. In this connexion, it is important to mention here that excepting the Babri Masjid no other mosques spread all over India were demolished.

By two such acts there leaves no cause for consternation by the Muslim community. India is a secular country which is upheld always. Constitution of India has also guaranteed equal rights and privileges to all the people of India professing different religions. In pursuance of the call of Shahi Imam if at all it materialises to form a separate national party to protect the interests of the Muslims there will be a division between the Muslims and the non-Muslims in the secular country of India, which under no circumstances could be accepted.

It is most likely that Shahi Imam's call for floating a separate national party was that he wanted to take advantage of the fact that India is the second largest Muslim populated country in the world.

Q.48. What is all about Sarkaria Commission?

Ans. The purpose of upholding Centre-State relations lies in maintaining unity and strength of the nation. But, what is the basis of the strength of the nation and of the centre? There are two alternative views such as:

(a) The strength according to one view lies in only making the centre strong concentrating on legislative, administrative and financial powers in the hands of the centre.

(b) The other view is to maintain the strength of the nation and of the centre basically in the strength of the people who live in the states. For solving their problems and thus gaining in strength people residing in any state should turn primarily to the state government for discharging responsibilities in economic and administrative spheres. Simultaneously, there is also a requirement of the interaction between the centre and the states. Strength of the total nation thus logically lies in (a) developing the strength of each state, (b) making the centre perform in its own specific areas, and (c) fostering a healthy relationship between the state and the centre. A realignment only in this direction can form the basis of a strong nation.

The Sarkaria Commission report, however, has taken other view. It has stressed upon that without making the centre more powerful, the nation cannot be made powerful. It has recommended by and large status-quo in the centre-state relations, especially in the areas relating to legislative matters, role of the Governor, use of Article 356 and Central Reserve Police etc. Apart from the above, on financial matters, there are some minor reallocation recommended in the Sarkaria Commission report for the states. Also the Sarkaria Commission upheld the need for decentralisation of powers as well as the responsibilities which should be expected to be discharged by states for the purpose of maintaining Centre-States relations.

Q.49. What are the ways out to cool down the tension between India and Pakistan?

Ans. Stability in South Asia has been seriously at stake arising out of Kashmir tangle, which has no doubt resulted in retardation of rapid development of the two countries—India and Pakistan devoting more attention to manoeuvring military superiority over each other country in the event of armed confrontation. It was proved in the past that all the wars with India could not benefit Pakistan to annex even an inch of Jammu and Kashmir territory from Indian yoke. Still then Pakistan has been frantically amassing sophisticated military arsenal from every source with the sole purpose of taking on with India on Kashmir issue once again to regain its deference from the ignominy of discomfiture in all the wars with India. But, military adventurism is not in any way going to bring honourable solution to Kashmir tangle rather the temperature in the sub-continent will go on continuing to be heated up.

The international concern about the strained relations between India and Pakistan with the result of another possible armed conflict was shown by the U.S., Britain, France and even the biggest regional player, China, even when the war in Iraq was continuing. Immediately after Nadimarg incident on 23rd March, 2003 in which 24 Kashmiri pundits were brutally killed by the Pakistan sponsored terrorits, the U.S. State Department stated that violence would not solve Kashmir's problem.

The concern of the international community seemed to be to find a permanent solution to the Indo-Pakistan tensions so that the two neighbours were neither able to blackmail and threaten each other nor destabilise the region. With this purpose in view, in one of his telephone conversations with Shri Atal Bihari Vajpayee, the then Prime Minister of India in the month of March, 2003, the U.S. President, George W. Bush had apparently said that U.S. was looking at LoC as possible solution to the Kashmir dispute. Therefore, a broad consensus on this issue between India and Pakistan taking into consideration their domestic political constraints was of paramount necessity to bring lasting peace and prosperity in South Asian region.

Q.50. Under what circumstances, Pakistan has a bent of mind towards militarism?

Ans. Since its birth on 14th August, 1947, Pakistan has been pursuing the policy of militarism at the cost of country's developmental process. The tendency of militarism in Pakistan was due to the fact that for half of the years ever since its independence there was the military governments, installed by Field Marshall Ayub Khan, General Yahya Khan, General Zia-ul-Huq and finally General Parvez Musharraf (may be again by another military ruler after Parvez Musharraf). Therefore, their bellicosity towards India was nothing but inborn. When the militarism is the life-blood of political leaders of Pakistan, they have made Azad Kashmir as the safe haven for training of the terrorists aimed at India. If terrorism is there in any country of the world, it is Pakistan which has taken birth out of militarism.

Although Pakistan incurred discomfiture by the mighty military forces of India in all the wars, yet they want to remain complacent by warning India of massive retaliation if it tried to launch a pre-emptive strike on Pakistan arguing that Islamabad had a more advanced missile programme than New Delhi. Even Pakistan had gone to the extent of telling that in five minutes time New Delhi and Mumbai could be completely annihilated. These are nothing but all irresponsible utterances by Pakistani military junta against a powerful country like India.

Under such war-like attitude of Pakistan which is mixed up in the blood of Pakistani military junta, it should be the absolute policy of India not to react to such irresponsible utterances of Pakistan, rather India has to pursue a policy similar to that of China who are progressing by leaps and bounds both economically and militarily without exposure to the world.

Q.51. Was it in the fitness of things on the part of the Government of India to pass Resolution in the Parliament criticising the U.S. military action against Iraq?

Ans. India is a natural ally of the U.S. Ill-timed Resolution criticising the U.S. military action against Iraq passed by the Indian Parliament and that too on the day the American troops had marched into Baghdad and when it was evident that the Saddam Hussein regime would crumble without much resistance, obviously antagonised the Bush Administration. On account of this, there were clear indications that the Government of India would find it difficult to be considered Washington's "natural ally". Moreso, New Delhi's chances of bagging significant contracts for reconstruction in post-Saddam Iraq appeared to have been jeopardised.

It was no doubt a rude shock to Washinton on account of passing of the Resolution by the Indian Parliament, deploring the American action after keeping quiet for more than a month and just when world-wide criticism of the U.S. had significantly ebbed. The Bush Administration argued that the Indian Resolution was not even matched by most Islamic nations and the Arab world. After passing the Indian Resolution, the U.S. State Department was seriously considering to step back from their South East policy.

In the matter of Iraq war perpetrated by the coalition forces, when the Government of India decided initially to maintain neutral policy, it was not of course expected of India shifting its stand at the fag end of the war. It was likely that the ruling NDA government had to succumb to the extreme pressure of the opposition to pass such Resolution. If it was so, the ruling NDA government should have been resolute in its stand looking to the future repercussions of such Resolution, although there was much deliberation in the matter of language of the Resolution.

Under the circumstances, it was now for the Government of India to be on the correctional course to cool down the temperature built up in the bilateral relations between New Delhi and Washington particularly in view of the fact that India came much closer to Washington during the last few years as also Indian economy is largely dependent on loans from countries like the U.S. It is always recommended that India has to take stock of its economic and military strengths before taking on the lone superpower in the world.

Q.52. It was the desire of Parvez Musharraf, President of Pakistan, that India should not have interference in Afghanistan. Why?

Ans. India evinced to take part in the economic rehabilitation of war ravaged Afghanistan after the fall of Taliban Government consequent upon the U.S. attack, and so in a very consistent and transparent manner with the purpose of maintaining traditionally good and quite developed ties with Afghanistan.

In fact, Pakistan did not want that there should be bonhomie in the relations between India and Afghanistan with the purpose that India should have an ally in the region of Indian sub-continent to fight terrorism jointly with Afghanistan. While Musharraf had been complaining about Indian interference in Afghanistan (which was of course not his lookout), Washington discreetly advised New Delhi to go slow on Afghanistan in order not to agitate Islamabad on the issue. As U.S. Deputy Secretary of State, Richard Armitage prepared to leave for India, Pakistan and Afghanistan in the month of May, 2003, who was likely to face a new problem in India-Pakistan relations while sojourning in the sub-continent, Vyacheslav Trubnikov, Russian President, Vladimir Putin's pointman for Afghanistan warned Armitage not to come in the way of India's traditionally good and quite developed ties with Afghanistan.

It was the perception of Parvez Musharraf that in the event of closer relations between India and Afghanistan, there would be disengagement of Afghanistan from nurturing terrorists, which would be advantageous for India putting Pakistan in difficult situation, as Pakistan would not be in a position to strengthen the terrorist movement furthermore from the soil of Azad Kashmir only, duly supported by al-Qaida group originating from Afghanistan in order to strike Jammu and Kashmir in a bigger way. This would also deny Pakistan to prove to the world that Pakistan was not the only country where terrorists were active but also Afghanistan and that India's contention that Pakistan was the hotbed of terrorism would be belied.

In order, therefore, to fulfil the objective in this direction, Pakistan made the Durand Line an issue to come closer to Afghanistan. Pakistan unilaterally erected border posts along the Durand Line which had been agreed upon in November, 1893 between Abdur Rahman Shah, the then ruler of Afghanistan and Sir Mortimer Durand, the Foreign Secretary of Colonial India as the border between Afghanistan and the British Indian empire in the part which became Pakistan in 1947. That Agreement expired after a century in 1993 and Afghanistan renounced the Durand Line in 1949. The erection of border posts by Pakistan unilaterally along the Durand Line was to exert pressure on the Karzai Administration in Afghanistan so that it would take Pakistan's interests more fully into account than those of some other participants in the anti-terrorist coalition.

Q.53. In what way India has attained global status?

Ans. Global status of a country is determined only when it takes part or has a say in the affairs of other countries in recognition of its being one of the major powers of the world. That India has expanded its horizon as a major power thus attaining global status is based on its political will and maturity in the comity of nations which the major world leaders have already recognised.

India's ties and relations with other major powers of the world in particular regulating the world order apart from other countries—both big and small, are commendable. It was the established conviction expressed by George W. Bush, President of the United States of America after holding parleys with Shri Atal Bihari Vajpayee, the then Prime Minister of India, within 10 days after the end of the 57th U.N. general meeting at New York, that nothing would stand in the way of cementing Indo-U.S. relations despite India's nuclear and missile programme as also earlier slow pace of India's economic reforms. This was a clear indication how the U.S. President evaluated the importance of India as a global status.

India's involvement with the ASEAN countries not being part of the same displayed the matured foreign policy of Shri Atal Bihari Vajpayee in binding all the ASEAN countries into one fold facilitating India to come in close contact with the member countries.

India's contribution in concluding peace process between Sri Lankan government and the LTTE has brought perennial peace in Sri Lanka after about 20 years of internecine war in the island.

The then Indian Prime Minister, Shri Atal Bihari Vajpayee was involved in the global diplomacy when he arrived in Berlin for talks with German Chancellor, Gerhard Schroeder on 27th May, 2003.

After attending the Berlin parleys he again reached St. Petersberg on 30th May, 2003 where he met the world's most important leaders who gathered in the home town of President Vladimir Putin for its tercentenary.

India evinced to take part in the economic rehabilitation of war ravaged Afghanistan after the fall of Taliban government consequent upon the U.S. attack, and so in a very consistent and transparent manner with the purpose of maintaining traditionally good and quite developed ties with Afghanistan.

Taking into account India's global status, the French President, Jacques Chirac invited Shri Atal Bihari Vajpayee to be part of the G-8 summit of the world's riches nations which was held in Evian-les-Bains, France, from 1st to 3rd June, 2003, although India is a non G-8 nation.

All these facts in brief are a clear testimony that India has already attained global status.

Q.54. What was the problem with Nagaland that India had been facing?

Ans. Nagas claimed that they were never a part of India either by consent, conquest or accession. Naga territories conquered by the British could not become an India heritage. The Representatives of the Nagas had told the 1929 Simon Commission on constitutional reform in India that the Nagas wished to be left alone. On the eve of the Indian independence, the Nagas asserted their right to be free and declared independence on 14th August, 1947. The struggle of the Nagas with the Government of India was for the recognition of 'unique history and situation of the Nagas.' Their only legitimate claim was to have a government of their own. Apart from armed suppression, the Government of India had tried unsuccessfully to come to terms through several agreements with the Nagas to end the insurgency in the region.

The National Socialist Council of Nagalim (Isak-Muivah) under the leadership of Isak Chisi Swu as Chairman and Thuingaleng Muivah as General Secretary had been waging protracted battle for a greater "sovereign Nagaland" till a truce was entered into with New Delhi in August, 1997. After lapse of five years of truce, the Nagas wanted from New Delhi a lasting and honourable settlement to the Nagaland problem. Indian government gave preference to hold political parleys with NSCN (I-M), because it was the largest, strongest and most organised and disciplined group of Naga insurgents. The other faction of Naga insurgents which was not of much importance as that of NSCN (I-M) was NSCN (Khaplang). They also represented, the Naga 'national interest.' The NSCN (K) has its support base mainly among the Hemi Nagas of Burma.

New Delhi engaged Shri K. Padmanabhiah, former Home Secretary as the Centre's interlocutor in preparatory talks with NSCN (I-M) for possible solution of Naga problem politically. The peace talks aimed at ending one of the country's oldest separatist movements, while the parleys in respect of Nagaland issue were held in other countries time to time in the past, the substantive negotiations took place only on Indian soil. The substantive discussions in the peace talks were expected to revolve round the thorny issues such as flag, citizenship, defence, trade and currency, list of which was submitted by the two leaders of NSCN (I-M) to the Government of India. The crux of the intention of the Naga insurgents was to establish a greater "Sovereign Nagaland" (Nagalim).

When the Government of India took keen interest in putting an end to the age-old Nagaland problem, there is a clear expectation that the issue would be sorted out once and for all in the not too distant future.

Q.55. What are the evidences of China's intention of establishing sprawling hegemony over Asia *vis-a-vis* India's position?

Ans. In fact, China's dream following the collapse of the Soviet Union was to become the sole Asian military and economic hegemony. China has also global strategic ambition which is likely to affect American authority and influence. Following are the evidences of China's ambition to have sway over the Asian continent, in particular:

(a) Chinese nuclear and missile supplies to Pakistan.
(b) The demand for Indian nuclear disarmament.
(c) Naval activities in LOCO islands and in Gwador.
(d) Building of military airfield in Manually.
(e) Buildup of rail and road links in Tibet.
(f) Chinese possession of more than 5000 sq. kms of part of occupied Kashmir gifted by Pakistan.
(g) Signing of a deal with the ASEAN to give birth to the biggest free trade zone comprising 1.7 billion consumers.
(h) Flooding of Indian market with its cheap goods with the sole purpose of capturing Indian market.
(i) Signing of Dhaka-Beijing defence deal on 25th December, 2002 with the purpose of wooing Bangladesh and aiming at opening another front against India in the East.
(j) Pakistan as an extension of the China policy to maintain and develop a line of military and diplomatic pressure against India and furthermore Pakistan is the gateway to the Middle-East including Saudi Arabia.

These are the evidences as to why China has a bent of mind to establish its hegemony in Asia by giving rebuff to India's strategic and diplomatic importance in the region, India's position as a global power and military strength as also its alignment with the United States of America and other friendly Asian powers like Japan.

As a counter rebuff to the Chinese growing influence in Asia, the Vajpayee-NDA coalition's pragmatic attitude to economic reforms has increased Indian economic energies and confidence in the ability to treat China's economic growth as a challenge. Warm Indo-U.S. relations have revealed that the U.S.A. is now very much interested to see that India emerges as a big power in Asia by helping to resolve Kashmir tangle with Pakistan honourably in the interest of maintaining peaceful co-existence between India and Pakistan so as to enable India to hasten its journey towards attaining all-round developments at the quickest possible time.

As per Aristotelian drama, when "action is the ruling law of drama", the Indian drama is revealed by its nuclear and missile developments. From other defence point of view, India has naval deployment in the Indian ocean area. The U.S.A. feels that the China's global strategic ambition can affect American authority and influence in Asia, the Pacific and Indian ocean regions. Therefore, the U.S.-India defence cooperation is a policy of the U.S. government that India should be made stronger furthermore in Asia and hence the U.S. government has okayed supply of sophisticated defence equipment by Israel to India but not to China.

With Indian manufacturing base, its export trade is growing and it attracts Western attention. Now India has an upward tilt in the strategic and economic spheres and this points to a long term competition between India and China.

Pragmatic analyses of the above facts have revealed that India has been continuing to vie with China's growing influence in the region being saddled in international centres of importance. Military build-ups, alliances, agriculture, industry, software, economic developments through privatisation and other scientific and high tech fields are the themes of prosperous India.

Q.56. How are the relations between India and Israel?

Ans. India which restored full diplomatic relations with Israel in the year, 1992 did not move any anti-Israel resolutions at the U.N. since 1994, though India has been one of the most vocal and consistent supporters of the Palestine cause. India owes Israel a debt of gratitude for standing by it during the Kargil war of 1999. During this war, Israel stripped their own army of weapons and had them flown across to aid India. Apart from this, after the December 13, 2001 Parliament attack, Israel wanted to assist India again. These illustrate the kind of relations that India and Israel built over the course of the last few years.

Relations between India and Israel were cemented with the first official state visit of Israeli Prime Minister to India, Ariel Sharon from 9th to 10th September, 2003, which was cut short because of suicide attack by the Palestinian terrorists at a crowded bus stop near Tel Aviv on the night of 9th September, 2003. That India is one of the most important countries of the world was expressed by Ariel Sharon during his visit to New Delhi. This is no doubt how Israel attaches importance to India in the comity of nations. Sharon pinned the hope that his visit to India would help achieve many things together in many areas.

India and Israel have agreements on cooperation in science and technology, space, education, culture, health, agriculture and combating narco-terrorism. In a joint statement issued by the Prime Ministers of India and Israel on 9th September, 2003, the two countries condemned states and individuals who aid and abet terrorism across borders, harbour and give sanctuary and provide them with financial means, training and patronage. The two countries have a mutual interest in making the world a more secure place to live in.

Israel was keen to supply India electronic fencing sensors and gadgetry that could be put on the borders not only in Kashmir but also in the eastern sector (Bangladesh) where a lot of infiltration takes place.

As a close ally, Israel also supplied India sensitive technology. As per the repeated requests of Ariel Sharon, India assured him that the country had an impeccable record of non-proliferation and that the sensitive technology received from Israel would be kept secret and not to be leaked out to a third country.

For the purpose of strengthening defence of India further, Israel also sold to New Delhi three Phalcon air-borne early warning systems, Green Pine Radar, Arrow Anti-missile, submarine and other sophisticated military hardware. It is noteworthy to mention that Israel has emerged second to Russia in supplying military equipment to India.

From the above, it is a clear manifestation that the relations between India and Israel have become very much warm and cordial, although India consistently supports Palestine cause and also have close relations with Iran and Syria.

9

International Topics

Q.1. What were the circumstances leading to the outbreak of Israel and Palestine conflict?

Ans. In fact, the conflict between Israel and Palestine started only after the blatant aggression perpetrated by Israel on Palestine in 1967. Since then what is happening in Palestine is a virtual war between Israeli troops armed with tanks, helicopter, gunships and rockets on the one side and Palestinian civilians armed with a few guns and fire-bombs on the other. The wanton use of mighty forces by Israel against the Palestine embittered the Arab world. This direct and unprovoked attack by Israel was against the right of the Palestinians to have their own independent state. The world knows that if only the United States of America puts pressure on its ally, Israel, the Palestinians can hope for the restoration of their legitimate rights. The continued Israeli attack on Palestine has the tacit support of the U.S.A. and this was perhaps the most important reason of the attack on the World Trade Center and Pentagon on 11th September, 2001 as a revenge taken by Osama-bin-Laden against the U.S.A. When the war in Afghanistan was continuing George W. Bush, the American President suddenly changed tune by accepting the right of the Palestinians to have their own independent state. But, this was nothing but a diplomacy on the part of the American President to show to the Muslim world that the U.S.A. was actually interested in the solution of the West Asian crisis by guaranteeing the independent Palestine state and obviously this was not a fight against the Muslims when the Arab world tried to establish that in the name of Osama-bin-Laden, U.S. was bent upon annihilating the Muslims from Afghanistan by massive wanton bombings.

The Palestinians signed the Oslo Accord in 1993 with the expressed hope that they were now guaranteed self-determination and end to the military occupation of Gaza Strip and West Bank by the Israeli troops. But, most unfortunately, even after signing the Oslo Accord Israel did not cede control of Gaza Strip and West Bank. Israel now calls the Palestinians terrorists just because the latter are fighting tooth and nail to get back their lost land. There could be fragile cease-fire every now and then to get temporary relief from the gunfire. Israel has even gone to the extent of flouting every resolution of the U.S. Security Council over Palestine. What is now required most is that the key to the solution lies in the hands of Israel, which seems remote.

Q.2. What was the progress of development in Afghanistan after the ousting of the Taliban and installation of Northern Alliance government under the Chairmanship of Hamid Karzai?

Ans. Afghanistan was battered heavily by the ceaseless bombings of the U.S.A. and Great Britain to end the Taliban Government and annihilate the militant group, al-Qaida of Osama-bin-Laden who master-minded the havoc caused to the World Trade Center and Pentagon on 11th September, 2001. After fall of the Taliban Government transitional Northern Alliance Government under the Chairmanship of Hamid Karzai was installed in Afghanistan in the month of January, 2002 in pursuance of Bonn Agreement.

The stability and development of Afghanistan depended largely upon the foreign aid, as the economy of Afghanistan shattered completely due to this internecine war against the Taliban government supporting al-Qaida and Osma-bin-Laden. While millions of dollars were spent in ousting the Taliban, hardly any aid was flowing into Afghanistan even after eight months of installation of interim administration was put in place and also not a single labour-intensive project started in Afghanistan. After eight months of installation of Karzai government, more than 1.5 millions of refugees who fled the country during continuation of the war came back and another 60,000 refugees were expected to return in the first year of the government. But what would they do back home when the process of reconstruction was yet to commence. Although the U.S. and British governments assured reconstruction of the war battered country they did not come forward to implement their assurances. The donor countries claimed that there was no capacity in Afghanistan to absorb foreign aid. In this connexion, the Foreign Minister of Afghanistan, Mr. Abdullah asked, "But my question is—how will we even begin to build that capacity if we do not start receiving any aid?"

Afghanistan is no longer a centre of terrorism and threat to world peace or stability. Therefore, without a robust process of reconstruction, stability would not return to Afghanistan. For maintaining stability the Central Government in Kabul had to be helped to increase its capacity to govern and integrate its authority in the regions by appeasing the dominant ethnic group. Another important factor was to formulate a Constitution under which elections could be held.

While the other international community invested a lot in Afghanistan, the aid for reconstruction from the U.S.A. and Great Britain must be forthcoming for ensuring stable and prosperous Afghanistan, as had already been assured by them. India too committed to help in the reconstruction of Afghanistan in all possible ways and gifted three aircrafts to them for tiding over the problem of air communication.

Q.3. What led to the siege of Moscow theatre by the suicide squad of Chechnya on the night of 23rd October, 2002?

Ans. Chechnya demanded for autonomy through meaningful

dialogue. The Russian President, Vladimir Putin rejected the idea of independence of breakaway Chechnya in Southern Russia. He, therefore, took an uncompromising stand on the conflict in largely-Muslim Chechnya where the Kremlim had twice launched military pushes to crush separatists. Russia finally deployed its troops there in October, 1999 to suppress the demand of largely Muslim Chechnya for Independence. The Russian President implied the role of the international mujahedin fighting on Chechen separatist side. The hardline policy of Vladimir Putin was very much resented by Chechnya and they demanded complete withdrawal of Russian troops from its soil.

In the event of not complying with the demand for troops pull-out by Kremlin from Chechnya, Chechen suicide squad numbering around 50 guerrillas with heavy arms and explosives strapped to their bodies burst in the three-stored theatre in Moscow on the night of 23rd October, 2002, demanding immediate withdrawal of Russian troops from Chechnya, failing which they would kill all the 800 hostages held captive in the theatre by them. The main purpose of the Chechen militants was to use the hostages as the vehicle of their demand of troops withdrawal from Chechnya. Among the captives there were some 75 foreigners also.

The Palace of Culture *i.e.*, the three-storyed Moscow theatre was wired for in-house video. When the gunmen entered to siege the theatre, they were seen on the video screens and the audience thought that they were watching them as part of the show. It was totally unclear to them what was happening and who these men were. Within a moment the audience could realise that they were transformed into a terrifying siege by the militants inside the theatre and that they found themselves in a situation between life and death.

Vladimir Putin who rose to power on pledges to clamp down on the decade-old rebellion on Russian Southern fringe and boost public security said the main task was to secure the hostages' safe release from the clutches of the Chechen suicide squad. Information from the rebel's representatives confirmed that the terrorist act was planned abroad. Immediately after getting information about the siege of the theatre by the Chechen rebellions Russian troops and security forces cordoned off the area. The Chechen terrorists then warned that the Russian troops and security forces must be pulled out or they would start shooting the hostages.

After remaining in captivity for three days the hostages were rescued by the Russian special forces when they using gas to knock out Chechen guerrillas stormed the Moscow Theatre on 26th October, 2002 in a dawn raid that left 117 hostages dead along with most of the rebel captors who were around 50 in number including 18 women guerrillas.

With the release of the hostages, the nation breathed a sigh of relief. It was no doubt a great success to overpower the Chechen terrorists at the cost of death of 118 hostages for which Vladimir Putin asked forgiveness blaming the rebel attack of international terrorism which the world has to fight. He also lamented that lives of the 118 hostages could not be saved calling terrorism a strong and dangerous, inhuman and cruel enemy.

Even when the terrorists were perished, there was apprehension that the rebels would get entrenched and that there might be new terrorist attacks in much bloodier form than this.

Q.4. Who are the ASEAN members? What were the declarations in the Summit of the ASEAN held at Phnom Penh, the capital of Cambodia on 4th and 5th November, 2002. Apart from the ASEAN countries who were the other countries participating in the Summit of ASEAN and what global implications were there in attending the Summit by India?

Ans. The ten members of ASEAN (Association of South-East Asian Nations) are: Brunei, Cambodia, Indonesia, Laos, Malayasia, Myanmar, The Philippines, Singapore,

Thailand and Vietnam. Among these countries, Cambodia and Laos—the two tiny nations in Indo-China, were the latest members of ASEAN till the year, 2002.

In the Summit that was held on 4th and 5th November, 2002 at Phnom Penh, the capital of Cambodia, the following declarations/deals were made:

(a) The ASEAN signed a deal to have a free trade zone among the member nations, which was the biggest in the world, encompassing more than 1.7 billion people struggling to attain prosperity after centuries plunged in poverty.

(b) The member countries agreed that they would tackle militant violence which was a threat not only to mankind but to prosperity. Tackling of terrorism would also create an environment in which foreign investment could blossom in the ASEAN countries.

(c) They would call the international community to avoid indiscriminately advising their citizens to refrain from visiting the ASEAN countries in the absence of established evidence to substantiate rumours of possible terrorist attacks.

(d) The Summit aimed at boosting trade among the member countries and recognised the need for regional economic integration on an urgent basis, the sooner the better.

(e) The Summit recognised that security was an essential ingredient of prosperity and the member countries were united by fears of North Korea's nuclear weapons programme.

China, Japan, India and South Africa attended the two-day Summit on the side-lines.

China was very much interested in expanding trade to the south and increasing overseas investment and accordingly signed a deal with the ASEAN to give birth to the biggest free trade zone comprising 1.7 billion consumers.

Another landmark accord China signed with the Southern neighbours was to avoid conflict over the disputed Spratly islands in the South China sea over which Beijing came to the brink of war with Vietnam and the Philippines several times in the past.

By its presence Japan entered a new age of partnership with the ASEAN countries by signing a joint declaration in economic cooperation.

Attending the ASEAN Summit on the side-lines for the first time, Shri Atal Behari Vajpayee, Prime Minister of India proposed to create a Free Trade Area (FTA) with ASEAN and received strong approbation from the ASEAN countries. Shri Vajpayee announced that India too was eager to negotiate a free trade zone with the ASEAN. The Indian Prime Minister put forward a vision of India and ASEAN wedded together at the Summit. The Summit in Phnom Penh provided India an opportunity to establish its estimation in the ASEAN world. By attending the Summit Shri Vajpayee displayed his matured foreign policy in binding all the ASEAN countries into one fold facilitating India to come in close contact with the member countries.

India agreed to help Cambodia and Laos—the tiny ASEAN countries, in the following ways:

(a) India extended the Most Favoured Nation (MFN) status to Cambodia.

(b) A soft credit loan of $10 million was extended to Cambodia with payback period of 25 years, including a grace period of five years.

(c) Indian Institute of Technology, Mumbai, would provide help to build a technology institute in Cambodia.

(d) India pledged to provide expertise to Cambodia in dealing with WTO-related issues to help attain membership of the World Trade Organisation.

(e) India would build a railway network that would form part of a direct rail link between Singapore and Kuoming in South China.

(f) India would provide a soft credit lone of $10 million to Laos on long repayment terms for building a power transmission link in Laos to evacuate the excess hydel power to power-starved Cambodia.

The United States of America and other powers had minutely observed India's involvement in shouldering greater responsibility in strategically important regions of South-east Asia by dwarfing the influence of China in the region. This would no doubt facilitate India to take much greater responsibility for the management of the international system in future. Therefore, India's positive engagement with the ASEAN countries had had global implications.

Q.5. How was the peace process concluded between the Sri Lankan government and the LTTE?

Ans. The northern and eastern parts of Sri Lanka with habitation of Hindu majority Tamils were battered by the bloody civil war between the LTTE and the Sri Lanka government's military forces since 1983 which claimed 64,000 people and also the former Prime Minister of India, Rajiv Gandhi had to pay a heavy price of his life by the LTTE on the soil of India itself for his policy towards Sri Lanka which was considered antagonistic to them (LTTE). The Liberation Tigers of Tamil Eelam were firm in their demands for self-determination in establishing a separate state or eelam in Sri Lanka for the Hindu majority Tamils. Talks for peace process were brightening on the basis of the earlier indefinite ceasefire agreement signed between the Sri Lankan government and the LTTE which was a political breakthrough of immense significance, ensuring that the end of violence created the conditions for durable peace. This Agreement was based on the implicit recognition of the LTTE and Mr. Prabhakaran as the "sole spokesman" of the Tamil people.

In pursuance of the Agreement, peace talks between the Sri Lankan government and the Liberation Tigers of Tamil Eelam started as from 18th September, 2002 in Thailand with the initiative of Norwegian government's representative, Mr. Eric Solheim. The talks were led by Mr. G.L. Peiris, a legal expert, on behalf of the Sri Lankan government, and Mr. Anton Balasingham, the LTTE's chief strategist. From the initial talks held at a palm lined resort, west of the capital of Thailand, Bangkok, it transpired that the LTTE seemed to have accepted that it would not be possible to achieve an independent sovereign eelam in Sri Lanka and the Tiger's chief negotiator hinted that they were interested for 'substantial autonomy' within a homeland, but at the same time they would continue to fight for separate state "as a last resort" for the Tamils, if their demand for autonomy was not met. In turn Colombo also seemed to have realised that peace could not be achieved without making significant concessions including substantial devolution of powers and the unification of the Tamil majority—northern and eastern parts of island.

In the second round of peace talks held on 31st October and 1st November, 2002 in Thailand, the two sides agreed to set up a "political committee" to discuss Tamil claims for self-determination. Sri Lankan government chief negotiator, Mr. G.L. Peiris said the Committee would be led by himself and chief Tamil Tiger negotiator, Mr. Anton Balasingham. The purpose of the "political committee" was how to devolve power and what were the arrangements to resolve the ethnic questions.

It was felt by both LTTE and the representatives of Sri Lankan Government that since the violent and brutal war had been continuing since 1983 it was not expected of achieving speedy solution over the matter and it was decided that the next round of discussion would take place in Oslo, the capital of Norway.

At last Sri Lankan government and Tamil Tiger rebels made a breakthrough by ending a 19-year internecine separatist war and arrived at an unprecedented historic decision in an Oslo hotel on 5th December, 2002 with chief government negotiator, Mr. G.L. Peiris by agreeing to work out a self-rule and regional autonomy within a federal system than a separate state for the Tamils in Northern and Eastern part of Sri Lanka.

Q.6. What were the salient features of the Friendship Treaty signed by Russia and China on 16th July, 2001?

Ans. The Russian President, Mr. Vladimir Putin and the Chinese President, Mr. Jiang Zemin signed the Historic Friendship Treaty in Moscow on 16th July, 2001 valid for 20 years. This Friendship Treaty declared Russia and China "Friends forever, enemies never." The First Friendship Treaty which was concluded between these two countries expired in the year, 1980. During this intervening period between 1980 and 2001 border clashes soured the relations between the two great countries disturbing peace in Asia, which gave an advantage to the United States in contemplating to widen and establish their influence in the region.

This Historic Friendship Treaty guaranteed their cooperation in nuclear non-proliferation and encouraged all nations to join in the Nuclear Non-Proliferation Treaty as also called for an international pact to ensure de-militarisation of outer space. One important feature of this Treaty was that it did not form an alliance between Russia and China directed against any third country. The treaty also stipulated that the two countries would have no territorial ambition and gave solemn promise to respect each other's territorial integrity. This naturally enkindled the hope that the Treaty rebuffed the revival of border conflict that damaged Sino-Russian relations in the 1960s and 1970s.

The Treaty represented a culmination in the perennial sweet bilateral relations between Russia and China and called for mutual cooperation to curb U.S. sway in the world especially in the context of their determination to set at naught the ABM Treaty in flagrant violation of world opinion.

Signing of Historic Friendship Treaty between Russia and China had also a far-reaching effect in India. India has already age-old warm and cordial relations with Russia and at the same time it paved the way in maintaining a good relation with China by India after the terrorist attack on World Trade Center and Pentagon on 11th September, 2001. Obviously, maintaining hearty relations with all these three major countries, the continent of Asia has become efficacious and development process of India is destined to be quickened with the support and cooperation of Russia and China being friends of India and these big trio of Asia combinedly would come forward for putting resistance to any big power of the world to set their foot in any of the Asian countries for increasing their influence.

Q.7. Under what circumstances the United States of America entered into hostility with Iraq?

Ans. Iraq invaded Kuwait in 1990. The coalition led by Washington forced invading Iraqi troops out of Kuwait. In an apparent reference to the U.S. military presence in Kuwait, Iraqi President, Saddam Hussein apologised to the Kuwaiti people on 7th December, 2002 for his 1990-1991 occupation and urged them to struggle against foreign armies. The apology letter from Saddam Hussein reads as under:

> "We apologise to God for any deed that angered him in the past, which we might not have known of and is blamed on us, and on this basis we also apologise to you."

The U.S. alleged that Baghdad had biological, chemical and nuclear weapons of mass destruction in violation of U.N. Agreements reached after the 1991 Gulf War when a coalition led by Washington forced the invading Iraqi troops out of Kuwait.

British foreign secretary, Jack Straw told BBC television that Saddam's disclosures about weapons had not been truthful and hence the declaration of Saddam Hussein was not accurate and it was a pack of lies. Straw told that the previous U.N. weapons inspectors team which left Iraq in 1998 found chemical and biological materials in possession of Iraq to make weapons of mass destruction.

On the basis of the reports of having weapons of mass destruction in possession of Iraq, Washington was bent upon freeing Iraq from possession of such deadly weapons with the help of U.S. led military action.

The fresh U.N. resolution had given Baghdad a deadline till 8th December, 2002 to provide a full account of any past and current programmes involving biological, chemical or nuclear weapons and as demanded in a U.N. Security Council resolution in November, 2002 the U.N. Arms Inspectors began searching Iraq for weapons of mass destruction.

Iraq handed over the declaration in a 12000-page dossier to the U.N. Arms Inspectors on 7th December, 2002 that it did not have any such weapons of mass destruction and challenged the U.S. to provide the U.N. Arms Inspectors with evidence to the contrary.

U.S. officials said that Washington had substantial evidence, including some not made public, that Iraq had retained and accelerated banned weapons programmes. The Bush administration said that they would take a few days more time to scrutinise the dossier handed over by Iraq to the U.N. Arms Inspectors and if they (Washington) were satisfied that Iraq still was in possession of weapons of mass destruction, war with Iraq was inevitable.

Q.8. What was the significance of Dhaka-Beijing defence deal?

Ans. Relation between India and Bangladesh started becoming bedevilled after the Bangladesh Nationalist Party under the Premiership of Begum Khaleda Zia came to power in 2001. The relation further worsened after the Indian leadership openly accused Bangladesh of harbouring terrorists who were responsible for violence in India. Bangladesh being a small country could not afford to think of remaining isolated from any strong country at times of any eventuality facing the country. During the visit of Parvez Musharraf to

Bangladesh in early part of the year, 2002, he expressed regret for the excesses committed by Islamabad to the then East Pakistani people which had led to the emergence of Bangladesh with India's military assistance and assured BNP Government of all support and assistance from Pakistan on all matters, since Pakistan could not heal up the wounds suffered after East Pakistan was separated from the western wing of Pakistan emerging as a new country in the name of Bangladesh with India's assistance. Pakistan and Bangladesh came closer to each other after the visit of Parvez Musharraf. It was likely that nurturing and supporting the terrorists directed against India by Bangladesh was possibly the sequel to the clandestine directives issued by Parvez Musharraf to BNP Government. In order to bolster the terrorist activities from the soil of Bangladesh, I.S.I. and al-Qaida group received impetus from Pakistan. The attempt of Parvez Musharraf was nothing but to rupture the relation between India and Bangladesh.

The Chinese leadership, aware of the hostile relations between India and Pakistan might be deliberately trying to open a front against New Delhi in the east at the opportune moment when the relation between India and Bangladesh was not cosy. China's close links with Pakistan was a known fact. Beijing contributed to more than 80 per cent of Pakistan's military hardware and ammunition and also secretly helped Islamabad develop nuclear and missile programmes.

Defence preparedness by any country—whether big or small, is an artifice to display to the world that such country is not weak. The defence agreement signed by China and Bangladesh on 25th December, 2002 was, therefore, a sign of renewed vigour with which China was wooing Bangladesh and that it might be aimed at opening another front against India in the east. China's attempts to woo the Bangladesh Nationalist Party government and broadbase its relations with Dhaka became apparent from Beijing's financial loan, trade concessions and assurance to help infrastructure.

But, the most significant step was the agreement on defence cooperation. This defence deal helped enhance cooperation in defence training and production in Bangladesh. Experts believed that the deal might be China's attempt to open another front against India to keep it preoccupied in South Asia at the cost of fulfilling its ambitions as a key international player.

While the defence deal between China and Bangladesh sparked concern in New Delhi, Bangladesh would surely heave a sigh of comforts by coming into the folds of one of the stronger nations in Asia. For Khaleda Zia, the defence agreement was no doubt an opportunity to thumb her nose at India and proved that Bangladesh had stronger allies to fall back on and Dhaka would not hesitate to cooperate with the stronger ally in the face of any strong arm tactics by New Delhi.

Q.9. Pakistan has become an irresponsible state after possessing nuclear weapon. How could it be justified?

Ans. No country other than Pakistan possessing nuclear weapons has threatened to go nuclear, because they know how to keep their nuclear capabilities under control, taking into account the holocaust which would ensue by the use of nuclear weapons. On the contrary, by acquiring nuclear weapons, Pakistan had been most irresponsibly acting in such a manner as if India would be afraid of losing large chunks of territory from the mainland in the event of going nuclear by Pakistan against India. To all intents and purposes, Pakistan proved itself an irresponsible state by the following utterances:

(a) Parvez Musharraf's utterances to a gathering of Pakistan Air Force officers on 30th December, 2002 were: "I personally conveyed messages to the then Indian Prime Minister, A.B. Vajpayee through every international leader who came to Pakistan, that if Indian troops moved a single step across the international border or the Line of Control, they should not expect a conventional war from Pakistan".

(b) Pakistan's Ambassador to the United Nations Organisation, Munir Akram, too, talked of using the nuclear option in the event of an Indian strike.

(c) During the military standoff across the border, Pakistan had deployed its nuclear-capable missiles. This indicated that Pakistan was fully prepared to strike India with the help of missiles with nuclear capability.

In a series of statements from Pakistan it was proved that Islamabad was ready to flex its nuclear muscle against India. By such threats from Pakistan, New Delhi painted Islamabad as an irresponsible state incapable of holding its nuclear status and expressed apprehension of a nuclear conflict in the subcontinent. General Sunderajan Padmanabhan on the day of his retirement as Indian Army Chief on 31st December, 2002 wondered that it was a misfortune for Pakistan that they had such a chief like Parvez Musharraf who went on threatening India with nuclear warfare. New Army Chief, Gen. N.C. Viz also branded Musharraf's actions and utterances as irresponsible.

Q.10. Pakistan has been branded as the most dangerous country in the world—How?

Ans. The U.S. journalist, Seymour Hersh elicited his opinion in the magazine, 'The New Yorker' that Pakistan was the 'most dangerous country in the world' and his opinion was based on the following facts:

(a) Pakistan, one of the Bush Administration's important allies in the war against terrorism, was helping North Korea build atom bomb not to the liking of the United States of America under Bush administration. Pakistan was closely but clandestinely associated with the Pyongyang regime of North Korea in their nuclear programme. Top secret CIA document said that since 1997 Pakistan had been sharing sophisticated nuclear technology, warhead design information and weapon-testing data with North Korea. Mr. Hersh in the magazine quoted a former Pakistani official telling him that the Pakistan Government's contacts with North Korea increased dramatically in 1997.

(b) Pakistan had provided some of the know-how to North Korea to manufacture missile.

(c) When the American war was continuing in Afghanistan to oust the Taliban government and wipe out Osama-bin-Laden of al-Qaida in retaliation to World Trade Center and Pentagon attacks on 11th September, 2001, Government of Pakistan under the military ruler, Parvez Musharraf gave refuge to the al-Qaida in Pakistan, fleeing from Afghanistan. 'The New Yorker' magazine said that Islamabad has supplied highly enriched uranium (HEU) to al-Qaida to help them manufacture atom bomb. Hersh said that there was al-Qaida sympathy within Pakistan's nuclear programme.

Nancy Powell, U.S. Ambassador to Pakistan urged Musharraf government of Pakistan to ensure its pledge to prevent infiltration across the line of control and end the use of Pakistan as a platform for terrorism.

Parvez Musharraf could of course decipher the changed attitude of the U.S. government that Pakistan became a dangerous country in the world by the above activities and accordingly cautioned his countrymen to be alert in future, as he could sense that the next target of U.S. government might be Pakistan after the possible war in Iraq.

Q.11. What was all about the U.S. Space-Craft, 'Columbia' and what was the reaction of Iraq after it exploded on 1st February, 2003?

Ans. It was another tragedy of extreme magnitude for the United States of America when the U.S. Space Shuttle, 'Columbia' exploded on 1st February, 2003 after the demolition of World Trade Center on 11th September, 2001, *i.e.*, within a span of 1 year and 5 months.

'Columbia' was NASA's (National Aeronautics and Space Administration's) oldest plane and the first of its orbital fleet. It was delivered to Kennedy Space Center in

March, 1979. The Space Shuttle, 'Columbia' was launched from Kennedy Space Center, Florida, to begin the first shuttle mission on 12th April, 1981 for three days upto 14th April, 1981. Its primary aims were to accomplish a safe ascent into orbit, check all light systems and carry out a safe landing. The 22-year-old Spacecraft underwent more than 100 modifications upto September, 1999 at Rockwell International's Palmdate, California assembly plant. Columbia undertook orbital missions for a total of 26 times till 1st February, 2003.

The ill-fated 'Columbia' was launched for the last time on 16th January, 2003 for 16 days mission trip from Kennedy Space Center, Florida, with seven-member crew on board including Kalpana Chawla of Indian origin and Col. Ramon, Israel's first astronaut, others being all Americans. While returning to earth on 1st February, 2003, communication and tracking of the Shuttle was lost at 9.00 A.M. (Eastern Standard time) with the Mission Control at an altitude of about 203,000 feet (61,900 metres) in the area above north Central Texas. At the time when the communication with the Spacecraft was lost, it was travelling approximately at a speed of 12,500 miles (20,100 kms) per hour and within a minute's time of losing the communication there was conflagration with huge vibrating sound just about 16 minutes away from the earth. The fragmented parts of the exploded Spacecraft scattered covering an area of 200 kms around Texas with no signs of life of all the seven astronauts on board. Thus, the U.S.A. had suffered another colossal loss at the explosion of the Space Shuttle, 'Columbia' and this loss was not only for the U.S.A. but to the whole world. The world leaders including the U.N. Secretary-General, Kafi Annan were deeply mortified and expressed profound condolences for the colossal loss.

It is pertinent to mention here that the number sixteen was a bad omen in the case of the Spacecraft in point of the fact that it was launched on 16th January, 2003, it was for 16 days in orbit and it exploded 16 minutes before the scheduled touchdown.

The immediate popular reaction in Iraq to the loss of the U.S. Space Shuttle and its seven-member crew including the first Israeli astronaut was that it was the retribution of the Almighty God. He wanted to show that His might was greater than the Americans. Bush administration encroached on Iraq for no fault of theirs and hence God imposed penalty on them.

Q.12. Under what circumstances Pakistan was barred from re-entry to the Council of Commonwealth?

Ans. Pakistan was suspended from the Council of the Commonwealth in November, 1999 for the military coup that overthrew democratically elected Nawaz Shariff government and brought Musharraf to power on 12th October, 1999.

The meeting of the Commonwealth Ministerial Action Group (CMAG) comprising of the Commonwealth foreign ministers was held in London on 1st November, 2002 to decide whether Pakistan should be allowed re-entry in the Council of the Commonwealth. The CMAG were of the opinion that the general election in Pakistan held on 10th October, 2002 had not completed the transfer of power from military to civilian rule but helped Musharraf perpetuate his dominance in the country's affairs. In fact, the election strengthened Musharraf's own position as military dictator by trampling the constitution in his favour.

Commonwealth foreign ministers, however, agreed to maintain Pakistan's suspension from the Council of the Commonwealth—the decision making bodies of the 54-nation Organisation, until they had a clearer picture of the role and functioning of democratic institutions after formation of the government. They said it was too soon to judge how much control Musharraf, whose 1999 bloodless coup triggered Pakistan's suspension from the group of mainly ex-British colonies, would hand over to parliament. Musharraf was strongly criticised for amending the Constitution before the election to ensure a major role for the military in overseeing the work of a future government and giving him the power to dismiss parliament if it became unruly and to appoint a military dominated National Security Council to oversee civilian rule.

After the election held on 10th October, 2002, Mir Zafarullah Jamali, a pro-military politician, who vowed to continue Musharraf's key policies and is a Muslim League (Quaid-e-Azam) nominee, who is in proximity with President Parvez Musharraf, was sworn in as Pakistan's first Prime Minister on 23rd November, 2002. The military ruler, Musharraf's election as President of Pakistan as well as appointment of Jamali as Prime Minister of Pakistan was a clear testimony that Pakistan did not opt fully for the installation of civilian government.

Under the circumstances, the Commonwealth Ministerial Action Group (CMAG) decided unanimously to debar Pakistan from re-entry to Commonwealth till democratic form of government is restored in Pakistan in true sense of the term.

Q.13. The U.S. has exposed itself as a country having tendency of militarism. How could it be justified?

Ans. Charter of United Nations is that it protects all nations against military actions. Therefore, George W. Bush's use of decisive coalition force to attack Iraq on 20th March, 2003 was a flagrant violation of the Charter of the United Nations. This is nothing but a distinct indication that the United Nations have become a failure in maintaining world peace by avoiding war. The support of 35 nations extended to George W. Bush to wage war against Iraq was also obviously against the United Nations' Charter. The effectiveness and credibility of U.N. in the war against Iraq has no doubt been dwindled to a great extent and it is now a matter of conjecture how far United Nations would be able to mobilise world support to maintain world peace in future years to come by avoiding wars in the presence of the United States of America as the only super power of the world when other developing nations have leanings towards such a great power, as their developments largely depend upon the financial assistance of the USA.

The commencement of war against Iraq led by the combined forces of the U.S. and its ally seriously impaired the authority of the U.N. system. It denigrated the Security Council, flouted international Law and caused grave injury to the concept of national sovereignty. The war was initiated without the U.N.'s approval and it testified that the U.S. has acquired imperial ambitions and wanted to reshape the world according to its likes and dislikes through military adventurism.

America's pre-eminence in today's uni-polar world has emboldened it to demonstrate its hyper-power status in conflicts after conflicts since Gulf War-I in 1990-91, the campaign against Serbia in Kosovo in 1999, war on Afghanistan in 2001 and now war on Iraq in 2003. Growing unilateralism in the conduct of U.S. foreign policy was never in evidence in the past as in the case of the ultimatum issued by President Bush to Iraqi leader, Saddam Hussein to leave his country within the deadline of time fixed or face imminent military attack.

The U.S. pressed ahead with the development of the National Missile Defence system by abrogating the 1972 Anti-Ballistic Missile Treaty with Russia and also pulled out of international discussions aimed at effectively monitoring the 1972 Biological Weapons Convention.

The belligerent attitude of the U.S. is obviously a step towards breeding of anti-American sentiments by majority of the world community. President Bush may end up winning war against Iraq but losing peace.

Q.14. What is the global policy of the United States of America?

Ans. After disintegration of the U.S.S.R., the United States of America emerged as the sole super power of the world. This cleared its channel to forge ahead to assert suzerainty over a number of countries of the world.

Being the only super power, the U.S.A. has won patronage of many developing as well as underdeveloped countries of the world by extending to them fabulous financial assistance and as such countries have naturally leaned and shown allegiance towards the United States, as they have understood that their development process largely depends upon the U.S. financial assistance only. By such tactical methods, the U.S.A. has exerted influence all over the world. Thus, having attained initial success in implementing its global policy of bringing the developing and the underdeveloped countries under its fold, the U.S. has turned its eyes to other aspects as a global power, which are analysed below.

The United States of America has a global policy of establishing military bases at different points of strategic importance. They have made military base at Diego Garcia which is an island situated in the midst of the Indian Ocean. It is a naval base which was established in the year, 1973. The purpose of the U.S. is to have full use of Diego Garcia for bombing raids against Iraq.

When Kuwait was invaded by Saddam Hussein in 1991, the American troops came to Kuwaitis help to oust the military adventurism of Iraq. Even after termination of the Kuwait war, the American soldiers have been stationing on the Kuwait soil as part of their military base there.

Also for the cause of fighting terrorism in Afghanistan after the attack on the World Trade Center on 11th September, 2001, the U.S. set up a military base in the North West Frontier Province of Pakistan adjacent to the border of Afghanistan.

All these U.S. military bases, as it appears, are aimed at the gulf countries, which are rich for their oil reserves.

Apart from the above military bases, the U.S. also established network of other bases world-wide, such as Pearl Harbour (in Pacific Ocean), South Korea, Guatemala, Japan and Guantanamo Bay (Cuba) as part of their global military supremacy. Setting up of these additional military bases is also another global stratagem of the U.S. to have sway over the countries when occasion arises.

As far as global military power is concerned, America's pre-eminence in today's uni-polar world has emboldened it to demonstrate its hyper-power status in conflicts after conflicts since Gulf War-I in 1991, the campaign against Serbia in Kosovo in 1999, war in Afghanistan in 2001 and now war on Iraq in 2003. The U.S. pressed ahead with the development of the National Missile Defence system by abroagating the 1972 Anti-Ballistic Missile Treaty with Russia and also pulled out of international discussions aimed at effectively monitoring the 1972 Biological Weapons Convention. Demonstration of hyper-power status has helped the U.S. to push sale of its sophisticated war equipment in large scale to a number of its allied countries. This is also a tactical policy of the U.S. for sale of war equipment globally and hence the loss of weapons in wars in terms of dollars is made good by such sale to countries.

American troops attacking Iraq were looked upon as invaders rather than liberators. The "shock and awe" tactic of a massive bombardment of Iraq's capital was nothing but to decapitate the Iraqi leadership. Bush administration attacked Iraq on 20th March, 2003 without any provocation whatsover. The U.S. along with Britain moved against Saddam Hussein for his inaction to destroy weapons of mass destruction, although no evidence was found by the arms inspection team deployed by the United Nations. On the other hand, contradictory reason was that their attack on Iraq was to bring democracy to the country after years of tyrannical rule of Saddam Hussein. Naturally question arose, since when American government actively promoted democracy in other countries. The glaring example was Pakistan when Parvez Musharaff seized power from the democratically elected Nawaz Shariff government in 1999 and the U.S. did not come forward to revive democracy in Pakistan at that time. If later version of the U.S. was the reason for the attack of Iraq what mattered them if actually it was a rule of tyranny of Saddam Hussein. From all these analyses there was transparency of fact that the absolute U.S. policy of attacking Iraq was to have full control of oil supplies from Iraq which is the second highest oil producing country next to Saudi Arabia.

In order to have easy sway over the gulf countries possessing fabulous oil reserves, it is also one of the global stratagems of the U.S. Government to exert its influence over some of the Muslim countries in the region and in this direction the U.S. was crowned with success to woo Pakistan and Afghanistan on the ground of stamping out terrorism.

From the pragmatic facts and circumstances as narrated above, the U.S. global policies are not hidden to the world.

Q.15. What were the reactions throughout the world arising out of the war against Iraq initiated by the Bush administration?

Ans. It was absolutely unjust on the part of the coalition forces led by the Bush administration to attack Iraq in defiance of UN charter. By the invasion of Iraq, the Bush administration set a new record in alienating its friends. It created a rift in the North Atlantic Treaty Organisation, brought the United Nations into disgrace, provoked a chain of anti-war mass protests throughout the world and induced thousands of young men in the Islamic world to join suicide squads and fight the aggressors.

The terrorist suicide bomb attack on the fortified three complexes in Riadh on the night of 12th May, 2003 in which 34 people including at least 8 Americans were killed, just a few hours before the arrival of Kolin Powell, U.S. Secretary of State at Saudi Arabian metropolis, seemed to indicate the upsurge of anti-American sentiment in the aftermath of the war against

Iraq. This incidence of terrorist attack is likely to translate into increased violence in the days to come.

Unlike in the war against Osama-bin-Laden, the war against Saddam Hussein of Iraq did not command a global consensus. Powers like France and Germany and members of the North Atlantic Treaty Organisation (NATO) did not support U.S. intervention in Iraq. Other major powers like Russia and China also expressed their resentment and disapproval of the attack on Iraq. Even the country like India needing U.S. support for its war against Pakistan-sponsored terrorism, expressed its displeasure at the high-handedness of the U.S.

The fallout of the Iraq war and the U.S. victory led to the emergence of a new kind of cold war. In the new cold war, the U.S. was without some of its traditional partners like France and Germany and was pushed back to a kind of isolationism. U.S. victory strengthened and consolidated the forces of Islamic fundamentalism as well as terrorism of which the U.S. has to be alert always from another attack like World Trade Center and Pentagon. The Iraq war thus changed the international relations even more than it did on that fateful day in September, 2001.

The war in Iraq has led to the belief that the existence of Arab League which was formed in the year, 1945 with the purpose of unifying the Arab world, has become infructuous as it has failed to avert war against their own member country. Therefore, question has cropped up as to how the Arab League has to be reconstituted completely again.

Consequent upon the Iraq war the world has been divided into two poles—one with the American pre-eminence in uni-polar world and the other forming unity among some of the European countries consisting presently of France, Germany, Belgium, Luxembourg, Italy and Greece. These countries have vowed to strengthen their defence unitedly so that they could check the influence of the U.S. to spread in the European countries in future. For this purpose, these countries arranged a summit in Brussels on 29th April, 2003 to arrive at a stratagem to protect their countries from the growing influence of the United States of America. Therefore, although the U.S. has become the only super power after the break-up of the Soviet Union, another combined power opposed to the U.S. has started emerging in Europe and possibly in Asia with the combined countries of Russia and China, who are already united by virtue of friendship treaty signed by them on 16th July, 2001 valid for 20 years.

Q.16. Is there any weakening of terrorist activities in the world after the wars in Afghanistan and Iraq?

Ans. George W. Bush, American President vowed to wipe out terrorism in order to make the world a habitable place for the humanity to live in peace and tranquility from the menace of terrorist activities. Wars in Afghanistan after the catastrophe of 9/11 and Iraq to wipe out Saddam Hussein who appeared dangerous to the U.S.A. having possible clandestine link with al-Qaida, the deadly terrorist group, have failed to crush terrorism. Repeated warnings from George W. Bush are hardly of any consequence to the terrorists. The horrific attacks at the expatriate housing compound in Riadh on the night of 14th May, 2003 reminds us of the fact that terrorism has not in fact weakened rather it has been getting impetus with renewed vigour and strength to take revenge against the U.S. by consolidating its network of organisations especially in the Muslim world.

Some of the most prominent countrymen of the U.S. urged George W. Bush repeatedly to restrain the energy he has squandered on the war on terror and not to open so many other dangerous fronts to counteract the terrorists. But, he refused to listen to them apparently under intense pressure from the Israeli lobby. It is of course hilarious when George Bush tells in all seriousness that the war on terrorism will prolong and that Osama-bin-Laden and all those responsible for terrorism shall be brought to justice. This is because of the fact that there seems to be no end to terrorism. Terrorists are still waiting to seize any opportunity to strike out against the West. The frequency of terrorist attacks is a great cause for concern. The counter terrorism tactics adopted by the U.S. Administration has simply exposed the lack of credibility of George W. Bush, because terrorism has since doubled activities to exhibit its determination to strike in bigger ways in future posing challenge to the U.S. actions to curb them.

10

VIVA VOCE

Q.1. What do you mean by labour surplus and disguised unemployment?

Ans. Sir/Madam, labour surplus means the existence of such a large population in the rural sector that the marginal product of labour has fallen to zero.

Labourers may appear to be doing work of one sort or another but they are so crowded on the land that if some of the labourers are removed, total product would remain unchanged. This condition is called disguised unemployment.

Q.2. Suppose, as an employee you have been discharging your duties honestly and sincerely as per your assessment. But, how could you understand that your boss feels happy about your performance?

Ans. Sir/Madam, after giving greater responsibilities to me and allowing me total independence in my work by my boss, when he trusts and has confidence in me, I shall naturally feel that my boss feels happy about my performance of working. In such case, my interest in the discharge of my duties will be heightened to pave the way for shouldering higher responsibilities upto the organisational expectations in future.

Q.3. Do you agree that sufficient academic qualifications only will help an employee ascend to the higher position in service?

Ans. Sir/Madam, sufficient academic qualification is not the only criterion to ascend to the higher position. With sufficient academic qualification, if any employee has aptitude, personality traits and interest commensurate with the profession, he is destined to rise high in service. Also an employee must believe in himself, in his own abilities and focus on achieving a well planned objective through sustained effort.

Q.4. It is understood from your Resume that you have done a language course in French. But, what for have you done this language course?

Ans. Sir/Madam, French is the most popular language and is spoken by over 120 million people all over the world. This language has a rich heritage. Knowledge of this language is also very much useful in the fields of travel and tourism, public relations and mass communication. Needless to mention, I have also felt elated in learning this language especially for its sweetness.

Q.5. Suppose in due course of your working in an Organisation as an Executive you have been asked by the Management to put down your SWOT. Could you please tell us what this is all about?

Ans. Sir/Madam, SWOT stands for 'Strength', 'Weakness', 'Opportunity' and 'Threat'. In order to make a SWOT analyses, I have to ascertain my strength *i.e.*, plus points as also my weaknesses *i.e.*, minus points in relation to my job related performance, team work, innovativeness, leadership, responsibility, job knowledge, decision making and competence. While analysing SWOT I, have also to put down new opportunities in my work environment. As far as threat is concerned I have to underline that it is an out-dated knowledge arising out of the redundancy in the new economy confronting with global competition.

Q.6. Suppose, while working as an Executive in an Organisation you have decided to quit your employment for better placement elsewhere. In this case, what will be your role to play during the last few days of your employment in the Organisation?

Ans. Sir/Madam, in such case I have no doubt to handle the situation sensitively. I have to finish my pending job and train my successor for handing over of responsibilities. I will also not give vent to the name of the Organisation where I am going to join, else it may have adverse effect. Finally, I must take my leave-taking in good taste and leave a good impression in the minds of the Management staff and their employees with my jovial and cooperative attitude as also with humour.

Q.7. MBA Campus Interview was held for the freshers for selection in providing employment. But, why could you not be selected for employment in the Campus Interview?

Ans. Sir/Madam, Campus interview does not guarantee employment to each and every fresher by virtue of academic achievement, presentation of skills and result of aptitude test. Unfortunately, I was one of such freshers not getting employment in the campus interview

Q.8. What for did you study Sociology?

Ans. Sir/Madam, since I am interested in the behavioural pattern of the people, their culture and customs, Sociology is an interesting field for me. Although Sociology is not essentially a job oriented subject, yet the students of Sociology are benefited for civil services or can join anthropological and environmental movements. With this purpose in view, many students join TATA Institute of Social Sciences (TISS) or any other well reputable Universities offering master in Social Welfare and go for social work, research or teaching.

Q.9. In your present Organisation you have been working as Territory Sales Incharge. Now you are desirous of working as Sales Development Officer in this Organisation. But why?

Ans. Sir/Madam, every prospective employee has the propensity to rise high in service career step by step by dint of his sincerity and hard working. My working as Territory Sales Incharge has of course given me opportunity to study the markets in field, trend of sale of commodities as also the behavioural pattern of the dealers. My working as Sales Development Officer in your Organisation being in officer's cadre will help me widen my knowledge further about the nerve of the market for sale and when my knowledge about the market after working in such position will be saturated, my case for further promotion for the post of Sales Manager will be favourably considered by you, of which I am very much optimistic. The post of Sales Development Officer is a prelude to Sales Manager.

Q.10. In what way your post graduation in Political Science is going to help you discharge your duties as Administrator/Administratrix in civil service?

Ans. Sir/Madam, it is a universal fact that an Administrator/ Administratrix studying Political Science is by far an able Administrator/Administratrix in the discharge of his/her administrative functions. Study of Political Science helps a person understand the various aspects of Constitution of a country, different systems of governance of a country, ways and means of implementation of governmental plans and fundamental rights and duties of the citizens of democratic countries. If an Administrator/Administratrix is ignorant of these aspects without studying Political Science, he/she will be lacking in administrative acumen. Therefore, study of Political Science has direct link and cohesion in his/her administrative functions. In plenty of cases, Civil Service Administrators have also been elevated to the exalted positions in Ministry as Secretary and the like by virtue of his/her competence and mental acumen which he/she acquired on account of studying Political Science.

Q.11. Why are you interested in Civil Service Post?

Ans. Sir/Madam, I personally feel that I will be well fitted in civil service, which requires mental acumen, wide knowledge and ideas of things, practical approach and above all spot decision. Immediately after completion of my academic education, I started preparing myself for this type of job. This job has its own charm and flavour. It is by far a dignified job and commands respects from society. There is self-satisfaction in this type of job. Persons in civil service can serve the country better. Moreso, the diversity and the challenging nature of the job, direct role in policy implementation and the opportunity it offers to work at the grassroot level for the masses have urged me to have a leaning towards civil service.

Q.12. Although salary and other benefits offered by a company are attractive, yet a few officers do not enjoy job satisfaction in discharging their duties. Why?

Ans. Sir/Madam, apart from financial satisfaction, one can derive job satisfaction in any Organisation by way of fulfilling expectations with regard to job content, learning opportunities, responsibilities, work environment, interaction with higher management, colleagues and other staff members, opportunities to contribute and to utilise one's capabilities and growth possibilities. Moreso, an officer can also enjoy satisfying career if his/her personality traits, aptitude and interest match the professional opportunities. If all these things are not analysed through introspection, an officer of a Company cannot think of attaining job satisfaction.

Q.13. Do you feel that the women getting educated and employed will add to the unemployment problem in the country?

Ans. Sir/Madam, in order to contain unemployment problem in the country what is needed most is to reduce the growth rate of population. Women getting educated and employed will not in fact add to the unemployment problem in the country but actually solve it by bringing down the rate of growth of population. When the women are educated and employed the rate of growth of population is reduced.

Q.14. What impact do you visualise owing to application of VRS?

Ans. Sir/Madam, most of the educated youths have been groaning under the pangs of unemployment problem, which is being precipitated further for ever rising educated youths coming out of the colleges and universities every year. It is being observed that everywhere there is squeeze in employment potentiality in the country and hence aspirations of most of the educated adolescents are being rapidly belied when they look to their bleak future. They are now suffering from frustrations. When this is the clear-cut scenario in the arena of employment, application of VRS at the same time has deepened the crisis. As for simple instance, when the SAIL authorities alone what to talk about other Organisations have already decided that they would reduce their total employees strength from 1,48,000 to 1,00,000 in three years' time under VRS effective from the year, 2002, it is a direct pointer to the educated unemployed youths of the country that their future career in the field of employment is not guaranteed, as the squeeze in employment is the direct result of VRS. Viability in the employment position is directly linked with sound health of economy in a country. VRS has been felt a necessity when the overall health of economy is emaciated, arising out of fall in the production level. Under the circumstances, application of VRS has no doubt impaired the quality of the educated youths who are desperately searching for employment and in consequence the social fabric is destined to affect seriously and the lawlessness amongst the educated unemployed youths will be the order of the day.

Q.15. You have aspiration to cling to civil service post. Could you please tell us in what way you are fully equipped with the required qualifications to work in such position?

Ans. Sir/Madam, such position demands an individual to be harnessed with requisite educational qualification as also necessary soft skills like communication and inter-personal skills, team building ability, initiative, creativity, human resource development and information technology. Such position also requires different types of personality traits, intelligence, analytical skills, assertiveness, resourcefulness, practicality and emotionality as also aptitude. My aspiration to cling to civil service post has been determined by analyses of my personality, aptitude, inherent potential and inclination, strengths and weaknesses based on results of personality, aptitude and EQ tests.

Q.16. Do you agree that there should be certain percentage of job reservation for different communities of people of India?

Ans. Sir/Madam, I must say that it will not be at all wise to set certain percentage of job reservation for different communities of people of India. India is a unity in diversity and our Constitution guarantees equal rights to all people irrespective of caste, creed and religion. The nation belongs equally to all citizens and communities, not more to some and less to others. Therefore, in the matter of employment it will be suicidal to set job reservation for different categories of people because it will discriminate people to people and foment discontent amongst the contestants for employment. Employment should be provided on the basis of suitability and merit of the candidates only.

Q.17. Please opine whether it would be a step in the right direction amending the Factories Act to allow women employees to work in night shifts in factories.

Ans. Sir/Madam, work place conditions for the women employees to work in night shifts are not the same in all the factories of the country. Taking into consideration this factor, there is every possibility that security of the women employees working in night shifts may be at stake. Moreso, our country is not akin to the behavioural pattern of the Western countries where men and women employees can work in night-shifts shoulder to shoulder, as in the case of working in general shifts. In my opinion, women emancipation should not be reflected in their working in night shifts in factories together with their male counterpart under the present Indian conditions. It is of course true that in many establishments women employees are working in night shifts under congenial circumstances, but these establishments are not covered under Factories Act.

Therefore, it should not be a step in the right direction amending the Factories Act to allow women employees to work in night shifts.

Q.18. Please justify that unemployment problem aggravates owning responsibility to instability of government of a country.

Ans. Sir/Madam, for all developmental purposes a government ought to be stable. Now, the present trend in political arena is that due to emergence of multiplicity of different political parties no single political party expects to get 2/3rds majority in the election to form government and as such it becomes government of conglomeration of different parties forming 2/3rds majority. Such government as is the experience does not become stable for full term of five years in most of the cases and, therefore, without stability of the government developmental process is impaired and also foreign investments for setting up industries generating scope for employment opportunities wither away, because the foreign investors do not feel security for their investments for instability of government. Hence, stability of government is an essential ingredient for development of a country and without development employment opportunities cannot be expanded.

Q.19. Do you feel that ST/SCS and OBCs should be given certain percentage for providing employment?

Ans. Sir/Madam, my personal opinion is that it will not be a wise policy on the part of the government to fix up certain percentage for providing employment to the STs/SCs and OBCs. It is an admitted fact that till now they are not equalising in standard with the general category of the job seekers. The purpose of interview is to gauge the best lot of the candidates for providing employment. Therefore, if the government wants to give preference to the STs/SCs and the OBCs for providing employment even if they are not suitable for the job, it will be an injustice to the general category of the candidates seeking employment. I, therefore, personally feel that in order to avoid any discrimination between STs/SCs/OBCs and the general category of job seekers, the government should pay special attention first to ameliorate the status and standard of the STs/SCs and the OBCs by providing all facilities and opportunities so that they can come in parity with the general category of the job seekers to compete in the field of employment equally. It is pertinent to mention here that with the privatisation of Public Sector Units as per the policy of the government of India the question of fixation of certain percentage for providing employment to the STs/SCs/OBCs will be out of question.

Q.20. What is an interview in the Interview Board?

Ans. Sir/Madam, interview in an Interview Board is not conducted with the sole purpose of asking questions on varied nature by the interviewers and getting replies thereto from the interviewees *i.e.*, it is not purely a question-answer session. Right or wrong answers of the candidates are not the criteria to evaluate the candidates' competence to the job. In fact, interview is a personality test of the candidates based on their views, opinions, reactions, comments and attitudes which measure the suitability justifying the candidates to get employment of which they are interviewed in the Interview Board.

Q.21. Is it justified that a Company can issue termination letter to its employees giving three/one months' notice, as the case may be, as stipulated in the appointment letters, without assigning any reason thereof. In such case, can the employee fight it out?

Ans. Sir/Madam, as per Article 226 of the Constitution, an employee can of course challenge the arbitrary decision of the employer in terminating his services without assigning any reason. This will be in the case of the employee working in Public Sector Company, as such Company cannot deal with its employees in arbitrary manner, although in the appointment letter it may be written clearly in one of the clauses that the services of the employee can be terminated after confirmation of his services by giving three/one months' notice or pay in lieu thereof without assigning any reason thereof.

In the case of working in a Private Limited Company, unless the employees are protected under the Industrial Disputes Act, it may not be possible to win success in filing case against the employer in the above situation. The basic reason is that the employee has accepted the terms of employment and the service rules of the company by signing the duplicate copy of the appointment letter. The only consolation is that such a clause in the appointment letter is contrary to public policy and so it may go in favour of the employees other than those working in managerial capacity.

Q.22. In what way the terms of V.R.S. could be amended to make it more effective?

Ans. Sir/Madam, Voluntary Retirement Scheme (VRS) is called the 'Exit Policy' or 'Golden Handshake' or 'Separation Scheme'. It is of paramount necessity to make some changes in V.R.S. policy to get overwhelming response. When the number of educated youths are inflating in the country by leaps and bounds, who are aspiring for getting gainful employment, it will not be in the fitness of things to squeeze the employment potentiality by the application of V.R.S. with no substitution by way of denying fresh appointment. Otherwise, it will have tremendous ill effects on the society. V.R.S. should not be made compulsory for all the employees in general working in establishments. From the pragmatic point of view, V.R.S. should aim at retiring the de-motivated and inefficient employees aged above 50 and replacing them with fresh hands. The V.R.S. scheme should also be made as an exit option to people who do not want to work any more. The objective of the scheme should not be to reduce manpower but improve its quality by infusing fresh blood without increasing its payroll cost to be able to match the new generation. This way of application of V.R.S. will weed out the unproductive and inefficient employees of establishments and increase the efficiency in the working system with new blood who would be working side by side with the efficient employees even crossing 50 years of age.

Q.23. What are the unemployment statistics of India?

Ans. Sir/Madam, according to the National Sample Surveys for 1993-94 and 1999-2000, the rate of unemployment increased by about one per cent per annum during the above period as against the growth of population by about two per cent per annum. India's population as in the year, 2002 was 104 crores with an increase of about 1.6 crores per year. The unemployment figure in the above year *i.e.*, in 2002 was 10 crores and it is likely to increase at the rate of 40 lakhs per year due to increasing population and squeeze in the employment potentiality. Since India is compelled to use modern technologies designed to minimise human employment, population control emerges as the only solution to the unemployment problem and minimise poverty in the country.

Q.24. What are the factors leading to the existence of child labour?

Ans. Sir/Madam, child labour in India between the age of 8 and 14 years is mostly found to work in tea-stalls, restaurants and houses as domestic servants. The link between child labour and lack of education is undeniable. As long as children remain out of School, they are at a greater risk of being forced to work. It is poverty which causes child labour. Even if there are adequate opportunities for the children of poor families for schooling in their areas, the parents of poor families will not allow their small children to go to schools in majority of the cases as long as they remain hungry. Such children are forced to work primarily as child labour because their parents' income is not sufficient to make both ends meet.

Q.25. It is presumed that you might have come by taxi for attending to this interview. Could you please tell me what was the number of the taxi which you hired?

Ans. Sir/Madam, yes, I have come by taxi but I did not take note of the taxi number, as taking note of the same is not in any way related to the working after my appointment. But, since you are interested in knowing the taxi number, I obviously entertain the notion that you must have 2/3 taxis of your own plying in the city for business purpose and, therefore, you have wanted to confirm from me whether it was one of your own taxis which I hired for attending to this interview.

Q.26. Could the services of an employee remaining on unauthorised leave for a number of occasions be terminated?

Ans. Sir/Madam, an employee remaining on leave for long periods on several occasions without sanction is liable to be sacked, the Supreme Court has ruled.

The Bench said: "If after giving repeated opportunities to the delinquent officer to improve, he proves to be incorrigible and found completely unfit to remain in service, then in order to maintain discipline in the service appropriate punishment can be given".

Q.27. Do you feel that in a country like India development of regional language will help the candidates get employment in a better way?

Ans. Sir/Madam, if the development of regional language is stressed upon by any state for the purpose of enlarging the scope of employment, it will be a retrograde step. Different states of a vast country like India are linked with a common language and this common language is used as a means of interstate correspondence and business contacts. Use of regional language will shrink employment potentiality, as the prospective candidates cannot think of competing for employment on all-India basis. Entrepreneurs also will find it inconvenient to employ persons in all categories of posts, knowing the regional language only. Therefore, setting up of new industrial establishments by the entrepreneurs of other states will pose a great problem and this will obviously shrink employment potentiality in a state. Hence, development of regional language for the purpose of broadening the scope of employment will be a step in the wrong direction.

Q.28. What are the differences between the male and female members working in managerial capacities?

Ans. Sir/Madam, women are not intellectually inferior to their male counterparts. They are good academic record holders. A woman is sensitive and it is worth saying that women are patient and always ready to lend their ears. They are even hard working. Slogan has always been raised that men and women are equal. Woman is a good strategy analysist. It is no doubt a recognised fact that by virtue of positive attitude and compact knowledge women bosses are as good as their male counterparts, especially in air conditioned chambers.

With the voice of the feminists heard more and more everyday and with the active participation of women in every sphere of work, women folk still fail to make better bosses than their male counterparts. She is more likely to yield to the pressure than her male counterparts. She cannot handle physical exertions settling disputes between labour unions and the Management, or visiting factory of the Company at odd hours of the night in case of emergency becomes impossible for her and here lies her minus point as an administratrix. A woman does not possess strength and will power with which she can handle her professional problems always.

Q.29. What is all about logistics management?

Ans. Sir/Madam, the dictionary meaning of 'logistics' is the branch of military art concerned with transport, housing and supply of troops. In the domain of commercial world, the term 'logistics' is regarded as one of the most important management functions and is associated with raw-material sourcing, delivery to production line and distribution to the end customer at optimized resource utilisation. Logistics is called the 7 "R"s which is explained as the process of getting the Right Goods, in the Right Quantities, in the Right Condition, at the Right Time, to the Right Place, at the Right Cost with the Right Information. Logistics is a process which begins when raw materials leave the supplier and ends when the final product is delivered to the end user/ customer. Tracking and Tracing are integral part of Logistics.

Q.30. What is the reaction of the male subordinate staff members when their boss is a female member?

Ans. Sir/Madam, this question would not have arisen if the ratio of male and female bosses working in offices would have been balanced and that the subordinate male employees were familiar to work under their female bosses, as in the case of other developed nations of the world—both oriental and occidental.

However, at the present situation of Indian work culture, as far as the reaction of the male subordinates working under their female boss is concerned, from the psychological point of view they get impetus to work sincerely and diligently especially when their female boss knows the technique of superintending in the working of the male subordinates through tender-heartedness. Female bosses are by nature soft spoken and by their sweet words the male subordinate employees feel inclined and devoted to work. Female bosses are also at the same time quite efficient in their working and this generates the sense of respectability amongst the male subordinates towards their female bosses. The question of their indiscipline while working under a female boss is conspicuous by its absence because it is a misconduct and is subject to disciplinary action.

There is of course no denying the fact that there exist handful of male subordinate employees who are not prepared to accept the authority of female bosses, as they nurture the conception that male members play upper-hand always as compared to their female counterpart. But, ultimately the attitude of these employees will be softened when there will be balancing in the ratio of male and female bosses in most of the Indian offices.

Q.31. Is the Management of Organisation liable to pay E.S.I. contributions of both employees and employer on overtime allowance earned by the employees?

Ans. Sir/Madam, as per the ruling of the Supreme Court of India, overtime allowance paid to an employee is an integral part of his salary/wages within the meaning of Section 2(22) of the Employees' State Insurance Act. Therefore, the Management of Organisation is statutorily required to pay E.S.I. contributions of both employees and employer on the basis of enhanced salary/wages arising out of overtime allowance paid.

Q.32. Under what conditions an industrial unit could be termed as sick unit?

Ans. Sir/Madam, there are different perceptions of the symptoms of industrial sickness. To an investor a sick unit is one which cannot pay dividends. To an industrialist a sick unit is one which is on the brink of closure for inefficient running on account of sustaining financial losses. In terms of the definition of the Reserve Bank of India an industrial unit is considered as sick if it has incurred financial loss for one year and is likely to continue to incur such loss in the next two years also. This definition of the Reserve Bank of India is only for the registered companies which are in existence for at least seven years.

Q.33. What is ICICI and what are its objectives?

Ans. Sir/Madam, the full name of ICICI is Industrial Credit and Investment Corporation of India Limited established in the year, 1955. The purpose of its establishment was to encourage and assist industrial development in India. Its objectives are:

(i) Encouraging and promoting industrial investment as also expansion of investment markets.

(ii) Providing assistance in the creation, expansion and modernisation of industrial enterprises.

(iii) Encouraging and promoting participation of private capital in such enterprises.

The primary purpose for which assistance is extended by ICICI is purchase of capital assets in the form of land, building and machinery.

In pursuance of its above objectives, ICICI provides financial assistance in the following forms:

(a) Providing loans in rupees repayable over a period of 15 years.

(b) Providing similar loans in foreign currencies for payment for imported capital equipment and technical services.

(c) Providing credit facilities to manufacturers for promoting sale of industrial equipment on deferred payment terms.

(d) Guaranteeing payments for credits made by others.

Q.34. What is your idea about FERA?

Ans. Sir/Madam, the Foreign Exchange Regulation Act (FERA) came into being in the year, 1973. FERA is an instrument for implementing the national policy on foreign private investment in India through Reserve Bank of India. Trading, commercial and industrial activities in India of persons resident abroad, foreign citizens and foreign companies (other than Banking company) are regulated by FERA. They have to obtain permission from the RBI for carrying on in India any activity of trading, commercial or industrial nature; opening branches/offices or other places of business in India; acquiring any business undertaking in India; and purchasing share of Indian Companies. Apart from this, the foreign Companies have also to obtain permission from the RBI to acquire or hold any immovable property in India incidental to any activity undertaken by them.

According to FERA, non-resident (including Indian citizens), foreign citizens resident in India and foreign companies require the permission of the RBI to accept appointment as agents or technical management advisers in India of any person or Company or permit the use of their trade marks.

Q.35. Please enlighten your ideas about BIFR.

Ans. Sir/Madam, the most important piece of legislation dealing with industrial sickness is the Sick Industrial Companies Act (SICA), 1985. The SICA provides for the establishment by the Central Government of a Board for Industrial and Financial Reconstruction (BIFR).

The BIFR consists of a Chairman and not less than two and not more than fourteen other members, duly appointed by the Central Government. The Act also provides for the establishment of an appellate authority called the Appellate Authority for Industrial and Financial Reconstruction consisting of a Chairman and not more than three other members for hearing appeals against the orders of the BIFR.

When an industry becomes sick, the Board of Directors of such Company can make a reference to the BIFR for determination of the measures to be adopted with respect to the Company. Such reference has to be made within sixty days from the date of finalisation of the audited accounts of the Company for any financial year.

On receipt of the reference, the BIFR may make an inquiry either directly or through appellate authority for determination as to whether the industrial company has actually become sick or not. If BIFR is satisfied that the sick industrial unit is not likely to be made viable within a reasonable time, it forwards its opinion to the High Court which in turn shall order the winding up of the Company in accordance with the provisions of the Companies Act, 1956.

However, before referring the matter to the High Court by the BIFR finally, it is the endeavour of the BIFR to find possibility of reconstruction of the sick unit by suggesting measures to be adopted.

Q.36. What are the causes of industrial sickness?

Ans. Sir/Madam, the causes attributed to make an industrial unit sick are:

(i) Mass indiscipline among the employees which includes impunctuality in attendance, leaving the place of duty without permission/information, disobedience to the reasonable orders of the superiors and regular absenteeism.

(ii) Low output of work by the employees/workers.

(iii) Reckless expenditure.

(iv) Poor working condition.

(v) Dissatisfaction prevailing in the minds of the employees/workers.

(vi) Sordid employee-employer relations.

(vii) Managerial deficiencies/mismanagement.

(viii) Marketing constraints/competitive market.

(ix) Sporadic power cuts.

(x) Labour trouble.

(xi) Raw material shortage/non-availability.

(xii) Frequent breakdown of plant and machinery due to their obsolescence.

(xiii) High cost of production.

(xiv) Under-utilisation of plant capacity.

(xv) Lack of timely modernisation/machinery replacement.

(xvi) Infrastructural bottlenecks.

(xvii) Recession.

Q.37. What are industrial licence and letter of intent?

Ans. Sir/Madam, a licence is a written permission issued by the government to an applicant desiring to manufacture specific items included in the schedule. A licence contains particulars of the industrial establishment, licenced capacity of the plant and machinery, its location and the items to be manufactured. In the licence there is the mention of specific period within which production has to be started.

As far as letter of intent is concerned, government conveys its intention to grant licence subject to fulfilment of certain conditions. This means that letter of intent is a prelude to the issuance of licence. The conditions are: approval of foreign investment proposal, import of capital goods and equipment, taking steps to control pollution etc. On fulfilment of the prescribed conditions, the holder of the letter of intent would approach the concerned ministry for getting the letter of intent converted into industrial licence.

Q.38. What is the difference between a Holding Company and a Subsidiary Company?

Ans. Sir/Madam, a Company is called a Holding Company when it controls the affairs of another Company. In this case, the said another Company over which the control is exercised must be subsidiary to the controlling/holding Company.

A Company shall be considered a subsidiary Company if it fulfils any of the following:

(a) When one Company holds the majority of the shares in another Company, the latter forms the subsidiary of the former.

(b) When one Company controls the composition of the Board of Directors of another Company, the latter forms the subsidiary of the former.

Q.39. Please enlighten about SEBI.

Ans. Sir/Madam, The Securities and Exchange Board of India (SEBI) was formed in the year, 1988 under a resolution of the Government of India. It was subsequently made a statutory body by the Securities and Exchange Board of India Act, 1992. According to this Act, SEBI consists of a Chairman and five other members appointed by the Central Government. Out of these five members, two members represent the ministries of Finance and Law and one member from the Reserve Bank of India. With the coming into being of the Securities and Exchange Board of India Act, 1992 some of the powers and functions exercised by the Central Government in respect of the regulation of the stock exchanges were transferred to the SEBI.

Objectives and functions of SEBI are:

(i) To promote the development of and to regulate the securities market and

(ii) To protect the interests of investors in securities.

On 25th January, 1995 the government promulgated an ordinance to amend the Securities and Exchange Board of India Act, 1992 so as to arm SEBI with additional powers for ensuring the orderly development of the capital market and to enhance its ability to protect the interests of the investors.

Q.40. What is your idea about MRTP Act?

Ans. Sir/Madam, The Monopolies and Restrictive Trade Practices Act, 1969 came into being from 1st June, 1970. The objectives of the MRTP Act are:

(i) Control of monopolistic, restrictive and unfair trade practices, prejudicial to the public interest and

(ii) Prevention of concentration of economic power.

The MRTP Act was amended in 1982, 1984, 1985 and 1991.

1982 Amendment

Goods exported out of India were excluded from the calculations for the purpose of determining market dominance.

1984 Amendment

It empowered the Central Government to direct severance of inter-connections between undertakings.

1985 Amendment

It raised the asset of undertakings from Rs. 20 crores to Rs. 100 crores.

1991 Amendment

The main thrust of the MRTP Act was to achieve prevention of monopolistic, restrictive and unfair trade practices.

The above are the salient features of MRTP Act.

Q.41. Can the employer issue notice to the employees asking for pre-mature retirement?

Ans. Sir/Madam, premature retirement is a permissible means for reducing staff strength for the purpose of attaining efficient running of the Organisation in line with its financial status. While issuing notice to certain section of the employees for pre-mature retirement from service, their overall efficiency status is assessed, *i.e.*, whether they are found unsuitable for further service. It can, therefore, be construed that an employer has wide powers to issue orders for pre-mature retirement from service provided they are not in breach of rules.

Q.42. In a number of Organisations one of the terms of specialised employment carries a clause to the effect that after leaving the services of the Company the employee is debarred to take up employment with a competing Company. Under the circumstances, can the Company take legal action against the concerned employee joining the competing Company in terms of the said clause?

Ans. Sir/Madam, there is no denying the fact that such restrictive clause is common in respect of employment contract in specialised position and is legally permissible. Leaving of the Company by an employee may be on two counts—one by way of resignation and the other by way of termination of the services of the employee. While the Company is within its right to take legal action against the employee joining the competing Company after resigning from the parent company, in terms of the clause, as mentioned in the letter of appointment, the terminated employee will be outside the purview of the said clause and, therefore, taking legal action against such employee by the Company will be void.

Q.43. Government employees were not in fact in support of the privatisation policy of the Government of India. Why?

Ans. Sir/Madam, depending upon the provision of holidays/ leave enjoyed by the government employees, they work only for 164 days in a year of 365 days which is only

45 per cent of total working. Working of 164 days is also further interrupted by bandhs, pen-down strike, go-slows and holidays under Negotiable Instruments Act. Availing of too much of holidays/leave by the government employees has an adverse effect in their efficient working. Divestment/privatisation of Public Sector Units means that the employees have to put in maximum efforts to work efficiently in the interest of viable running of private sector units. Otherwise, their services may be at stake. Therefore, since the government employees are not accustomed to work efficiently in most of the cases on account of enjoying more number of days of holidays/leave, they were not at heart in support of privatisation of PSUs.

Q.44. How could you evaluate team work in an Organisation?

Ans. Sir/Madam, overall efficient running of an organisation of today does not depend upon individual performance but it is the output of total working group that matters *i.e.*, overall corporate performance is a factor. It encourages cooperation amongst co-workers. In the new dispensation, team players have the edge. It is the psychological effect in the minds of the employees in general that they do not take in good taste when handsome increase in salary is granted on the basis of individual performance and in consequence it becomes a retrograde step in the overall efficient running of an organisation. Therefore, it is always recommended that there must be uniformity in the increase in the pay-package depending upon the output of total working group and this will ignite team spirit and the organisation in turn will prosper.

Q.45. Is it in order to go on occupying Company's quarters by an employee even after retirement from service pending finalisation of dues?

Ans. Sir/Madam, occupation of Company's quarters by an employee after retirement from service has nothing to do with the settlement of dues by the Company. Occupation of Company's quarters by an employee beyond certain time limit has a criminal consequence under the provision of Section 630 of the Companies Act. The Management can, however, consider request in writing of the retired employee to retain the Company's quarters for a certain extended period of time at an increased rent.

It is of course the responsibility of the Management to settle the dues of the employee in full and final within the extended period of holding of the Company's quarters, if not earlier. Even if the employee does not relinquish possession of the quarters during the extended period of occupation of the same pending receipt of his dues, the Company can of course file a criminal case against the employee concerned as per Section 630 of the Companies Act. It is also within the right of the employee to file a case against the Company for non-payment of his dues.

Q.46. Under what compulsions Exit Policy has been felt a necessity?

Ans. Sir/Madam, Exit Policy in other ways is called Voluntary Retirement Scheme (VRS), 'Golden Handshake' or 'Separation Scheme'. Exit policy refers to the policy regarding dispensation of the services of the excess manpower in business enterprises before they are actually superannuated.

The following are the compulsions under which Exit Policy has been felt a necessity:

(a) Exit Policy is taken when the overall health of economy is emaciated, arising out of the fall in the production level.

(b) Today's business world has become too much competitive as a result of which profitability of a number of organisations has been slashed down which does not justify keeping a battalion of employees in roll of the organisation. This necessitates trimming of employees strength through Exit Policy in order to attain cost efficiency improvement and cost reduction in every possible way for the purpose of survival of business enterprise.

(c) On account of improved technology, restructuring and modernisation of business establishments employees become surplus in certain units necessitating adoption of Exit Policy.

(d) New economic policy may also create unemployment at the enterprise level in a large number of cases by adopting Exit Policy.

Therefore, under the above conditions if Exit Policy is not taken in time, it may eventually lead to the closure of the business establishments throwing all the employees out of employment.

Q.47. In your managerial capacity if you are given too much of workload how would you handle the situation?

Ans. Sir/Madam, when I will be saddled with too much of workload, it would indicate that I am a competent manager of the organisation. Needless to mention, competency does not imply that my capacity to work is beyond limit, since I am a human being. Under the circumstances, I would prioritise the work in order of importance and urgency. At the same time, I would not give wrong signals to my higher management that I am trying to evade work.

Q.48. Is it in the fitness of things that there should be job reservations for the domiciles of the states of India?

Ans. Sir/Madam, India is a unity in diversity. Communalism has no place for a country like India. In the case of employment there should be right persons for the right job irrespective of variation of states. Then only efficient running of organisations will be a possibility. Fixation of job reservations for the domiciles of states of India will only foment hatred and acrimony towards the job aspirants of other states coming to alien states in quest of employment. In the matter of employment there must not be taboo differentiating people to people residing in other states, since India is one in diversity. Job should be offered on merit of the case. Bond of fraternity will be intensified when there will be free accessibility to employment by the job aspirants of all the states of India without any discrimination and that all the states of India must follow the same principle of offering employment equally—neither more nor less.

Q.49. After having opted for VRS by an employee, the Management of the Company subsequently stopped release of the said employee under VRS. In such case, can the Management of the Company terminate the services of the employee already opting for VRS earlier, by giving him one or three months period, as the case may be, as per the terms of employment?

Ans. Sir/Madam, release of employees under Voluntary Retirement Scheme as well as subsequent stoppage of release of the employee under VRS is absolutely at the discretion of the Management and the employees have no say in the matter. But, terminating the services of the employees in particular who opted for the VRS, as per terms of employment contract *i.e.*, by giving one month or three months notice or pay in lieu thereof is not surely in order on the part of the Management, if the employees concerned are covered under Industrial Disputes Act. The arbitrary decision of the management in terminating the services of the employees could be challenged in the court of law, as such termination is opposed to public policy.

As far as the employees not covered under Industrial Disputes Act, the terminated employees going to the court of law for redressal are not likely to get favourable ruling by the court in favour of them, as in such cases the judicial authorities are in favour of the management.

It may be noted that termination of services of the employees under VRS or otherwise is a different issue and should not be clubbed together.

Q.50. Is it in order that there should be big disparity in the salaries of the managers and those other than managers?

Ans. Sir/Madam, it is always recommended that the ambitious employees should join organisations and sectors where the disparities in salaries of managers and those other than managers are the maximum. From the psychological point of view, disparities in salaries will inspire the ambitious employees to attain efficiency in their performance of work in order to get rapid promotions and increase in their salaries. It has been the experience that disparity in salaries of the highest and the lowest employees in an organisation motivates the newcomers to perform better. If all the employees in a company are high fliers, it would come crashing down very soon. It is, therefore, suggested that the ambitious employees should start off as a small fish in a big pond and ultimately they will be big fish in a big pond.

Q.51. What benefits are accrued by way of privatisation of state owned establishments?

Ans. Sir/Madam, privatisation of SOEs is an important strategy of economic rejuvenation. Privatisation helps solve fiscal crises of state and usher in a new industrial democracy. The benefits of privatisation are enumerated as under:

(a) Privatisation of SOEs enables the government to mop up funds.

(b) It reduces the fiscal burden of the state by relieving it of the losses of the SOEs and reducing the size of the bureaucracy.

(c) It enables the government to concentrate more on the essential state functions.

(d) Privatisation helps the state to trim the size of the administrative machinery.

(e) Privatisation helps accelerate the pace of economic development as it attracts more resources from the private sector for development.

(f) Privatisation results in better management of the enterprises.

(g) Privatisation encourages entrepreneurship.

The trend towards privatisation has been observed in developed and developing countries including communist countries such as China, former USSR, East European countries and Cuba. By nationalisation, the countries like the United Kingdom have testified how it could help solve the fiscal crunch of the state.

Q.52. What is G.M.T. (Greenwich Mean Time)?

Ans. Sir/Madam, before I explain the full form of Greenwich Mean Time, I would like to Inform that 'Mean Time' is the time as given by the position of the mean sun. Greenwich Mean Time is the solar time at the Greenwich mid-day. This mid-day time is formally known as Universal Time.

Q.53. Do you feel that Human Resource Development of India is a success?

Ans. Sir/Madam, Human Resource Development is a valuable asset which should be nurtured and developed. I feel that some hurdles are standing in the way of its development in the true sense of the term. Language, literature and culture have an important bearing on the unity, integrity and development of a country, which will only be possible through a strong national language. 70 per cent of the people of our country speak and understand Hindi. A feeling of cordiality and oneness is required to be generated through this language only. But, unfortunately, people living in the Southern parts of the country are not willing to accept Hindi as national language, although Hindi has a vast literature in the country. Therefore, it is posing a challenge to the development of human resource on account of non-acceptance of Hindi as a common language throughout the length and breadth of the country, as a result of which many talented and promising students of the villages are being denied high posts in services.

Q.54. What do you mean by 'laissez faire'?

Ans. Sir/Madam, 'laissez faire' is a French word. The word meaning of this word is 'let alone'. But, the broader meaning of the same is permitting things to look after themselves without interference by the Government in economic affairs.

Q.55. What is your idea about 'Renaissance'?

Ans. Sir/Madam, the word, 'Renaissance' is a French word, which means rebirth or revitalisation. It is a transition period between the middle ages and modern ages covering the years, 1350 to 1650, during which period spectacular metamorphosis took place. In the fields of arts, scholarship and science wonderful and surprising accomplishments took place. The invention of printing and discovery of new world by Columbus were the events during Renaissance. The Renaissance movement first started in Italy.

Q.56. Why is the power of vehicles measured in terms of horse power?

Ans. Sir/Madam, in 17th century A.D. and even before that, horses were the important means of transportation of men and material. In 1769 James Watt, a Scottish Engineer made improvements in the design of steam engines. The term 'horse power' was first used by James Watt to compare the power of steam engine to the power of horses. The term is also now used to express the power of car engines, electric motors and nuclear reactors. The metric unit of power is watt. One horse power is equivalent to 746 watts.

Q.57. What do you mean by Habeas Corpus?

Ans. Sir/Madam, Habeas Corpus is a writ asking an arrested person to present before the court of law with the purpose of investigating the righteousness of his/her detention. This way of investigation ensures that imprisonment of the person cannot take place without legal hearing.

Q.58. What is the difference between the role played by the judge and jury?

Ans. Sir/Madam, a judge is a public official who hears and decides cases brought before a court of law for the purpose of administering justice. A judge hears both civil and criminal cases, in the latter, not only do the judges decide if the accused is innocent or guilty, but also pronounce sentence in case if the accused is found guilty.

A jury consists of 12 or more private citizens summoned by law and sworn to hear and deliver verdict upon a criminal case presented in the court. In case of finding a person guilty, they cannot sentence the accused, which must be done by the judge. In some countries judges have to accept the jury's verdict, in other they need not.

In some places, the jury's decision has to be unanimous, in others majority verdict will suffice the purpose.

A judge's statement is guided by law but the jury's law is decided by sentiment.

Q.59. What do you mean by Contempt of court?

Ans. Sir/Madam, contempt of court is a flagrant violation of norms requiring to maintain the prestige and honour of the authority of a court of law. Disrespect to the court of law which is tantamount to contempt of court includes infringement of court order, improper use of legal documents and breach of injunction and interfering with court proceedings. Punishment imposed by a court in such cases is either a fine or imprisonment.

Q.60. What are the Union Territories and their capital cities?

Ans. Sir/Madam, the Union Territories and their capital cities are:

Union Territories		*Capital Cities*
(a) Andaman & Nicobar	-	Port Blair
(b) Chandigarh	-	Chandigarh
(c) Dadra & Nagar Haveli	-	Silvassa
(d) Daman and Diu	-	Daman
(e) Lakshadweep	-	Kavaratti
(f) Pondicherry	-	Pondicherry

I may mention here that Delhi is the National Capital Territory and not Union Territory.

Q.61. At the opening ceremony of the Olympic games which country leads the march-past and which country comes last?

Ans. Sir/Madam, in the case of a march-past at the opening ceremony of Olympic games, Greece comes first and the team of the host country comes last. As far as teams of other countries are concerned, they come in alphabetical order.

Q.62. Which are the largest and second largest undersea tunnels of the world?

Ans. Sir/Madam, the Seikan Tunnel of Japan which was built in 1988 is the longest undersea tunnel of the world. Its total length is 53.90 kms. The undersea Tunnel beneath the English Channel connecting between Folkestone (England) and Calais (France) which was built between December, 1987 and December, 1990, the total length of which is 49.94 kms. is the second longest undersea tunnel of the world.

Q.63. Which was the first Japanese loan to India after lifting of post-Pokhran sanction?

Ans. Sir/Madam, the first Japanese loan of Rs. 350 crores to India extended by Japan Bank of International Cooperation after lifting of post-Pokhran sanction was for the infrastructural development of Ajanta-Ellora Complex in Maharashtra.

Q.64. Why do the judges break the nibs of pens after signing death sentences?

Ans. Sir/Madam, death sentences are the extreme punishment which is imposed on the convicts by the judges who think that such decision is in fact against their conscience. They therefore, break the nibs of the pens after signing the death sentences on two counts—firstly, they express their conscience by breaking the nibs and secondly, they do not want to reuse the pens as the same signal the end of lives of human beings.

Q.65. In what way glass was first manufactured?

Ans. Sir/Madam, in 368 B.C. when a particular ship anchored on the bank of a river in Syria, a crew got down from the ship and spent all their time on the beach where they planned to prepare food to eat. Accordingly, they brought a few big lumps of soda-ash from the ship's cargo for the purpose of holding the pots of food over the fire. When the preparation of food was completed, it was observed that some of the sand under the fire was converted into liquid substance, which was nothing but liquid glass. This liquid glass was formed due to the reaction between soda-ash and sand. This way glass was manufactured for the first time in 368 B.C.

Q.66. How could you measure the length of a rope given to you without the help of tape, scale or hand?

Ans. Sir/Madam, depending upon the length of the rope I will make it either half-fold, three-fold or four-fold or more. This will facilitate me to surmise each folded length of the rope by comparing it with the length of hand which is normally 18" long. By this way, the approximate total length of the rope in respect of the number of folds could be arrived at without measuring it by hand, tape or scale. It will not be out of place to mention here that by such method of measuring the rope, exact measurement of the same will not be a possibility.

Q.67. What was the type of rocket launched by India on 12th September, 2002?

Ans. Sir/Madam, an Indian Space Research Organisation (ISRO) rocket named as Metsat was blasted off successfully from Sriharikota, 100 kms from Chennai on 12th September, 2002 and placed into orbit at 36,000 kms above the earth. The weight of the Metsat is over 1,000 kgs. By launching this satellite India took a giant leap towards accurate weather forecasting and cyclone warnings. This satellite could also be used as a platform for the moon mission probe.

Q.68. What are the shortcomings in the Indian Cricket team?

Ans. Sir/Madam, the shortcomings are summarised as under:

(a) The first and foremost shortcoming in the Indian cricket team, as was observed in the number of games played by India with other world teams, is that when the important wickets start falling, the rest of the batsmen lose their morale and cannot stand for a longer time in most of the cases to score comfortable runs for surging ahead to the winning stage of games. This means that they suffer from nervousness.

(b) The performance of all the players from beginning

to end while batting should not be of fluctuating standard.

(c) Indian team has to improve upon the back-foot play.

(d) Another embarrassing display in Indian team is mindless batting.

(e) Indian players are unwilling to learn any lessons from their previous failures and bat poorly to inflict humiliating defeat on themselves.

(f) Over-confidence to win games is another draw-back of the Indian team.

If these shortcomings are overcome, Indian Cricket team will surely rank as the No. 1 team in the world.

Q.69. Internal brain drain has been caused in Indian science. How?

Ans. Sir/Madam, closely linked to the bureaucratic culture in Indian science is the disturbing phenomenon of internal brain drain. The gains so achieved in Indian science during the past half a century cannot be consolidated if internal brain drain did not stop. Misconception has generated in the minds of the talented scientists that career in science is not considered worthwhile and hence it is noticed that there has been diversion of talent from research careers to non-scientific fields in government and private sectors. This is what is called an internal brain drain.

Prime Minister, Atal Bihari Vajpayee after opening the 90th session of the Indian Science Congress at Bangalore on 3rd January, 2003 vowed in his address to over 300 scientists to free science and technology institutions from the clutches of the bureaucratic culture in Indian science. He also announced that the government would formulate pragmatic and flexible scheme to enable the expatriates to return and work in Indian science and technology institutions by ensuring that scientific institutions did not become afflicted by the culture of government agencies.

Q.70. What are the reasons for the population explosion in India?

Ans. Sir/Madam, although India started its family planning programmes right from the year, 1951 and spent colossal amount of money on the same, the objectives have not been crowned with success. The main impediments to the success of population control programmes in India are: lack of education (not merely literacy), poverty, high infant and child mortality rate, preference for male kids, caste and communal politics, lack of political will, non-participation of men in family planning, poor management of family planning programmes, religious fundamentalism and unrealistic national population policy.

Q.71. How could you account for the rise in prices of commodities in relation to the rise in prices of imported crude oil?

Ans. Sir/Madam, crude oil price is the direct determining factor to regulate prices of commodities. Production of crude oil in India accounts for only 33 million tonnes per year. It is too insufficient to meet up the domestic requirements. Based on an estimated demand of 112 million tonnes of crude oil per year for a country like India having population of more than 100 crores in the year, 2002, the import bill was destined to be to the tune of $19 billion in 2000-2001 compared with $9.6 billion in 1998-1999 because of the hike effected in its price by OPEC (Organisation of Petroleum Exporting Countries), which obviously leads to the substantial increase in the prices of petrol, diesel and kerosene. This leads to the increase in freight charges and accordingly carrying cost of the items is bound to increase and so the increase in prices of commodities becomes inevitable. Side by side with this increase there becomes sympathetic rise in the prices of other commodities also, although they have no direct bearing with the increase in oil prices. Thus, increase in crude oil prices leads to increase in the prices of commodities.

Q.72. As far as the important events were concerned in the year, 2001, what were those major events in the said year?

Ans. Major events in the year, 2001 were as under:

(i) Dreadful earthquake of Gujarat on 26th January, 2001, *i.e.*, on the day of Republic Day celebration.

(ii) Tahelka Episode. Mamata Banerjee quit the Railway Ministry on this count. George Fernandez was compelled to quit Defence Ministry.

(iii) Bloody fight between BSF and BDR of Bangladesh.

(iv) Failure of Agra Summit between Atal Behari Vajpayee, Prime Minister of India and General Parvez Musharaff, President of Pakistan, which led to worsening of Indo-Pak relations.

(v) Massacre of the members of Royal family of Nepal.

(vi) Attack on World Trade Centre of the United States of America on 11th September, 2001.

(vii) War started in Afghanistan on 7th October, 2001.

(viii) Attack on Assembly House of Jammu and Kashmir at Srinagar on 1st October, 2001.

(ix) War between Israel and Palestine.

(x) Attack on Indian Parliament by the Pakistani sponsored terrorists on 13th December, 2001.

(xi) Death of Madhav Rao Scindia in Plane crash.

(xii) Killing of Phoolan Devi by gun fire.

(xiii) Collapse of Taliban rule in Afghanistan due to internecine war conducted by the United States of America.

(xiv) Spread of Anthrax in the United States of America and other parts of the world.

Q.73. What do you understand by Balance of Payment?

Ans. Sir/Madam, Balance of Payments relates to the statement of all transactions of a country with other countries of the world during a specific period. These transactions are in the form of imports and exports of goods and services; movements of short-term as well as long-term investments; currency and gold remittances. The Balance of Payments are grouped into current account, capital account, unilateral transfer account and gold account.

Q.74. What are the measures which could be adopted to revamp economy of the country?

Ans. Sir/Madam, the important steps which could be initiated to revamp the economy of the country are:

(a) Fall in savings rate, particularly, public savings is a pointer that the economy is not viable. Therefore, in order to strengthen economy steps are to be taken to boost savings, which is possible by granting tax incentives for savings and raise rate of interest to the senior citizens and pensioners in particular.

(b) The Finance Ministry has to see that there is no cut on the percentage of tax exemptions for various kinds of investments including National Savings Certificates and Public Provident Fund.

(c) There should be lifting of the freeze on leave travel assistance given to the government employees, as this will encourage spending on tourism resulting in the revival of hotel business in the country.

(d) People should be discouraged from unproductive saving on gold holdings. In order to achieve this purpose, the government should work out a successful Portugese model of 1950s which saw a large number of Goans depositing gold in banks.

(e) The Government should consider overhauling the Foreign Investment Promotion Board (FIPB) so as to attract significant foreign investment flows.

Implementation of the said steps in particular initiated by the Government will no doubt revamp the economy of the country.

Q.75. What were the dangers faced by India from the beginning of the 21st century?

Ans. Sir/Madam, although India is determined to be treated as one of the big powers of the world in spite of heavy odds and ends, for which she has already made strides in the number of fields, India was beset with multifarious problems especially from the beginning of the 21st century in a big way, such as: terrorism, unemployment, corruption, poverty, over-population, global recession, education, crime, environment, globalisation, health and drug abuse.

Q.76. How important is health for a country?

Ans. Sir/Madam, healthy nation is a secure nation. Sick and weak citizens cannot be the source of strength for a country. Hard labour put in by the citizens helps develop a country and this hard labour is the outcome of disease-free health of the people. Therefore, in the interest of progress of a country it is the responsibility of the government to see that people pay more attention to remain healthy and for this purpose the Health Ministry has to prioritise maintenance of health of the people and provide health services at reasonable cost so that the citizens are made health conscious.

Q.77. What did the then Human Resource Development Minister, Dr. Murli Manohar Joshi tell about the need to improve upon the quality of education at New Delhi on 19th February, 2003?

Ans. Sir/Madam, while delivering the inaugural address at a seminar, "Excellence in Education: The Golden Journey" organised by Confederation of Indian Industry (CII) and Ashray Hastha Trust at New Delhi on 19th February, 2003, Dr. Murli Manohar Joshi, the then HRD Minister called for a holistic vision of education. He emphasised that education must be imparted with a clear-cut vision. The entire education system must aim at excellence and quality which would only be possible when there was marriage between the two. The entire community should not treat education as a mere classroom activity between the teachers and the taught. Dr. Joshi told that it should be the intention of the educators to create various skills through education among students and the ingredients of the skills should include development of body, mind, intellect and souls and then only the students would hold them in good stead in the job market.

Q.78. What is the difference between "Deportation and Extradition" of criminals?

Ans. Sir/Madam, deportation depends entirely upon the government and is the sovereign right of a country. Usually, a person is not deported as a fugitive, but is requested to leave by the host Government for any number of reasons.

Extradition is a request by other country, which is examined by the court and can be stopped by the judge or magistrate even if the administration wants to accept the request of another country.

Q.79. What are the average number of suicide cases per lakh of people per year in India and the probable reasons thereof and which state is topping in suicide cases?

Ans. Sir/Madam, the average number of suicide cases in India are ten per one lakh of people per year. Growing incompatibility between income and requirements, break-up of joint families, unchecked alcoholism and drug abuse as well as love affairs are the factors contributing to the suicides in India. Disparity between income and needs is the prime factor that drives people to kill themselves in most cases.

Kerala is topping in the matter of suicide cases which touched 31.5 per one lakh of people per year. Although Kerala made strides in health education and achievement in service sectors is spectacular, its reflection is conspicuous by its absence on the economic front. Steadily dwindling industrial investment and an ever shrinking agricultural bases over the last more than three decades had an impact on the income profile of the state which leads to suicides in most cases.

Q.80. What were the total number of NRIs living in different countries and the quantum of remittances made by them to India per year? What was the reason for the balance of payment crisis faced by India in 1990-91?

Ans. Sir/Madam, till the year, 2002 there were 20 million non-resident Indians living in 110 different countries of the world and their per year remittances to India were $14 billion.

The NRIs invested in India through portfolio investments rather than FDI. The balance of payment crisis could not have been faced by India in 1990-91 had the NRIs not withdrawn their deposits in the said year.

Q.81. Do you agree that the NRIs should be invited in the interest of the country?

Ans. Sir/Madam, NRIs are the financial giants. India is a developing country and the NRI's contributions in setting up big enterprises will go a long way in hastening development of the country and consequently solving unemployment problem to a great extent. But, what is needed most is that in order to attract them, extending all infrastructural facilities to them is to be guaranteed. Apart from this, militancy in trade unionism is to be done away with completely so that the NRIs feel complacent that once they set up industries, they are not closed down subsequently on account of labour problem. Industrialisation of the country means elevation of standard of living of the people and maintenance of social order. For such massive industrialisation, the Government will also be benefited immensely by way of receiving sales-tax, excise duty, export duty and income-tax from such industries. Therefore, the NRIs must be invited in the interest of the country as a whole.

Q.82. In what way the NRIs could be tempted to invest a good amount of their money for setting up industries in India.

Ans. Sir/Madam, NRIs are the financial giants. Their contribution in setting up industries in India is of paramount importance, which will hasten industrialisation of the country and easing unemployment problem to a great extent. While the Government of India is setting up industries in pursuance of the programmes laid down in the Five-Year Plans, the combined effort of both the government and the NRIs in the field of industrialisation of the country is most welcome. Therefore, it has been felt an imperative necessity to attract the NRIs to India, for which they are to be given all facilities.

The then Prime Minister, Shri Atal Bihari Vajpayee announced in New Delhi on 8th January, 2002 that the government has decided to grant dual citizenship to the NRIs which would facilitate Indians settled abroad to extend their contributions in the rapid progress of the country. Granting dual citizenship would be within the framework of the Citizenship Act and no amendment in the Constitution would be necessary. Initially the government has decided to implement the dual citizenship to the NRIs who are settled in the United States of America, Great Britain, Canada, Australia, New Zealand, a large part of Europe and Singapore. Granting dual citizenship to the NRIs will surely inspire them to industrialise India in a big way side by side with the setting up of industries as per Five-Year Plans initiated by the Government.

Q.83. What is the difference between the Japanese and Indian work culture—whether Indians have work culture or not.

Ans. Sir/Madam, to all intents and purposes work culture is the determining factor for development and prosperity of a nation. Salaries and wages are paid to the employees/workers in return of their work, but when the employees think of their monthly salaries/wages only without putting in sincere services, the Organisations are destined to emaciate and ultimately such Organisations become sick and finally are closed down. So has been happening in the case of many of the Indian Organisations arising out of lack of work culture amongst the employees. If there would have been work culture amongst the Indian employees in general, Indian Organisations would have prospered at a faster rate, with bounties of resources available in the country.

In the case of Japanese people, work culture is completely opposed to that of Indian people. They owe complete allegiance to the organisations where they work. Any loss sustained by Organisations is considered by the Japanese people as their own loss and the loss of the nation as a whole. The output of work of the Japanese people is measured on hourly basis and as such there is keen competition amongst the employees to increase productivity for enticement of high remuneration. By this way, hard working and work culture of the Japanese people have automatically increased. This work culture has prospered Japan by leaps and bounds. At no point of time, they slacken work at the cost of productivity. Strikes, gheraos and go-slow are foreign to them. According to the report published by the Asian Productivity Organisation, the productivity of the average Japanese worker was about 33 times more than that of his Indian counterpart.

This is the difference of work culture in respect of Indian and Japanese people.

Q.84. Which combined states of India are called "the Seven Sisters"?

Ans. Sir/Madam, the states combinedly of Arunachal Pradesh, Assam, Meghalaya, Mizoram, Manipur, Nagaland and Tripura are called "The Seven Sisters" of India.

Q.85. What is the difference between Mrs. (Dr.) Ganguly and Dr. (Mrs.) Ganguly?

Ans. Sir/Madam, Mrs. (Dr.) Ganguly means she is the wife of Dr. Ganguly and Dr. (Mrs.) Ganguly means Mrs. Ganguly herself is a Doctor.

Q.86. What is brain drain and how does it affect the country's development?

Ans. Sir/Madam, brain drain is the migration of talented persons like doctors, engineers, scientists, technicians and educationists from their home country to foreign countries for higher remuneration, better living and better working environment.

It is an admitted fact that brain drain is creating a void to a great extent in the development of India. India has been producing galaxy of intellectuals. But, to the utter dismay, these intellectuals mostly have inclination to leave their parent country for settlement in other affluent countries, especially the United States of America where they are assured of better placement befitting to their capabilities and qualifications. The exodus of such intellectuals has denied their utilisation in the field of speedy progress and prosperity of India where bounties of resources are already there. India could have achieved much speedier progress like other fast developed countries of the world had such creamy people would have stayed for serving their own country considering that they are the sons of the soil.

Q.87. What were the causes of the outbreak of riot in Nigeria connected with the Miss World contest of the year, 2002?

Ans. Sir/Madam, the Miss World contest which was to be held in the Nigerian capital, Abuja, in early December, 2002 was repudiated at the said venue owing to an extraordinary outbreak of sectarian violence which compelled the organisers of the Miss World contest to shift the venue to London, where the contest went ahead on 7th December, 2002 as scheduled.

It was a riot between the Muslims and the Christians, killing, looting and arson, erupted in Northern Nigeria which is inhabited mostly by Muslims with a sizeable Christian minority. The riot spread from the cosmopolitan city of Kaduna to other cities in the north of Nigeria including its capital, Abuja. The conflict had started with some clerics denouncing the contest as sexually degrading and immoral. The rioting in Kaduna began as a protest against an article published in the Kaduna based newspaper, "This Day" on 16th November, 2002, that offended the Muslims, because it (the article) said that the Prophet Mohammad would probably have married one of the Miss World contestants were he alive. The holy *Quran* has clearly stated that whoever insults Prophet Mohammad should be killed.

Consequent upon the outbreak of riot the death toll rose to more than 200 and more than 500 people were seriously injured.

Q.88. Do you agree that taking into account the base year, 2001, the poverty of the people of the country will be eliminated in 20 years time?

Ans. Sir/Madam, the proposition will no doubt hold good if the growth of population is checked first, which seems to be a distant dream for the specific reason that the life span of the people has increased supplemented by the application of Malthusian theory of population. Even if the implementation of Family Planning Scheme is strengthened, total population of the country is estimated to be to the tune of one hundred and thirty crores after 20 years. With this massive growth of population stalling increase in per capita income with ever increasing price structure compatible with global trend, it is definitely an extremely hard task to alleviate poverty from the country in 20 years time. Elimination of poverty can be expected to be achieved in 20 years time when there are combinedly rapid industrial growth, generation of employment opportunities, increase in food production with no possibility of imports, implementation of Family Planning Scheme, increase in per capita income of the people and spread of education.

Q.89. What were the main reasons for the sluggish development of India in earlier years?

Ans. Sir/Madam, the Nobel Laureate and the great economist Dr. Amartya Sen advocated that the principal reasons for India's sluggish development lay in the neglect of education and health. The Nobel Laureate was always critical of India's high budget allocation to defence rather than to the social sector. It was his belief that the human resources development index in the country would continue to be low till the government prioritised education and health. The political administration of

India believed that India needed to keep up its high budgetary allocation to defend in the interest of national security. However, since India had already armed itself quite satisfactorily to meet the challenge of external threat, she should now prioritise development of education and health without of course neglecting defence preparedness for speedy development of the country. Needless to mention, rapid development of those countries was possible because such countries prioritised health and education of their countrymen.

Q.90. Who are G-8 nations? What are the objectives of the Summit of G-8 Nations? Is the Summit a success?

Ans. Sir/Madam, G-8 Nations are United States of America, Great Britain, France, Germany Canada, Russia, Japan and Italy.

The objectives of the G-8 nations are:

(a) To look after the plight of the poor and heavily indebted countries.

(b) To boost global trade.

(c) To intensify efforts to promote food safety.

(d) To protect agriculture sector against foreign competition.

(e) To maintain health fund to fight AIDS, malaria and tuberculosis.

As has been noticed, the Summit of the G-8 nations is not very much effective. The Summit arranged for the G-8 Nations is also very much expensive. Practically, it is a lavish gathering by thousands of officials and journalists. No follow-up action is taken in the next Summit. The G-8 Nations have not attained any success in any direction so far.

Q.91. Why did George W. Bush, President of the USA consider that war against Iraq was absolutely necessary?

Ans. Sir/Madam, George W. Bush, President of the United States of America considered Saddam Hussein, the then President of Iraq as the second biggest enemy of the world next to Osama-bin-Laden. Iraq's weapons programme was a grave and growing threat to the

United States of America. Bush asserted that Iraq had stockpiled biological and chemical weapons of mass destruction in defiance of the United Nations and was building facilities to make more. Saddam Hussein had also longstanding ties with terrorist groups capable of and willing to deliver weapons of mass death. He was a cruel and dangerous man who had deceived the world about his weapons of mass destruction. Bush clearly asserted that the peace and security of America could not be left in the hands of this cruel and dangerous man. It was, therefore, absolutely necessary that in compliance with the demands of the world and in terms of new resolution of UN Security Council members Saddam Hussein should immediately disarm. Otherwise the USA would go to war with Iraq with the purpose of ending Saddam Hussein regime and terrorism in Middle East region also.

Q.92. What is EU (European Union) and what is its importance for India?

Ans. Sir/Madam, European Union is the largest economy after the US and Japan. It has the 15-member states. Of these members, France and the UK are permanent members of the Security Council. Germany also being one of its members is the strongest contender for the membership of the Security Council. Four other states are members of G-8 nations and all are among the most advanced economies in the world. The first EU summit was held at Lisbon in 2000, second summit at New Delhi in 2001 and the third summit at Copenhegen in 2002 in which the Prime Minister of India, Shri Atal Behari Vajpayee attended.

The Ambassadors of EU at New Delhi were fully satisfied with the way the assembly election in Jammu and Kashmir was conducted in 2002. They unanimously voiced that the election there was free, fair and transparent and that they even went to the extent of telling that they were astonished by the keenness of the people of Jammu and Kashmir to vote. The EU is sensitive to the issue of criminals with international terrorists links.

Q.93. What were the sentiments expressed by the people of Jammu and Kashmir in the state elections held in 2002?

Ans. Sir/Madam, the polls in Jammu and Kashmir held in 2002 were successfully conducted and were widely seen as being the freest and fairest in the state's history. The level of popular participation in the elections confirmed that most Kashmiris were willing to join the democratic process of India and rejected the politics of terror and violence perpetrated by Pakistan.

Q.94. Jammu and Kashmir is an example of unity and secularism in India—How?

Ans. Sir/Madam, total population of Jammu and Kashmir was recorded as 1,00,70,000 as per the census of 2001 after a growth rate of 29.4% during the period, 1991-2001 in the state. Muslims in India are living in peace and amity with the Hindus since inception of partition in 1947. The state of Jammu and Kashmir acceded to India immediately after partition and the Muslims forming more than 75% of the total population of the state as citizens of India have been living in peace and amity with the Hindus as brethren. India is a secular state as the second largest Muslim populated country in the world. Since the inception of accession, the people of Jammu and Kashmir never displayed their resentment of remaining within the secular state of India, India is a unity in diversity and obviously Jammu and Kashmir is united with India in spite of diversity. Under the circumstances, Jammu and Kashmir is truly an example of unity and secularism in India. The only thing is that the government of Pakistan out of their frustration are fomenting cross-border terrorism in Jammu and Kashmir to prove to the world powers that the Kashmiri people have revolted against India and, therefore, Jammu and Kashmir is an apple of discord between India and Pakistan.

Q.95. Why is there the necessity of holding free and fair poll in Kashmir?

Ans. Sir/Madam, firstly, as in the case of holding assembly elections in other states of India, holding free and fair assembly election in Kashmir is also equally important, as Jammu and Kashmir is an integral part of India. Such election in Jammu and Kashmir is being conducted as usual ever since the partition of India.

Secondly, after post-September 11, 2001, apparently, all elements of Islamic fundamentalism are in full display to counter Indian democracy that is seeking to survive through a free and fair poll. The Western world focuses their attention on the Kashmir election with great interest. They apprehend that if the elections in Jammu and Kashmir fail, the subsequent takeover by Islamic fundamentalist forces would result in an inevitable clash between India and Pakistan that could eventually become nuclear, a spectre horrifying to the United States of America and the rest of the world. It is with this objective in mind that the West is taking keen interest in the poll process in Jammu and Kashmir.

Q.96. Is the bifurcation of Jammu and Kashmir the way out for permanent settlement between India and Pakistan?

Ans. Sir/Madam, two-nations theory as propounded by Mohammad Ali Jinnah, that Hindus and Muslims cannot live together no longer exists with the already birth of Pakistan in the year, 1947. The division of the state of Jammu and Kashmir on religious lines will lead to disintegration of India. India is a unity in diversity. India occupies a second position in the world in the matter of habitation of Muslim population, first being Indonesia. The politics of dividing people on religious lines will result in catastrophe. Therefore, under no circumstances, there should be bifurcation of Jammu and Kashmir as a possible way-out for permanent settlement between India and Pakistan, especially when Jammu and Kashmir is an integral part of India. Now, the task lies on the part of the Government of India to liberate Pakistan occupied Kashmir from the hegemony of Pakistan.

Q.97. Could you please tell us what was the purpose for which more than 5000 sq. kms. of Pakistan occupied Kashmir was gifted to China by Pakistan?

Ans. Sir/Madam, the answer is very simple. Obviously, there are two principal factors of gifting more than 5000 sq. kms. of Pakistan occupied Kashmir to China by Pakistan.

(i) When India was partitioned in 1947 Jammu and Kashmir was a princely state and subsequently in the same year Maharaja Hari Singh signed the instrument of accession of Jammu and Kashmir in favour of India. But, Pakistan did not reconcile this accession and they occupied a part of Jammu and Kashmir in the year, 1948 declaring it as Azad Kashmir. Pakistan has been maintaining good rapprochement ever since 1962 *i.e.*, after Indo-China conflict, with China from where they have been receiving military hardware and nuclear technology and expertise apart from others to strengthen its military build-up to counteract with India in warfare. Hence, in order to please China for all the support received from them and to cement the bond of perennial relationship with them, more than 5000 sq. kms. land of Pakistan occupied Kashmir was gifted to China by Pakistan especially in consideration of the fact that the part of Jammu and Kashmir was an additional territory received by Pakistan through military operation. No country cedes its own territory to other country at will which was contrary to the fact in case of Pakistan occupied Kashmir.

(ii) By ceding a part of Pakistan occupied Kashmir it was the intention of Pakistan to maintain direct territorial link with China for transportation of arsenals through road communication which China constructed upto the gifted land of Azad Kashmir.

These are the two factors for which a part of occupied Kashmir was gifted to China by Pakistan.

Q.98. There was escalating Indo-Pak tension on the border with both countries deploying massive troops with sophisticated war equipment. Under the circumstances, was there any possibility of nuclear war between India and Pakistan on Kashmir issue?

Ans. Sir/Madam, both India and Pakistan are nuclear powers, it is of course true that neither Pakistan nor India will be spared if nuclear war breaks out. As far as intensity of nuclear power is concerned, India is beyond doubt superior to Pakistan and hence the impact of nuclear war will be heavier on Pakistan than India. India already announced that it would not make first use of nuclear bomb, but it would be compelled to use the same with all fury if nuclear option was directed against India by Pakistan and in that case the destruction would be terrible in Pakistan as compared to India. I am, therefore, of the firm opinion that chance was bleak of the outbreak of nuclear war between India and Pakistan on Kashmir issue which is not the solution to nuclear warfare.

Q.99. To your opinion, what should be the positive solution to Kashmir tangle between India and Pakistan?

Ans. Sir/Madam, Jammu and Kashmir has become the bone of contention between India and Pakistan. There must be an end to this problem once and for all in the interest of speedy development of India. There is no iota of doubt that Jammu and Kashmir is an integral part of India by virtue of its accession to India in the year, 1947. Nuclear warfare between India and Pakistan is also not the solution to Kashmir tangle, as in that case existence of both India and Pakistan will be at stake—what to talk of Jammu and Kashmir. Pakistan had occupied a portion of Jammu and Kashmir in the year, 1948 declaring it as Azad Kashmir, from which more than 5000 Square kms. of land was gifted to China. World powers are not interested in the mediation of Kashmir dispute. They have clearly opined that Jammu and Kashmir is a bilateral issue between India and Pakistan and, therefore, Pakistan is obviously denied support even from its allies, the U.S.A. and China in the matter of solution to Jammu and Kashmir. Under the circumstances, since it is very difficult on the part of India to get back Azad Kashmir including the gifted territory to China, the only solution, to my opinion, lies in the division of Jammu and Kashmir on the present LoC by converting it into international border. This is also very necessary due to the fact that China will never part with the more than 5000 sq. kms. territory of Azad Kashmir gifted to them by Pakistan.

Q.100. There is a secret clause in the Simla Agreement entered into by Indira Gandhi and Zulfiqar Ali Bhutto prohibiting use of air power by either side along the Line of Control (LoC). But, still then under what circumstances, Indian force had to use air power during the Kargil war along LoC?

Ans. The Army Chief, General Parvez Musharraf during the Nawaz Sharrif Government of Pakistan attempted to occupy Point 3610 in Kashmir during the continuance of Kargil war in 1999, miscalculating that India would not use its air force against the intruders. Musharraf's calculation was that the occupation of the vital Point 3610 in Kashmir would help him domestically, as he could have claimed that Nawaz Sharrif's betrayal over Kargil had been avenged by such occupation. The Indian army was determined to keep the Point unoccupied by Pakistani forces at any cost and hence used Mirages to bomb Pakistani intruders at Point 3610 in Kashmir, evicting them from Indian territory, destroying their bunkers and causing heavy casualties to the Pakistani army.

Q.101. During SAARC Summit in Kathmandu held on 5th and 6th January, 2001, Gen. Parvez Musharraf, the Pakistani President shook hands with A.B. Vajpayee, the then Indian Prime Minister. By this handshake did Gen. Musharraf achieve diplomatic or political success over Vajpayee?

Ans. Sir/Madam, by such handshake, Gen. Musharraf tried to impress upon the world how sincere he was in his efforts to have cordial relations with India. His extending hand for a handshake was nothing but a hypocrisy. But, seasoned political leader, Mr. A.B. Vajpayee could instantly understand the artificiality of Gen. Musharraf in his approach for a handshake and categorically stated that mere handshake would not suffice the purpose unless Pakistan displayed positive evidence to take action to quell terrorism perpetrated against India by his country. Mr. Vajpayee stated that he undertook bus journey to Lahore on a peace mission. But, what was the reward? The rewards were hijacking of IA plane to Kandahar and Kargil war. Again when Gen. Musharraf was invited to Agra Summit there was terrorist attack on Jammu and Kashmir Assembly complex on 31st October, 2001 and another on Indian Parliament on 13th December, 2001. Therefore, such a handshake by Gen. Musharraf was nothing but a drama and evidently he did not achieve any diplomatic or political manoeuvre over the then Indian Prime Minister, A.B. Vajpayee by such a handshake.

Q.102. Was it a correct decision on the part of India to release the three hard-core Kashmiri militants including Azhar Masood for the safety of the passengers on board the hijacked Indian Aircraft IC-814?

Ans. Sir/Madam, it is beyond the contradiction of doubt that there was flagrant security lapse on the part of the Kathmundu Airport Authorities which led to the easy passage of the air pirates to board the Indian Aircraft IC-814 at Kathmundu Airport on 24th December, 1999 and accordingly the Government of India was helpless in the matter. When the lives of the passengers of the ill-fated aircraft were endangered in the hands of the air pirates threatening to kill all of them provided the demands of the air pirates including the release of the hard-core militants along with Azhar Masood were not met, the Government of India had no other option but to release the militants in exchange for the safety of the lives of the passengers on board the hijacked aircraft. The lives of the passengers were precious and the government was under tremendous pressure from their relatives to ensure safety of the passengers which the government could not ignore. Therefore, under the compelling circumstances, the release of the hard-core Kashmiri militants in exchange for the safety of the passengers on humanitarian ground was not an incorrect decision on the part of the Government of India.

Q.103. India is a peace loving country being a land of Mahatma Gandhi. Do you think that India is being disturbed to maintain her peaceful co-existence thus thwarting developmental activities?

Ans. Sir/Madam, India has no design of territorial aggrandisement and wants to live in peace and amity with all the countries of the world by her matured foreign policy, especially with her neighbours, thus paving the way to attain developments undeterred on all fronts at a faster rate. Since Independence, India's development has become an eye-sore especially to one of our neighbouring countries, as it is not desired by them that India becomes one of the powerful countries of the world especially in Asia. In order, therefore, to thwart and destabilise developments, cross-border terrorism, proxy war and unprovoked firing by armed forces across the western border and I.S.I. activities have become a regular feature for years together, which culminated in the attack of the Parliament House on the ill-fated 13th December, 2001 by the Pakistani sponsored terrorists. Such nefarious design was meted out with the obvious reason to eliminate Political leaders thereby weakening India. Under the circumstances, India can never be a silent spectator being a peaceful country and she has definitely to counteract to crush such activities with all strength and vigour even at the cost of suspension of developmental activities for the time being. But, whatever may be the tribulations and severe afflictions, India is poised to go ahead in attaining all round developments in the not too distant future.

Q.104. In spite of pressure from the Western leaders President Musharraf of Pakistan does not want to stop infiltration into Jammu and Kashmir completely. What, in your opinion, is the reason for the same?

Ans. Sir/Madam, President Parvez Musharraf appeared to be telling the West to either accept that he cannot fully stop the export of insurgency into Jammu and Kashmir or risk facing a new government that could be far less accommodative regime in Pakistan. The

General is believed to be playing on fears that his government would be replaced by a fundamentalist one if it totally cuts off support to the Kashmiri cause. The Musharraf government seems to be implying that it is at the limits of the steps it can take against extremist groups and that the West should tolerate cross-border insurgency operation in Kashmir under the circumstances.

Q.105. What should be the top priority for attaining peace in Indo-Pakistan relations?

Ans. Sir/Madam, the first step to cool down temperature between India and Pakistan is to respect the Line of Control and ensure zero infiltration into India from Pakistan. When Jammu and Kashmir is the apple of discord between India and Pakistan, it is important to convert LoC into international border. Since it is one of the foreign policies of the U.S. to cool down temperature between India and Pakistan, they should press Pakistan to stop infiltration and dismantle its terror apparatus. When it is implemented it will automatically pave the way for initiating meaningful dialogue for reaching solutions to the outstanding knots between these two countries including Jammu and Kashmir.

Q.106. What are the problems being faced by India with the I.S.I. and militant groups in North-Eastern states?

Ans. Sir/Madam, I.S.I. (Inter-Services Intelligence) of Pakistan has been heightening their activities by establishing their bases in Nepal, Bhutan and Bangladesh. The North-eastern states of India have become the hot-bed of militant activities. The cadres of separatist organisation such as the KLO (Kamtapur Liberation Organisation) are being trained and armed by the ULFA (United Liberation Front of Asom) and the National Democratic Front of Bodoland and are supported by the I.S.I. There are as many as 14 ULFA camps located inside Bhutan where KLO militants are given training and shelter. Bangladesh government is also clandestinely harbouring support to the ISI and other militant groups to act against India. Between November, 1996 and December, 2002, West Bengal state administration arrested 125 persons for spying, carrying weapons and explosives. Hard evidence was available with the West Bengal government showing that many of those arrested were operating from outside West Bengal.

This way the Government of India has been facing problems with the ISI and militant groups in its North-eastern states including West Bengal.

Q.107. What was the necessity of formation of a Review Committee to take a comprehensive view of the Prevention of Terrorism Act (POTA), as announced by Shri L.K. Advani, Deputy Prime Minister of India.

Ans. Sir/Madam, Prevention of Terrorism Act was adopted on March 26, 2002 and since its adoption it has been grossly misused all over India. It has been observed that identifying the draconian provisions of POTA even many innocent people have been detained under this Act in different states of India. At present, the definition of terrorism under POTA is so vague that the police can take any suspect into custody. Under the POTA, the government is judge, jury and prosecutor. It can even declare an organisation a "terrorist organisation" without furnishing evidence or specifying the grounds for doing so.

Under the circumstances, formation of a Review Committee was felt an absolute necessity to soften the draconian provisions of POTA. Shri L.K. Advani; the then Deputy Prime Minister of India announced that the Review Committee would lay special emphasis on ensuring that the provisions of POTA were not used against ordinary criminals or those who were not terrorists or whose acts were not considered as terrorist act.

Q.108. Why is the national flag hoisted on the Red Fort?

Ans. Sir/Madam, our brave countrymen suffered inhumanly during their long struggle for Independence and sacrificed their lives for the cause of their motherland. Many of the freedom fighters were imprisoned in this historic Red Fort. In fact, it is a symbol of the golden days and also a symbol of Independence of India. Netaji Subhas Chandra Bose declared that when India would become independent from the clutches of the foreign yoke, national flag of India would be hoisted on the Red Fort in commemoration of the golden days of India. In keeping with his wishes, the first Prime Minister of India, Pandit Jawaharlal Nehru hoisted the national flag on the Red Fort on 15th August, 1947—the first day of the observance of independence of India and since then every Prime Minister has been hoisting the national flag on the Red Fort on 15th August of every year.

Q.109. What were the points of agreement and disagreement in passing the women's reservation bill?

Ans. Sir/Madam, there is no inkling of doubt that women are in no way inferior to men. They are now holding exalted positions in banks, industries, the media and so on by virtue of their intelligence, education, merit and mental acumen and also discharge their duties efficiently and honestly. It is an admitted fact that reserved number of seats for the women in parliament and the legislatures will help improve the status of women. In a democratic country like India men and women have to work shoulder to shoulder. Women are undoubtedly as competent as men in political representation. Therefore, taking into consideration the merits of the case, it is of paramount necessity to have women's reservation bill passed.

Passing of the women's reservation bill was contradicted and vehemently opposed by unruly acts of some parliamentarians. The practical problem facing the male legislators was the possibility that they would have to vacate 180 seats for the women representatives from their respective constituencies. They were of the opinion that the seats were not required to be kept reserved for women but encouragement was to be given to women through free and subsidized education and the raising of awareness of their rights. Also the male-dominated political system in the Indian democracy did not want to share power with women leadership. In the light of the above arguments some of the parliamentarians could not accept that women should have 33 per cent seats in the two houses.

Q.110. Under what circumstances/conditions the Article 356 of the Indian Constitution could be imposed in a state?

Ans. Sir/Madam, Article 356 is an emergency provision which grants the centre sweeping powers to dismiss state governments. The question of imposition of Article 356 arises only when there is the breakdown of law and order situation in the state and that it is imposed as a last resort. Before any action is taken in this regard, a show cause notice has to be issued to the state government and time for a reply. Within two months of issuing the order to dismiss a government, the matter should be placed before Parliament for consideration.

In case of constitutional breakdown, the Governor's report must be a "speaking document", which means it should have facts and figures to corroborate its views.

Q.111. What are the benefits of holding Lok Sabha and Assembly elections simultaneously?

Ans. Sir/Madam, expenses in conducting elections in a big country like India are no doubt enormous. When such a huge amount of money is spent to maintain Indian democracy in all the 28 states and also for installation of union Government through elections, India's speedy development obviously suffers a setback. Therefore, combined Lok Sabha election and Assembly elections which are particularly of close duration with the holding of Lok Sabha election will have far-reaching advantages such as:

(a) The administration and the political parties will be able to focus on development and reduce expenditure.

(b) Holding of simultaneous polls will strengthen democracy.

(c) The electorates have become fed up with frequent

elections and they would welcome just one election in five years.

(d) There will be anti-incumbency wave in holding simultaneous elections.

In this connexion, one important point to be noted is that while the simultaneous Lok Sabha and Assembly elections are held, governments at all levels in general should be allowed to complete their full five-year terms in order to avoid holding of interim elections due to falling of governments. Continuation of governments for full term will also ensure good governance, development and performance.

Q.112. Do you agree that conglomeration of different political parties is the only way out to govern India now?

Ans. At present there are multifarious political parties in India. In the election votes are shared by all the political parties thereby leaving practically no chance for a single political party to emerge victorious with two-thirds majority to form government singly. Under the circumstances, the only way-out left is to form government with the conglomeration of other political parties constituting two-thirds majority. Now, in order to ensure unity among other political parties taking part in the government, the Prime Minister has to be very much tactful in keeping unity among other political parties forming the government. Otherwise, the government will fall before full term of five years is completed and fresh election is to be held again involving crores of rupees as also stalling development of the country.

Q.113. Some political leaders of India held the view that Mrs. Sonia Gandhi is not a citizen of India challenging her election as Congress President. Is it correct?

Ans. Sir/Madam, there is no inkling of doubt that Mrs. Sonia Gandhi is truly and legally a citizen of India and that her election as Congress President is validated. Delivering the judgement on September 2, 2001, Mr. Justice, R.C. Lahoti, on scrutiny of the pleadings in the case, said that it must be held that the respondent,

Mrs. Sonia Gandhi by virtue of the Certificate granted to her under Section 5(1) of the Citizenship Act on April 30, 1983 was a citizen of India and hence there was no illegality of her enrolment in the electoral rolls.

Q.114. What is the full name of SIMI and on what ground Government of India has banned it?

Ans. Sir/Madam, the full name of SIMI is Students Islamic Movement of India. The Government of India had ample evidence at its disposal of this Organisation's links with al-Qaida group of Osama-bin-Laden. As per the contention of the Union Home Secretary, SIMI had also collusion with other militant groups and pan-Islamic outfits. Home Ministry had been receiving constant reports from number of State Governments and also other agencies about the nefarious activities of SIMI which were injurious to the maintenance of communal concord and territorial integrity. Under such circumstances, the Government of India had to ban SIMI.

Q.115. What benefits India would start getting after the Bush administration lifted sanctions.

Ans. Sir/Madam, the sanctions imposed by the U.S. Government on India in the wake of blasting of nuclear bomb at Pokhran (Rajasthan) had barred economic and military aid to India. The sanctions were lifted by the U.S. President, George Bush on 23rd September, 2001 on account of the changed world situation after the terrorist attack on America.

As a consequence of lifting of the sanctions while India would again start getting the economic and military aid from the U.S.A., there is every possibility that the long delayed project to manufacture light combat aircraft would be expedited, as India will be able to procure several equipment including radars and control system from the U.S. for the project.

Q.116. How could the Britishers conquer India?

Ans. Sir/Madam, the very simple thing is that when the people of a country are united and there is strong

Government, the enemy and the invader find it a very difficult task to conquer a country. For this reason, even the mighty Americans could not prevail over Vietnam even after several years of war because of the mass resistance of the people of Vietnam. But, it was not so in the case of India. The rulers of the then India were not strong and united and the people were indifferent and not politically conscious. Although the Britishers set their feet on the soil of India with the sole purpose of doing trade and business, they could sense the weaknesses of the then rulers of India and the fragmented nature of the people and this facilitated the Britishers to have hegemony over India. But, ultimately when the mass movement was initiated in an organised manner at the helm of Mahatma Gandhi the Britishers had to quit India.

Q.117. Please enlighten the role of Commonwealth and justify India's joining the Commonwealth.

Ans. Sir/Madam, Commonwealth is an association of democratic countries of the world. 54 countries are the members of Commonwealth comprising 29% of the total population of the world. Commonwealth is the conglomeration of the world community by uniting the developed and the developing countries. It is an effective forum to foster international relations for the benefit of mankind especially its own member countries. It is a driving force in international efforts to secure exoneration from indebtedness of the poorest countries of the world. Commonwealth is a legacy of the British colonial past. The pre-requisite for becoming membership of the Commonwealth is past political association with the United Kingdom of which India is not immune. This justifies as to why India has become one of the members of Commonwealth countries.

Q.118. Please enlighten the role of CHOGM.

Ans. The full name of CHOGM is Commonwealth Heads of Government Meet. The member countries of CHOGM are from the members of Commonwealth. CHOGM is a watchdog for functioning of democracy in its member countries. It penalises the erring members for derailing democratic process. At the 32nd CHOGM meet in Durban in November, 1999, Pakistan was placed under suspension from its membership because of military takeover in October, 1999. CHOGM promotes economic and educational cooperation among the member countries. It condemns global terrorism and corruption. CHOGM has also to play a major role to promote world peace.

Q.119. How could you justify that India should become one of the permanent members of Security Council?

Ans. Sir/Madam, India's case to have permanent seat in the Security Council is pending before the UN for a long time. India has been emerging as a big power. There is very good rapprochement in the international relations with other countries of the world by its progressive foreign policy. India represents one-fifth of the total population of the world. India is a nuclear state. India is also a leading country amongst the SAARC nations. India, which has an increasingly global role to play, is a natural contender for the position. India's role in peacekeeping from Bosnia to Sierra Leone is laudable and it is a glaring example of the true international leadership India had demonstrated to the world. All these factors justify India's entry into the United Nations Security Council as a permanent member. India's entry into the Council will also help create a multipolar world.

Q.120. Who are the members of SAARC and what are its objectives? Do you feel that SAARC is a success?

Ans. Sir/Madam, firstly, I would like to mention that the full name of SAARC is South Asian Association of Regional Cooperation. Its members are: India, Pakistan, Nepal, Bangladesh, Bhutan, Sri Lanka and Maldives. The objectives of SAARC are: (i) Development of industries and trade, (ii) Economic Cooperation, (iii) Elimination of poverty, (iv) Weeding out terrorism facing the SAARC nations, (v) Agricultural development and (vi) Social and political issues. In this connexion,

I would like to mention here that the venue of SAARC is not the forum of discussing bilateral contentious issues.

I feel SAARC has become a dismal failure. It has little to show by way of success, especially on economic front. Intra-SAARC trade is pathetic at less than five per-cent and prospects for the future remain bleak on account of the fact that in a world increasingly governed by rules of the World Trade Organisation, regional economic association is fractured. To all intents and purposes, achievements from SAARC also have been negated on account of India-Pakistan bitter relations and conflict.

Q.121. Why has India gone for nuclear bomb?

Ans. Sir/Madam, real development of a country without all-round defence preparedness has no meaning, especially when it is known that neighbouring countries either possess nuclear bomb or are in the process of possessing the same in the not too distant future. Possession of nuclear bomb by a country will bolster strength to counter any military threats especially from across the border. The purpose of going for nuclear bomb by a vast and fast developing country like India is very simple. A country is considered weak from military point of view, if she does not possess nuclear bomb. The countries possessing nuclear bomb will pose a constant threat to the sovereignty of such country without possessing nuclear bomb. In this modern era countries with nuclear bomb will think twice to go for war and if nuclear war breaks out the world as a whole will be completely destroyed, which nobody wants. Therefore, as a means of guarding our country from nuclear threats from other countries, India has gone for nuclear bomb and by possessing such bomb she has displayed that she is one of the powerful countries of the world, especially from military point of view.

Q.122. Do you feel that it is a wise decision of the Union Government to throw open defence equipment production to the private sector with permission for foreign direct investment also?

Ans. Sir/Madam, it was decided by the Union Government on 9th May, 2001 to allow the private sector to manufacture defence equipment within the country if necessary with foreign direct investment of upto 26% with the permission from the Union Government. The manufacture of ammunition and other defence-related products by the private sector will have to be cleared by the Defence Ministry. The Government of India has justified this decision by telling that India is importing most of its defence equipment from abroad. The decision of the Government in this direction seems to be of great consequence. If my personal opinion is sought in the matter of manufacture of ammunition and other defence-related products by private sector, I am of the opinion that it does not warrant manufacture of the same by private sector, when the government has been continuing to manufacture them in their own Gun-Shell factories all over the country. Import of most of the defence equipment by India from abroad does not justify that some of the defence equipment should be manufactured by indigenous private sector with foreign participation. Government of India is of course importing only those items which are very much sophisticated. Defence is a secret deal which should be kept within the control of the government itself. Shifting of manufacture of defence products from government establishments to private sector will cause lay-off and trimming of employees working in the Gun-Shell factories accentuating a further step of unemployment problem of the country, particularly when there is acute unemployment problem in the country as at present. This means that it will add fuel to fire, which is not desired at all.

Q.123. What prompted the Government of India to privatise the Public Sector Undertakings?

Ans. Sir/Madam, privatisation means transferring assets from the state to the private sector, instead of passing them from one arm of the government to another arm. Government of India has begun privatising its Public Sector Undertakings (PSUs) as part of liberalisation process. The major objective of disinvestment was to reduce the budget deficit. The government also claimed it had a desire to encourage accountability among PSUs. Apart from the above, privatisation policy of the government included the following objectives:

(a) Improving the efficiency and productivity of economic activities and facilitation of economic growth.

(b) Relieving the financial and administrative burden on the Government.

(c) Reducing the size and presence of the public sector.

(d) Helping meet national development policy targets.

Privatisation if correctly implemented can be a major instrument in transforming the economy of the country. Half hearted privatisation will never yield desired results.

Q.124. In what way the sale proceeds arising out of the disinvestment and privatisation of the government Organisations should be utilised.

Ans. Sir/Madam, to all intents and purposes, the sale proceeds arising out of the disinvestment and privatisation of PSUs should be earmarked for revitalisation of economic ills of the country. In this connexion, it is to be remembered, how the substantial sum of Rs. 10,000 crores raised under the voluntary disclosure of income scheme was squandered in paying increased salaries to government employees in pursuance of the directives of the Fifth Pay Commission despite pious intentions of using the money for infrastructural development of the country. Under no circumstances, this should be done in the sale proceeds arising out of the disinvestment of Public Sector Undertakings. Unless the government controls its fiscal deficit, disinvestment will mean an easy flow of cash to be spent on its employees for disbursing their salaries and meeting other current expenditures. If this is the purpose of disinvestment, the government will end up selling all the PSUs without any long term benefits, as had taken place in Argentina. Therefore, a method should be worked out whereby the disinvestment proceeds could be accumulated for its use to finance infrastructure projects or retire high cost debt. If it is not done in the matter of proper utilisation of disinvestment proceeds, it will be pernicious for the country to pursue economic growth.

Q.125. Do you agree that India is to be governed by a single party winning two-thirds majority or with conglomeration of different parties?

Ans. Sir/Madam, at the outset I would like to emphatically stress that at the centre there is no possibility of a single party government, as the seats are shared amongst all the political parties competing in the elections and hence the chance is absolutely remote on the part of any political party to bag seats forming two-thirds majority in order to form government under the present political scenario of the country. Under the circumstances, there is no alternative but to form government at the centre with conglomeration of different political parties with different ideologies and policies.

Even if there is slightest chance of formation of government by a single party, such government is not likely to be a popular government in the comity of the nation, by its actions, deeds and policies because of complexities in political scenario and ultimately the country may not forge ahead in right direction with the governance by a single party. Therefore, the advantage of the government with multiplicity of political parties is that the policies of such government are framed in line with the concurrence of all the parties forming part of the government, in consideration of the exigencies of situation and in such case the opposition party is also amenable to such policies in most of the cases.

Q.126. What is "Look East" policy of India?

Ans. Sir/Madam, India felt the extreme necessity of building stronger ties with the ASEAN (Association of South East Asian Nations) countries, especially for the specific reason that Bangladesh was not cooperating with India in dealing with the security needs of north-eastern states of India. Dhaka had been hosting insurgent groups which were active in India. The "Look East" policy of India aimed at maintaining cooperation with Myanmar which was dictated by geography and security interests as also with Thailand and Singapore. With South East Asia, India was rapidly developing close economic links as part of its "Look East" policy, which included Free Trade and Economic Partnership Agreements with Thailand and Singapore connecting transportation links with Myanmar, Thailand and Singapore.

The "Look East" policy harboured by India was prompted in view of Dhaka's intransigence towards its giant neighbour, India.

Q.127. Is bundh a solution to the problem?

Ans. Sir/Madam, I am of the firm opinion that bundh in any case is not the solution to the problems rather it heightens problems. It paralyses the normal lives of the people. In the event of the bundh offices, factories and industries are closed which entails heavy financial loss to the extent of crores of rupees and it becomes a retrograde step to the development of the state. It brings untold miseries to the daily wage earners as they find no source of earning. Dying patients who are required to be shifted to the hospitals for immediate treatment find it extremely difficult for want of any public conveyance. Public life comes to a stand-still. Bundh is not of course a yardstick that it has the total support of all the people. Bundh is nothing but a pleasure to the bulk of the office goers as they enjoy forced holiday for the day. It has been observed that by observing bundh for which it is invoked, no solution to the problems has been attained so far. Bundh is not at all a healthy sign for a developing country which has to be eschewed.

Q.128. The attack of Iraq spoke of George W. Bush's double standards. How?

Ans. Sir/Madam, Bush told Americans, "We cannot live under the threat of blackmail posed by the apparatus of terror in Iraq. The Terrorist threat to America and the world will be diminished the moment Saddam Hussein is disarmed". Bush argued that the key objective in invading Iraq in the face of international opposition was to bring democracy to Iraq, which would be possible only when Saddam Hussein, the Iraqi despot was removed.

But, in contrast Bush had pleaded with Atal Bihari Vajpayee, the then Prime Minister of India, that India should continue to exercise restraint and keep the LoC stable in the face of Pakistan's sponsorship of cross border terrorism which persisted as acknowledged by Washington.

Another contrasting feature was that Bush rewarded the strengthened dictatorship in Pakistan by lifting the coup-related sanctions against it. He also never urged upon the military dictator, Parvez Musharaff not to infringe upon the Constitution of Pakistan and the military ruler has continued to maintain his military suzerainty over Pakistan by amending the Constitution in his favour unilaterally.

These actions of George W. Bush were a clear testimony that the attack of Iraq spoke of the double standards of Bush.

Q.129. What is the purpose of appointment of a Lokpal?

Ans. Sir/Madam, every day when one opens the newspaper, he sees a scam. The purpose of a Lokpal is to look into corruption in public life. Once a Lokpal is appointed a major headache will be over as it would first go into the issue rather than litigants rushing to the courts.

The Government wanted that the appointment of Lokpal be expedited and hence moved a bill to that effect in the Lok Sabha on August 14, 2001. The bill was then referred to the Parliamentary Standing Committee, which gave its report in December, 2001 recommending drastic changes. The Government is considering the changes suggested by the Committee.

Q.130. Is it in order to pronounce death sentences on Mohammad Afzal, Shaukat Hussain and S.A.R. Geelani for their nexus with the terrorists and plotting the Parliament attack on 13th December, 2001?

Ans. Sir/Madam, the special judge, S.N. Dhingra read out, in the packed Patiala House special courtroom on 18th December, 2002, the orders awarding these three persons death penalty under the Prevention of Terrorism Act for their nexus with the terrorist outfits and plotting with them the Indian Parliament attack on 13th December, 2001.

The death sentence has been described as the rarest of rare cases. It is of course true that in many civilised countries of the world death sentences have been annulled. It is the contention of one school of thought that no man can take away what he himself cannot give. God creates human life and only he has the right to take it. A liberal society is based on the rights of individuals and everybody has the right to life. Therefore, taking away the life of an individual by another individual or group of individuals is a transgression of basic principle.

Whatever may be the argument disfavouring death sentence, it, the severest possible punishment, serves as an example and thus stops other persons from contemplating and/or committing the same heinous crime. The terrorists have no respect of their individual lives. By committing murder they forfeit their own right to life. When the terrorists have to take away lives of the innocent people, they have also no right to claim for their own existence in this world. They are the enemies of mankind, they deserve no leniency. The punishment to be given in such cases must be deterrent. Therefore, when the above three persons were branded as terrorists and that when they masterminded the attack of Parliament in collusion with other terrorists, it was perfectly in order that capital punishment was awarded to them.

Q.131. The then Prime Minister, Shri Atal Bihari Vajpayee announced dual citizenship for the people of Indian origin on 9th January, 2003 at a gathering of 1500 people of Indian origin at Pragati Maiden. What gains will India derive by such dual citizenship?

Ans. Sir/Madam, there are of course several considerations for which the Government of India thought it worthwhile to grant dual citizenship for the people of Indian origin. For the moment it applied only to NRIs in seven countries: The United States of America, the European Union, Canada, the United Kingdom, Australia, New Zealand and Singapore. The Government of India, however, made it clear that it would use its discretion in granting this status to NRIs. Dual citizenship would give the people of Indian origin the same rights as Indian citizens while doing business in the country.

Mr. Vajpayee's decision to grant dual citizenship was in the context of rejuvenating the Indian economy. One of the factors in this direction is the mobility of human resources. India will be benefited immensely by the riches of the people of the Indian origin doing business on the soil of India. It is the vision of the Indian leadership that India would be economically a prosperous country by the year, 2020 with the dexterity of experience gleaned by the people of Indian origin staying abroad on account of their global exposure. Overseas investment would no doubt get tumultuous momentum when the true picture of India was painted abroad in a credible and propitious manner.

People of Indian origin having been granted dual citizenship could project a positive image of India—not as a propaganda but as true reflection of reality. The country would also reap the harvest of the riches of their experience and the vision they acquired by their global exposure. Also when these people of Indian origin are conglomerated in their host country, it will have long-term significance for promoting the cause of India in the eye of the world.

Dual citizenship to the people of Indian origin would generate loyalty and sense of belonging to the country of their origin. Many Indians living abroad for professional and business reasons have opted for foreign citizenship, but in terms of culture and sensibilities they would see themselves as Indians when they would come back to the country of their origin after opening up of business investment opportunities for them.

Q.132. Which are the 'Bimaru' states of India and what are the problems with these states?

Ans. Sir/Madam, the 'Bimaru' states of India are Bihar, Madhya Pradesh, Rajasthan and Uttar Pradesh. There are specific problems for each of these four states, which have always lagged behind in health and education. The government was alarmed at the mushroom growth of population in these states which resulted in health problem as also education.

Q.133. What is the significance of Indian Republic Day celebration?

Ans. Sir/Madam, the momentous event of India was the achievement of independence on 15th August, 1947 after centuries of British domination. India became a Republic on 26th January, 1950 which is most important in the history of independent India.

On this day the Government adopted the National Emblem. This emblem, containing 4 Nos. Lions-Sarnath standing back to back, was preserved by Ashoka in the Sarnath museum at Sarnath—the metropolis of King Ashoka empire.

The National Anthem, 'Jana Gana Mana' the song of Rabindranath Tagore was adopted officially as the national anthem of India on 24th January, 1950.

'Vande Mataram' composed by Bankimchandra Chatterjee was taken as the national song and given equal status.

On every 26th January, Presidential Awards of Appreciation certificate for rendering distinguished record of service are distributed by the President himself.

The Constitution of India framed by B.R. Ambedkar was adopted on the 26th January, 1950.

Chief guest on the auspicious occasion of Republic Day is from the Head of State of other country. This gives India an absolute opportunity to cement perennial ties with such country.

January 26 is observed as International Customs Day. It is on this day that the Presidential Awards for the officers of Customs and Central Excise Department are announced. This coincides with the Republic Day celebration.

Q.134. What is the controversy in respect of Sonia Gandhi as AICC President and leader of the Opposition?

Ans. Sir/Madam, it is the contention of many of the political parties that although Sonia Gandhi has become an Indian citizen by virtue of the Certificate granted to her under Section 5(1) of the Citizenship Act on April 30, 1983 and there was no illegality of her enrolment in the electoral rolls, yet she is basically a woman of foreign origin hailing from Italy. The Bharatiya Janata Yuva Morcha which is a part of the BJP demanded that the Congress replace Sonia Gandhi as AICC President and leader of the Opposition Party in the interest of the country. Shri G. Kishan Reddy, President of the Morcha said that it was a crying shame on the part of the Congress Party to have their President with foreign origin and a pointer to the moral bankruptcy of the party. It is really tragic that the party which ruled the country for more than 50 years has chosen its leader who has foreign origin. This is really shameful to the Congress party, in particular and the country in general. Tamil Nadu Chief Minister, Jayalalithaa also opposed on 28th August, 2002 the idea of "foreigner" Sonia Gandhi becoming Prime Minister of India, if the Congress party could form the government at the centre. Her remarks against Sonia Gandhi gave an added impetus and sparked violence in front of Sonia Gandhi's residence on 29th August, 2002. What is smelled is that all these controversies have sprung up in the event of growing popularity of Sonia Gandhi as Congress President.

Q.135. Comparable to China how is the Indian economy?

Ans. Sir/Madam, possession of oil by a country determines the pace of development. China is self-sufficient in oil and a land of cheap fuel. On the other hand, India is deprived of possession of oil as compared to its requirement. India is thus the energy-starved nation in relation to its energy requirements. This is the single most important reason for India's lagging behind China economically.

Owing to changing technology it is not oil but gas which fosters growth of a country in the 21st century. Iran has offered to export 2.5 million tonnes of natural gas to India at a very economical price through pipeline. India has mooted out proposal that the flow of gas from Iran should be through an offsore pipeline laid in international waters well outside Pakistan's exclusive economic zone.

With the commencement of importing this natural gas from Iran, India would start making great strides in the not too distant future thus placing India's economy on par with China.

Q.136. Who discharges the duties and functions of the President of India when he is absent? In the case of resignation by the President to whom he will address such letter of resignation?

Ans. Sir/Madam, in the absence of the President of India on account of the reasons such as death, resignation, removal from office, as the case may be, Vice President acts as the acting President of India till such time a new incumbent is elected/appointed. If both President and Vice President remain absent from office on account of the above reasons, the Chief Justice of India or in his absence the seniormost Judge of the Supreme Court of India would act as the interim President till such time a new President is elected..

In the case of resignation by the President, he will address such letter of resignation to Vice President.

Q.137. What are the qualifications/eligibility to become the President of India and how President is elected?

Ans. Sir/Madam, the eligibility of the candidate to become the President of India are:

(a) He/she must be a citizen of India of any religious community.

(b) His/her age must be minimum 35 years.

(c) He/she must not hold office of profit under the Government of India or the Government of any State or under any local authority.

(d) He/she must be qualified for election as a member of the Lok Sabha.

Criteria for election as President

President of India is elected by an electoral College comprising the elected members of both House of Parliament as also elected members of the State Legislative Assemblies. The voting is conducted through secret ballot. The votes of electorate are so regulated that the total voting strength of Parliament is equal to the total voting strength of all state Assemblies together.

Q.138. In the Indian Constitution is there any statute scope for appointment of interim Vice-President?

Ans. Sir/Madam, there is no constitutional provision for appointing an interim Vice President in the case of a vacancy. Article 68(2) of the Constitution says, "An election to fill a vacancy in the Office of Vice President occuring by reason of death, resignation or removal or otherwise, shall be held as soon as possible after the occurrence of the vacancy." The most material function performed by the Vice-President is presiding over the Rajya Sabha. Until a new Vice-President is elected the deputy Chairman/Chairperson of the Upper House would chair the proceedings.

Q.139. What are the basic principles of Secularism as provided in the Constitution of India?

Ans. Sir/Madam, Secularism means that it will not differentiate whatsoever on the grounds of religion, caste and creed or community against any person professing any religious faith. Secularism does not permit preferential treatment or status and all citizens are equal in a state irrespective of professing different religions.

In view of the said principles of Secularism, the Constitution of India has provided that:

(a) While the state has secured every citizen the right to profess any form of religion, it will not permit any preferential treatment or status to anybody.

(b) No discrimination will be shown by the state against any citizen professing different religions.

(c) Every citizen irrespective or professing different religions will have the right to enter any office by virtue of his/her employment.

Q.140. Was it worthwhile on the part of the President of India, Dr. A.P.J. Abdul Kalam to inaugurate his presidential visits first to the riot-torn Gujarat on 12th and 13th August, 2002 after his coronation on 25th July, 2002?

Ans. Sir/Madam, the intentions of the presidential visits to Gujarat of Dr. A.P.J. Abdul Kalam were no doubt pious, as he wanted to offer his homage to the father of the nation, Mohandas Karamchand Gandhi and also to visit the house of his guru and mentor, Vikram Sarabhai. He also did visit simultaneously Naroda Patiya, one of the riot-torn localities to take stock of the situation personally from the riot affected people. There is a very strict code that governs the behaviour of the President of India. This code of course makes irrelevant the personal predilection and ideology of the individual who is President. This code says that the head of state should be above all controversy. Dr. Kalam during his Gujarat visit came perilously close to transgressing this code because of his good intentions. By his visit to Gujarat first he might have pleased the secularists but at the same time he could have avoided inauguration of his Gujarat visit immediately after his coronation to avoid any controversy.

Q.141. What are all about the sub-clause 1 and 2 of Section 22 of the anti-terrorism Act/POTA (Prevention of Terrorism Act)? How was sub-clause 2 of section 22 applied in the case of Anjum Zamarud Habib and Sabir Ahmed Dar?

Ans. Sir/Madam, sub-clause 1 of Section 22 of anti-terrorism Act says that a person commits an offence if he or she invites another person to give money for terrorist activities.

As far as sub-clause 2 of Section 22 is concerned, a person commits an offence if he or she receives money or "other property" with the intention to use it for the purpose of terrorism.

Anjum Zamarud Habib, Chairperson of Khwateen-e-Markaz, a Hurriyat Constituent, confessed to the Delhi police on 7th February, 2003 after her arrest that she had received Rs. 3 (three) lakhs from Jalil Abbas Jilani, Islamabad's Charge d' affairs at Delhi as gift for funding the Kashmiri militants which was to be handed over to the Hurriyat Chairman, Abdul Gani Bhat. Similarly, Shabir Ahmed Dar who is in charge of the Delhi-based Kashmir Awareness Bureau run by the Hurriyat was arrested on 7th February, 2003 by the Delhi police when Rs. 2.15 lakh was found in his Malviya Nagar residence at Delhi. The acts of both Anjum and Shabir were tantamount to sub-clause 2 of Section 22 of Anti-Terrorism Act.

Q.142. Do you feel that there may be rupture in the bilateral relation between India and Nepal if the Nepal Government implements the Supreme Court orders mandating work permits for Indians living in Nepal?

Ans. Sir/Madam, it is likely that the bonhomie between Nepal and India may turn out to be short-lived, if the Nepal Government implements the Supreme Court orders mandating work permits for Indians living in Nepal. The decision of the Apex Court, if implemented, will precipitate crisis over the future of million stateless people of Indian origin now living in Nepal. If New Delhi reciprocates by Imposing work permits on Nepalis living in India, the effect could be lasting. Any exodus of Nepalis from India as a result of reciprocity of New Delhi would add to the Nepal's economic woes. It is not, therefore, clear whether the Nepal administration would implement the court orders looking to their lasting economic woes damaging to the Kingdom's interest much more than adverse impact on India.

Q.143. What was the reason for the Maoist rebellion in Nepal?

Ans. Sir/Madam, Nepal is a monarchical country. King is the overall power to rule the Himalayan Kingdom. The Nepal Communist Party (Maoist) has been demanding for the establishment of republic in Nepal. They are of the opinion that monarchy in Nepal was outdated after the massacre of the members of royal family of late King Birendra on 1st June, 2001. They put forward two demands—one, the election of a constitutional assembly to draft a new constitution and the second, installation of interim government, but the Nepal government rejected both the demands of the Nepal Communist Party (Maoist). They then came to the conclusion that no fruitful objective would be achieved by holding parleys with the government for mitigating their two demands and accordingly took recourse to the path of violence and insurrection in a large scale to compel the government to come to terms with the rebel Maoist to yield to their demands. It is understood that the rebel forces of Maoist have been strengthened with the active support of China and I.S.I. of Pakistan and as such they are now indomitable to face any strong measures taken by the Government of Nepal. The uprising of Nepal is likely to continue till their objectives are fulfilled. The above facts are the clear-cut reason for the Maoist rebellion in Nepal.

Q.144. What is your idea about McMahon Line?

Ans. Sir/Madam, the McMahon Line which stretches 1500 kilometres long North Eastern frontier of India is the actual line of demarcation between India and Tibet. Sir Henry McMahon who was the Chairman of Simla Conference held with the representatives of China and

Tibet in 1913 and 1914 marked this line as the divide between India and Tibet. This McMahon Line became the apple of discord subsequently when China took over Tibet in 1959 as also during Chinese aggression in parts of Arunachal Pradesh of India in 1962. But, when China retreated from the occupied territory of Arunachal Pradesh India reaffirmed this McMahon Line as the traditional border and an agreement to this effect was signed between the Prime Ministers of India and China in September, 1993 to treat this Line as the actual line of control between these two countries on Permanent basis.

Q.145. Please tell about your idea in respect of Diego Garcia.

Ans. Sir/Madam, Diego Garcia is an island situated in the midst of the Indian Ocean. It is a strategic Anglo-American naval base which was established in the year, 1973. After establishment of the naval base, the inhabitants of Diego Garcia were evicted from their homes by the British and deported to Mauritius. Diego Garcia is a projection of the U.S. military power in the Indian Ocean and the Gulf. The U.S. made full use of Diego Garcia for bombing raids against Iraq.

Q.146. What are the factors on which the Indian industry could be made viable in global competitiveness?

Ans. Sir/Madam Indian economy being integrated, with the global economy, competitiveness is of paramount necessity for survival of Indian industry, for which three essential policy initiatives are needed, which are:

(i) Interest rates should continue at 5-6 per cent range similar to a number of developing and developed countries.

(ii) Exit policy for labour is equally important. There should not be any scope for redundant or unproductive labour in the industries.

(iii) Electricity should be made available without load shedding at a reasonable unit cost. For this purpose, all procedural and policy hurdles in the power sector should be removed with an iron hand.

Q.147. The West Bengal Chief Minister, Buddhadeb Bhattacharjee flayed lack of foresightedness in Tenth Five-year Plan. How?

Ans. Sir/Madam, the West Bengal Chief Minister, Buddhadeb Bhattacharjee said that the 10th Five-Year-Plan for the period 2002-2007 with the outlay of Rs. 15,92,000 crores was no doubt ambitious, but it lacked the foresightedness in the Plan, as there was no mention of any proposal on the burning issues like land reforms, disinvestment and employment generation. He accused the Centre of failing to initiate programmes for over the 15 crores unemployed youths in the Tenth Plan Mr. Bhattacharjee, therefore, wanted that there should be generation of employment in the Plan period. He reiterated that on account of pursuing the policy of liberalisation by the Centre, the people were scared of losing their jobs and hence the Tenth Five-Year Plan would have nothing to do to ease unemployment problem in the country.

Q.148. Indian democracy is based on certain principles. Which are those principles?

Ans. Sir/Madam, India's achievements in building a vibrant democracy have been recognised by all the major powers of the world. The principles of Indian democracy are based on the fact that it has successfully preserved its multi-cultural, multi-ethnic and multi-religious social fabric within a constitutional, democratic and federal framework. It has institutionalised freedoms, human rights and the rule of law. The change of governments in India is through a peaceful and non-violent expression of popular will and this has been possible because of the fact that Indian democracy is based on the above principles.

Q.149. Why did President George Bush want war against Iraq?

Ans. Sir/Madam, after Iraq's invasion of Kuwait in 1990 the United Nations declared that Baghdad was banned from possessing nuclear, biological or chemical weapons or missiles which could fly across 150 kms.

In order that Iraq ensured to destroy whatever weapons

stock it had, the U.N. set up a special commission (UNSCOM) to inspect the suspected sites and supervise destruction of the deadly weapons. According to Bush and Secretary of State, Colin Powel, Iraq did not cooperate in allowing UNSCOM to work and its illegal weapons were still secretly preserved in tact. As a result, they said that the regime of Saddam Hussein posed a great threat to the security of the United States of America and its allies. Moreover, Saddam Hussein was a brutal dictator and the Iraqi people needed to be liberated from his clutches. The U.S. also said that it had evidence that Saddam Hussein had links with al-Qaida and other terrorist groups. As long as Iraq possessed weapons of mass destruction, there was every possibility of the terrorists getting hold of the Iraqi weapons.

In view of the above facts and circumstances, the American leadership felt the absolute necessity of going for war against Iraq.

Q.150. What are the principles of NAM and how has it become effective in world forum?

Ans. Sir/Madam, NAM denotes Non-Aligned Movement. NAM is a 116-nation forum. The Non-Aligned Movement was founded on three fundamental principles: Disarmament, Development and Autonomy of Decision Making.

With the end of bipolarity and emergence of the United States of America as the sole superpower after fragmentation of the USSR, not to mention the globalisation of the market, all the three principles of NAM have virtually collapsed.

The CTBT (Comprehensive Test Ban Treaty) is dead and the U.S. is reported to be developing new generation of nuclear weapons. Development has long ceased to be a burning issue of NAM. With the collapse of bipolarity, autonomy in decision-making has been circumscribed all over the world.

Q.151. What are the objectives of WHO (World Health Organisation) and how does it work?

Ans. Sir/Madam, WHO is an World-wide Organisation looking after the attainment of maximum possible health by the undernourished people of the world. Since the prosperity of the people depends upon maintenance of disease-free health, its strategy aims at combined efforts of the Government and people for the successful implementation of the programme based on education with regard to existing health problems, availability of pure water and sanitation, balanced food supply, immunisation against infectious disease, family planning and proper treatment of common disease.

Q.152. Under what considerations Shri A.B. Vajpayee, the then Prime Minister of India advocated bilateral relations between India and Maldives.

Ans. Sir/Madam, Maldives is a SAARC nation and it took the lead in pushing for an additional protocol to the convention at the SAARC ministerial meeting in Kathmandu in 2001. India wanted to engage Maldives in the regional cooperation in the fight against terrorism for peace and regional stability. Shri Vajpayee promised on 23rd September, 2002 during his four-day visit to Maldives to continue and increase Delhi's support to defence training and equipment supply to Maldives. He also offered to set up facilities in Maldives for digital mapping of the islands and a remote-sensing centre. Although a small island country with a population of hardly thirty lakhs, Maldives is important to India because of its strategic location in the Indian ocean. The country's security relations with India have had a special significance since 1988 when the Indian military crushed an attempted coup in the islands in 1988 by the Sri Lankan militants.

Q.153. Who was Daniel Pearl and what was the probable reason of his murder?

Ans. Sir/Madam, Daniel Pearl was born in Princeton, New Jersey (the USA) and grew up in California. He was 38 when he was murdered. He was an American journalist.

The possible reason for his murder was that he was investigating links between Osama-bin-Laden's Al-Qaida network blamed for the attacks on World Trade Center and Pentagon on 11th September, 2001. Before his murder Daniel Pearl disappeared in Karachi (Pakistan) on 23rd January, 2002. British-born Islamic militant, Ahmed Omar Saeed Sheikh was charged in Pakistan with masterminding Pearl's kidnap and his murder subsequently.

Q.154. In what way Attorney General, Soli Sorabjee's opinion elicited by him on 20-1-2003 in the matter of denationalisation of HPCL (ESSO) and BPCL (Burmah Shell) without parliamentary approval was contradicted by the five India's most eminent jurists.

Ans. Sir/Madam, the Attorney General, Soli Sorabjee's advice was that there was no need to repeal the Acts of Parliament under which both HPCL and BPCL were taken over by the Government in 1970s. The Government said that it acted on the advice of the Attorney General who held that there was no need to refer the matter to Parliament.

In this connexion, the five of India's most eminent jurists severely criticised the Vajpayee government's decision to privatise HPCL and BPCL without parliamentary approval. In a joint statement issued on 10th March, 2003 justices V.R. Krishna Iyer, O. Chinnapa Reddy, P.B. Sawant, Rajinder Sachar and advocate Shanti Bhusan said the move to sell the two oil PSUs without amending the ESSO and Burmah Shell Acquisition of Undertakings Act is unconstitutional. The Government's decision to bypass Parliament on a matter of such public importance was against constitutional propriety and supremacy of Parliament. It showed an unhealthy contempt for Parliament and constitutional norms.

Q.155. Is it likelihood that another Warsaw Pact is likely to be formed after Iraq war?

Ans. Sir/Madam, Warsaw Pact was a military alliance of the former Soviet Union and its six socialist partners in Europe which was made infructuous with the disintegration of the Soviet Union. There was a presumption that the conquest of Iraq by the coalition forces of the United States in April, 2003 led to the sowing of another Warsaw Pact-II stealthily in the form in which it existed upto the time when Moscow-led East block collapsed. Of course, there was no formal alliance of any kind led by Moscow immediately after the war on Iraq was over. But, the seeds of another Warsaw Pact were not only sown, there were signs that those seeds were growing. Unrivalled demonstration of American military might as shown in the wars of Afghanistan and Iraq and the consequent expansion of influence of the US made it imperative to form an alliance under the aegis of Russia.

Q.156. Is the Delhi's relation with Washington like of the partnership or master-client one?

Ans. Sir/Madam, New Delhi's relation with Washington is definitely like that of a partnership and not master-client one, because of India's pride and size. There was a growing strength of the ties between the two large democracies. The U.S. with its global interests has much more to ask from India. With regard to Iraq war India had stuck to its position that it would not support any action outside the U.N. framework which was well understood by the U.S. Former U.S. President, Bill Clinton's visit to India in March, 2000 was the "turning point" in Indo-U.S. relations. The change in the Washington administration bringing the Bush government to power has not affected the momentum of intense engagement between India and the U.S. All these things are a clear testimony that partnership relationship is the basic theme between India and the U.S.

